UNEARTHING SHAKESPEARE

What can the Globe Theatre tell us about performing Shakespeare?

Unearthing Shakespeare is the first book to consider what the Globe, today's replica of Shakespeare's theatre, can contribute to a practical understanding of Shakespeare's plays. Valerie Clayman Pye reconsiders the material evidence of Early Modern theatre-making, presenting clear, accessible discussions of historical theatre practice; stages and staging; and the relationship between actor and audience. She relays this into a series of training exercises for actors at all levels.

From "Shakesball" and "Telescoping" to *Elliptical Energy Training* and *The Radiating Box*, this is a rich set of resources for anyone looking to tackle Shakespeare with authenticity and confidence.

Valerie Clayman Pye is an Assistant Professor of Theatre in the Department of Theatre, Dance, and Arts Management in the School of Performing Arts at LIU Post, USA.

UNEARTHING SHAKESPEARE

Embodied Performance and the Globe

Valerie Clayman Pye

LONDON AND NEW YORK

First published 2017
by Routledge
2 Park Square, Milton Park, Abingdon, Oxon OX14 4RN

and by Routledge
711 Third Avenue, New York, NY 10017

Routledge is an imprint of the Taylor & Francis Group, an informa business

© 2017 Valerie Clayman Pye

The right of Valerie Clayman Pye to be identified as author of this
work has been asserted by her in accordance with sections 77 and 78
of the Copyright, Designs and Patents Act 1988.

All rights reserved. No part of this book may be reprinted or
reproduced or utilised in any form or by any electronic, mechanical,
or other means, now known or hereafter invented, including
photocopying and recording, or in any information storage or
retrieval system, without permission in writing from the publishers.

Trademark notice: Product or corporate names may be trademarks
or registered trademarks, and are used only for identification and
explanation without intent to infringe.

British Library Cataloguing in Publication Data
A catalogue record for this book is available from the British Library

Library of Congress Cataloging in Publication Data
Names: Pye, Valerie Clayman, author.
Title: Unearthing Shakespeare : embodied performance and the
    Globe / Valerie Clayman Pye.
Description: Abingdon, Oxon ; New York : Routledge, 2017.
Identifiers: LCCN 2016032192| ISBN 9781138670259 (hardback)
    | ISBN 9781138670273 (pbk.) | ISBN 9781315617718 (ebook)
Subjects: LCSH: Shakespeare, William, 1564-1616—Dramatic
    production. | Shakespeare, William, 1564-1616—Study and
    teaching (Elementary) | Shakespeare, William, 1564-1616—
    Study and teaching (Secondary) | Globe Theatre (London,
    England : 1599-1644) | Theater—England—London—History.
Classification: LCC PR3091 .P88 2017 | DDC 792.9/5—dc23
LC record available at https://lccn.loc.gov/2016032192

ISBN: 978-1-138-67025-9 (hbk)
ISBN: 978-1-138-67027-3 (pbk)
ISBN: 978-1-315-61771-8 (ebk)

Typeset in Bembo
by Swales & Willis Ltd, Exeter, Devon, UK

For Thomas, Jolie, and Owen:

"my all the world."

(Constance, *The Life and Death of King John*, 3.4.104)

CONTENTS

List of illustrations	*ix*
Preface	*x*
Acknowledgments	*xv*

PART I
Excavating the foundation   1

1 Shakespeare's theatrical culture	3
2 Examining the Globe	16
3 Understanding the text	40
4 Creating character	85

PART II
Actuating practice   103

5 Activating the body	105
6 Awakening the listener	120

viii Contents

7 Energizing the language	130
8 Expanding the fiction	138
9 Developing and playing the Shakespeare score	153
10 Rehearsing the part	183

Afterword	*207*
Appendix A: Exercises for the classroom	*208*
Appendix B: Exercises for rehearsal	*210*
Appendix C: Exercises for solo practice	*212*
Index	*214*

ILLUSTRATIONS

Figures

1.1	Johannes DeWitt, illustration of The Swan, 1595	8
2.1	Stage at Shakespeare's Globe	19
2.2	Heavens at Shakespeare's Globe	19
2.3	Depth of stage perspective, Shakespeare's Globe	23
2.4	Illustration of elliptical energy	34
5.1	*Radiating Box*: initiation	110
5.2	*Radiating Box*: formation begins	110
5.3	*Radiating Box*: formation complete	110
8.1	Primary and secondary energy in a fourth wall paradigm	139
8.2	Illustration of elliptical energy	139
8.3	*Elliptical Energy Training Part I*	141
10.1	Prompt cards	185

Tables

10.1	Initials-only index card	185
10.2	Full-text index card	185
10.3	Initials-only index card for dialogue	186
10.4	Full-text index card for dialogue	186

PREFACE

If you have never been to the replica of Shakespeare's Globe, I can tell you, that just like Othello's handkerchief: "there's magic in the web of it." If you have been there . . . you know whereof I speak. And if you have never been to Shakespeare's Globe, and you have never seen one of Shakespeare's plays performed there, you must. I'm not kidding. (I'm not paid to tell you this. I promise, you have my word.)

There is magic in the web of Shakespeare's Globe. Like gossamer filament, intricately woven, it is, and it is not. We see, and we do not see. We are not "caught" in the web's magic, but we are suspended: poised willingly within its dynamic possibilities. The replica is a replication, and it is also a unique, contemporary site for performance. It shows us what performance might have been like, yet we experience the space and performance there within our own cultural expectations. As modern people, we straddle both worlds and enter into a hybrid mode of performance that looks to the past, but is entirely modern and meaningful to us today. The theatre itself is alive; it functions like a character in the performance. It is a vehicle for performance rather than a receptacle of performance. Shakespeare's Globe is "magical" because it serves as a catalyst: for performance choices, for relationships—both within and without Shakespeare's texts, and for community. I have been ensnared in that web, and it's radically changed the way I view and create performance.

Oh boy . . . am I gushing? It's possible, and I promise I'll keep it short lest this turn to Bardolatry. It's not though. Architecture-philia, perhaps?

Preface **xi**

Building-olatry? Definitely. What is it about that space that makes one want to wax poetic? Okay, makes me want to wax poetic? Why does it deserve to be the pilgrimage that Sam Wanamaker hoped it would be? And why should that matter to practitioners specifically? Later in this book I will discuss in detail what the space looks like and why we ought to pay attention to its unique qualities—that magical web. I will also show you how—just by paying attention to those qualities—you can cultivate a more intimate connection to Shakespeare's texts, regardless of where you perform them. You will understand how to "get into" Shakespeare like you've never done before, and how to let Shakespeare emerge through you.

Every one of us who is in the practice of speaking, performing, directing, or teaching Shakespeare must find ways of forging a personalized connection to Shakespeare's texts; one that makes our work meaningful for those with whom we share it. The actor longs to embody the text with integrity; the director longs to orchestrate a precise execution of artistic vision; the teacher or coach longs to facilitate these very moments of connection. Looking at the performance conditions at Shakespeare's Globe will help us do just that.

Whether you are a novice trying to find a tangible system for approaching and rehearsing Shakespeare's work, an established performer looking for a jolt to vitalize your current practice, a director or teacher hoping to inspire and galvanize your ensemble, or someone who simply loves and appreciates Shakespeare's language, I can relate to what you are going through. I have been through nearly every stage imaginable as a practitioner of Shakespeare's work. I have been a terrified young actor with no idea about how to approach the text; I have understood the mechanics of performing verse, but desired a way to bring more of myself to the material in order to work with greater honesty and spontaneity. I have experienced the exhilaration that comes from performing in that zone where you become one with heightened text and act as freely as you would with contemporary material. My own transformative journey moved me to uncover ways to inspire, support, and activate other actors to deepen their relationships to Shakespeare and, ultimately, to engage audiences in vibrant performances of Shakespeare's plays.

The archaeology of performance: "unearthing Shakespeare"

As craftsmen of performance, I consider the work we do akin to the work of archaeologists: to dig beneath the surface and brush aside the superficial layers in order to reveal and understand the underlying foundation, the world in which we study. Archaeologists uncover clues, details that teach us how

xii Preface

to appreciate the past. They provide us with a wealth of information with which we can formulate a comprehensive understanding of a given period of time. Although we cannot unearth artifacts that demonstrate the sentient, shared, ephemeral experience of performance, we can transform the "fossils" that can be recovered into fuel for creative, communal, embodied performances of our own.

As archaeologists of performance we will excavate the material evidence that can teach us about Shakespeare's theatrical culture. We will research the context from which Shakespeare's plays emerge, consider the clues present within the text, and enter into a relationship with those elements in and through practice. We will create a three-dimensional embodiment of the text that springs from a historically informed, spatially influenced muse: Shakespeare's theatre and his theatrical culture.

When we work as archaeologists of performance we empower ourselves to examine the vast scope of evidence and decide for ourselves those elements that ignite our creativity. I won't prescribe to you a singular way of working, an absolute set of rules you must adhere to. I also won't presume to tell you that we know exactly how Shakespeare was first performed—we don't know that with any certainty. What I will do is highlight the practical performance elements that formulate our foundation—our archeological "finds"—so that you can interpret how those components can help you to formulate your own personal connection to Shakespeare's text. My goal is to empower you with the tools you'll need to excavate the bones of the material you're exploring.

Becoming empowered

I need to be honest with you: I didn't always love Shakespeare. I know that may seem shocking—blasphemous—but it is true. I wanted to love it. I felt as though I should love it. How could I be a serious actor if I didn't love it? As a teenager, though, I just couldn't find my way "in" to the text; it felt completely inaccessible to me. I enjoyed reading it out loud in class, but most of the time I really didn't know what the text meant. I washed it with emotion to the best of my ability and waited with my classmates for the teacher to help us translate and comprehend it all. I longed to understand it for myself, but I had absolutely no tools to bring me any closer to that understanding. So I continued to read aloud, to try and grasp the content for myself, but it seemed only to instigate bigger feelings of failure when I didn't seize immediately the complexities inherent within Shakespeare's text. And then I began to fear that, perhaps, I couldn't do it on my own. What was I supposed to do with all of that language?

When I began to approach Shakespeare as an actor, those insecurities reared their ugly heads and roared like a mythological beast. I was filled with fear: Do I understand it? How do I speak it? Can I memorize it perfectly? How can I apply my actor skills to this text? Will the audience understand it? Will the audience be as bored as I sometimes was in English class? How can I be a living human being behind all of this poetry? Will I be too "big"? Am I too American? Will I just fake my way through it? Am I an imposter? Will it all just sound really nice and mean nothing?

Am I enough?

At the beginning of my work with a new group of actors, I ask them to write down their own fears about performing Shakespeare and then I collect them. I gather up all of their fears, and they are nearly identical to the ones I faced. I read them aloud to the group and everyone laughs. They laugh because they recognize themselves in those confessions and they realize that they are not alone. There is nothing unique about feeling somewhat removed from speaking Shakespeare's verse. We live in a very different world, and we use language differently than Shakespeare did. Our theatres are completely different from his. Our actor training is different. In fact, there are far more differences between Shakespeare and us than there are similarities. At our core, Shakespeare resonates with us because his work captures something profoundly honest about human nature—and that similarity is absolutely thrilling to be immersed in.

Embodied performance

The methodology laid out in this book synthesizes the historical and theoretical concepts surrounding Shakespeare in performance into a systematic way of approaching Shakespeare's plays that is meaningful today. Through a deliberate series of training, we will locate within the body-instrument elements that increase our connections to the text, to other actors, and to our audience. This awakens in us the presence we desire and grounds our creative impulses in a historically rich playground. Through this training, actors will gain a sense of what the reconstruction of Shakespeare's theatre can teach us about performing Shakespeare elsewhere today. Embodied performance is inspired performance.

How this book works

This book is divided into two parts. Part I does two things: it contextualizes the history surrounding theatre-making and theatre-going over the course

xiv Preface

of Shakespeare's career, and it also introduces the theories that underlie the practice you will encounter in Part II. Part I is the skeletal foundation, your archaeological "finds." Part II focuses on studio practice: the nuts and bolts of creating and developing performances. The structure of this book follows the parallel to archaeology: first, we will excavate the details of the past and consider the implications of their meaning, and then we will allow that information to inspire our imaginations in performance.

Throughout this book I will refer to the actor as single-gendered male for two reasons: Shakespeare's company was comprised only of male actors, and, many other vocational titles are used universally across gender—an individual is a doctor, a writer, a painter, an engineer, a teacher, an officer, a director. There is no reason why the same single-gendered usage ought not to be applied to the title "actor." By referring to an actor with the corresponding male pronoun, I hope to simplify any comparison to Shakespeare's company, and hope that readers of all genders, including transgendered and gender fluid readers, will identify with the actor's process under investigation. I hope that in future editions of this book, we will have an agreed upon inclusive single person pronoun that encompasses everyone. At the moment "an actor" and the plural pronoun "they" remain challenging grammatically. If only we had Shakespeare to coin the term for us . . .

Although Part I (the foundation) leads directly to Part II (the practice), you can certainly jump into a specific part of the practice if you have immediate questions that need answers. You can conduct your own excavation of the material as you see fit. However, the background provided in Part I will enhance and contextualize your experience with Part II.

Dig in!

ACKNOWLEDGMENTS

I consider my approach to performance one that is informed historically, and rooted in the body's somatic and kinesthetic awareness. I have spent the last 30 years in acting studios: for many of those years, as a facilitator and leader, for many others as a participant. I continue to train as an actor, and I keep at the ready a list of master teachers with whom I'd like to study next. My work is a creative imagining of possibilities. When I reflect back on my Shakespeare fears, I recognize that I was afraid because I was forced to face the differences between the text and me and I didn't have a way to process those dissimilarities. In many ways, the friction between what I believed I was capable of and what I was actually doing felt like I was trying to fit the proverbial square peg in the round hole. First, you exhaust the immediate possibilities that are readily accessible, and then an altogether different strategy emerges: a completely different tactic is needed to make this intersection and integration possible. I stopped trying to make Shakespeare conform to fit me, and began to transform my way of working with Shakespeare to fit myself to it.

Stanislavski talks of the "magic if"—the thing that enables the actor to unlock the circumstances of the play. My approach to performing Shakespeare is like an all-encompassing "magic if"—the key to unlocking, or in our case, unearthing Shakespeare in performance is to ask this important question: If I perform differently than I have been trained to do, what might I discover? If I look more deeply into all of the elements that could have been available when these plays were performed originally, could I unearth a whole new way of working that makes these circumstances come alive?

xvi Acknowledgments

I have had some brilliant teachers. I have also had some not so brilliant teachers who have equally taught me how I approach the art and craft of teaching. I am undoubtedly influenced by the years of studio practice that I have engaged in—both by my instructors and my fellow explorers. I am incredibly grateful to Patsy Rodenburg, Kate Wilson, and Judylee Vivier for encouraging me to embrace how my voice lives throughout my body, and for helping to put me more in touch with my body-instrument. My voice is free, resonant, and lives within me on a daily basis because of the work we have done together. I am also especially grateful to Charlotte Fleck, for helping me to understand the absolute beauty of a well-placed vowel and a crisp, clear consonant.

The roots of my work with Shakespeare are in the First Folio approach, although I am not a staunch enthusiast of the method above all else. I am keenly interested in how modern editors have interfered with what is on the page for the same reason that I am keenly aware that our current regimes for actor training have often impeded our ability to engage with Shakespeare's text rather than facilitated that engagement. Christine Ozanne first opened my eyes at LAMDA, and her partner, Patrick Tucker and his protégée, John Basil, have influenced me greatly. I have gone on to refine my own definitions and ways of looking at the text, but their work, along with Neil Freeman's, inspired me to look more closely—particularly with regard to punctuation, capitalization, titles, and adjoining sounds. They have built upon the scholarship of Richard Flatter, whose work in the mid-twentieth century preceded theirs. They all have books of their own, and I encourage you to look to them if you'd like an in-depth examination of their methods.

Some of the brilliant Shakespeareans who have shaped my work immeasurably are John Barton, Rodney Cottier, the late Tony Church, and the dear Peter Thomson, who always made me promise that I would write simply, with the reader in mind and for the reader's benefit. His books are the greatest example of his ideology.

I am indebted to the University of Exeter Drama Department, especially to Christopher McCullough and Lesley Wade, my doctoral supervisors, and to Jane Milling, Jon Primrose, and Gayatri Simons for their support and encouragement. I am equally indebted to the Globe Education staff: to Patrick Spottiswoode, and especially to Alexandra Massey and Madeline Knights for their support.

Although I have not worked with her directly, I am incredibly grateful for the legacy of Cicely Berry's work, which I believe has—without a doubt—informed in one way or another nearly all of what we practice in the Shakespeare studio.

Acknowledgments **xvii**

Catherine Weidner left an indelible mark when she put me in the hot seat in an improvisatory exercise involving snippets of Shakespeare's text (which, I must confess, I don't fully remember) that inspired me to pair improvisation and iambic pentameter. Joseph Olivieri's "Iambic Fairytale" led me to explore this idea further.

I am grateful to John Cameron and Deborah Mayo for the foundation they laid with Sanford Meisner's work, and especially to Deb for her encouragement and friendship over the past 25 years.

I have a deep appreciation for my colleagues at LIU Post, especially to Cara Gargano, Maria Porter, Jon Fraser, and David Hugo for their enthusiastic support.

I would also like to thank Ben Piggott and Kate Edwards at Routledge for their guidance and for making this book into a material artifact in its own right.

Rose Burnett Bonczek has been my mentor and dear friend, whose wisdom has guided me for the past fifteen years. Her year-long study in improvisation changed how I function as an actor, director, and teacher. I'm certain that I am not only a better artist and teacher, but I am a better person for having known her.

Actor training has always been a practical pursuit. I could not have developed new modes of training without the foundation of intellectual and creative curiosity I've cultivated throughout my career as a theatre-maker. I have done my best to acknowledge when I have been influenced and inspired by the work of others. I can assure you that any lapses in acknowledgement are "something of my negligence, nothing of my purpose" (*Twelfth Night* 3.4.125).

While I am quoting *Twelfth Night*, I must also say, "I can no other answer make but thanks, / And thanks; and ever thanks" (3.3.14–15) to the actors with whom I've worked, who have helped me to refine my teaching and my methodology over the years I've been developing it. Thank you for your willingness to play, to explore with me, and to push me to be even more articulate and specific about why—and how—we work as we do.

A huge "ever thanks" to my family—the ultimate cheerleaders— (especially to RoseAnn and Robert Clarke, Maxine and Jonathan Ferencz, and Shari and James Kerr); you have listened to me prattle on about this book for far too long. Your encouragement means everything, and I am so grateful for your support.

Finally, to my husband, Thomas, and my children, Jolie and Owen: "I thank you, good my Lord, and thank you all" (*Richard III* 3.1.19). This book simply would not exist without your unwavering sustenance. "I humbly thank you" (*All's Well That Ends Well* 3.5.69) for providing the context within which I appreciate the magnitude of Shakespeare's depth.

PART I

Excavating the foundation

1

SHAKESPEARE'S THEATRICAL CULTURE

While a lot has been said about Shakespeare being "of all time," "universal," and "timeless," the plays he wrote are the particular products of a very specific cultural landscape and reflect a time when theatre-making was undergoing radical changes. This panorama of theatre practice bears little resemblance to those practices we engage today—even in those companies dedicated exclusively to performing Shakespeare's plays in repertory. Shakespeare wrote his plays within a very specific moment of theatre history, and understanding this context and the differences between his practices and ours will help us to better understand the plays and how to explore and engage them in performance.

Before we begin to look at the texts of Shakespeare's plays, I'd like to examine with you the practice of making theatre in Shakespeare's time so we can understand the circumstances from which his plays emerged. At the time Shakespeare was writing, there was a seismic shift underway in theatre practices. Theatre was not yet the commercial enterprise it would eventually become. Early in Shakespeare's career, theatre companies depended on the support of wealthy patrons who commissioned performances at court, and these companies bore the names of those patrons. Shakespeare's own company was first known as the Lord Chamberlain's Men. They would later become The King's Men when King James I became their patron in 1603. These patrons provided the money for companies to develop their plays, and once these plays had been performed privately for an invited audience at court, they toured to the provinces where they were performed for the public at inn yards and other public spaces, like bear baiting arenas: spaces that

4 Excavating the foundation

were not dedicated exclusively to theatre performances. It is believed that Shakespeare would have been exposed to such a troupe of traveling players in his hometown of Stratford, where his father, John, was at one time the town bailiff, and the person responsible for organizing such performances.

Comprised only of men, these companies contained a dozen actors: eight or nine company members (depending on the year), along with three or four additional "hired men" as needed. That core group of eight or nine adult players was diverse, and was able to cover the basic "stock" characters you might encounter in any of the plays. Like any trade at that time, company members went through an apprentice system, where experienced mentors trained them on the job. Since each "player" (they weren't called "actors" at that time) played a particular type of role, it is safe to assume that apprentices were trained for that particular "line" in the repertory, each assigned to a specific senior company member. In fact, the relationship between players and their apprentices was an important one: players often made specific mention of their apprentices in their wills (like bequeathing them the musical instruments and costumes they would need) and apprentices were even known to have married their mentors' widows (OK, that part may not necessarily be relevant to theatre practices, but talk about commitment to the ensemble!). That roster of boy apprentices would also have played the female parts.

Like all budding enterprises, consumer demand for theatre "products" must have been great enough to prompt the building of spaces dedicated *just* for performing theatre. This is a pretty radical idea when you think about it. Up until this point, plays were developed for patrons, not for the public. They were shared with the public after the fact, but is it possible that the public was so hungry for more that playing companies could justify setting up shop in London where they could collect entry fees—and create for themselves a new model for generating revenue? Yes, apparently, and what ensued was a significant development of Elizabethan playhouses where there once were none.

One of the most important of these playhouses is known simply as The Theatre (1576). Built by James Burbage and his brother-in-law John Brayne, The Theatre is often recognized as the first permanent theatre, although this isn't entirely accurate. John Brayne had an earlier, albeit less successful, venture called The Red Lion (1567), which is often overlooked, perhaps due to its lack of financial success, perhaps because it lacked a permanent company of players, or perhaps because it lacked a connection to a particular player by the name of William Shakespeare. Who knows? James Burbage had a son, Richard, who was a member of the Lord Chamberlain's Men, and the leading man for whom Shakespeare wrote the first Romeo, the first Hamlet, the first Othello, the first Lear.

Shakespeare's theatrical culture **5**

There was a little squabble with the landlord of The Theatre, as the story goes, and in the winter of 1599 The Theatre was dismantled; its timbers were pushed across the frozen Thames River and reassembled in Southwark as The Globe. Since this was a Burbage venture, and Richard Burbage was the leading man and a shareholder in a playing company, The Globe became the home of that company, The Lord Chamberlain's Men. The Lord Chamberlain (Henry Carey) was a member of the Queen's Privy Council and one of Queen Elizabeth's inner advisors, as well as her first cousin. The Privy Council was the governing body in charge of public entertainment, which helped to position The Lord Chamberlain's Men for prosperity. Oh, and of course, they had that great playwright, which also helped.

We don't know how Shakespeare came to London, or how he acquired the capital to become a shareholder in The Lord Chamberlain's Men. Playing companies operated on a profit-sharing system, where each shareholder received a portion of the earnings, and the shareholders of The Lord Chamberlain's Men became very wealthy as a result of their venture at The Globe. This is a turning point, really. Up until this point, theatre is connected strongly to religion—first emerging (in the Western world) in conjunction with religious festivals (in ancient Greece and Rome) and religious pageantry (in Europe). For the first time, theatre is no longer used to relay religious dogma, as it was in the mystery and morality plays of the Middle Ages, but it emerges as popular entertainment, and this is truly remarkable. With its own dedicated venues, theatre is no longer connected to any larger governing body, like the Church—hence the need for the Privy Council to keep things respectable. Individuals of all classes could pay their hard earned money to be entertained—nearly every day of the week. THIS is the environment for which Shakespeare wrote.

While court audiences are fairly homogenous, audiences in the public playhouse are not. This newfound diversity is reflected in this new (and rather lofty) name: The Globe, and we can imagine the playwright in residence is writing in a way that reflects this fact. Furthermore, as someone whose financial success is directly dependent on that of the company, we might also imagine him writing in a way that keeps audiences coming back for more.

The Lord Chamberlain's Men were not the only company in town, though; they shared a duopoly with The Admiral's Men (whose patron, Charles Howard, was a member of the same Privy Council alongside Henry Carey), whose residence was the nearby playhouse run by Philip Henslowe, The Rose (1587). Henslowe was a meticulous record keeper, and his surviving diary provides us with a great deal of what we know about the

6 Excavating the foundation

practices of the time. The Admiral's Men were known to have performed a repertoire of plays that we could only consider absolutely absurd today— it's a body of work so vast that it is "such stuff that dreams are made on" except those dreams are closer to practitioners' nightmares. On average, we are talking about a different play every day, six days a week (Sunday was reserved for Church). Six *plays* a week. Just to compare, the average union contract today allows for eight performances of *one* play in a week. There were, of course, more than six plays in their repertoire; some plays were new, some plays recur more frequently than others, but by our standards this schedule is nearly unimaginable.

Even if we consider those few theatre companies with resident ensembles that are dedicated to performing Shakespeare (and his contemporaries) today, a company of actors may perform a handful of different texts over an extended period of time; that handful certainly doesn't keep shifting throughout the commercial season, as it did for The Admiral's Men. It's clear that the Elizabethans couldn't have worked the way that we do, and in fact, they didn't. Today it's pretty standard practice (when working with scripted drama) for actors to receive their scripts and to do their own analysis and homework on that script before getting together with the director and ensemble of actors to rehearse. Usually, the rehearsal period will begin with a presentation by the creative team of directors and designers to introduce their vision of the play and the world of the production. This may also include dramaturgical presentations where historical and other research is shared, followed by "table work": a period of intense reading to analyze details in the text. After this, actors will begin to investigate the play in practice under the director's guidance.

Given the amount of time and money available, this practice can vary, but this framework is fairly standard whether it takes place over a short period of time (days or weeks) or a longer one. In the Elizabethan playing company *none* of these practices would have occurred. First of all, scribes wrote the plays out by hand and as we all know time is money, so there would not have been multiple copies of each text to distribute. Instead, there was *one* full copy of the text, which belonged to the company itself. Each actor would only receive his own "part" of the play, hence our modern use of the term "part" to indicate the role or character in a play. In fact, "role" is another term we borrow from our Elizabethan predecessors. When players received their part of the play, they did so in a scroll: a rolled up piece of parchment that contained only the players' lines and the cues that prompt them. So the scroll was a "roll" with the part on it, and over time the "roll" containing the part transformed into what we now understand to mean the "part" itself: the "role."

Second, "directors" and "designers" had not yet become a part of existing theatrical practices. The director is a relatively modern invention. The Elizabethans had an "actor-manager" who helped to oversee things, but certainly not in the same capacity that a modern director would today. Given what we know about the rotation of plays, there would not have been any sort of scenic or production "design" as we might expect today; that would not come into play until the Italian development of perspective painting, and even then it was limited to only three locations: one for tragedy, one for comedy, and another for pastoral. So even when we begin to get a visual sense of place, it was not a design specific to a particular production, but was a standardized location according to the dramaturgical genre of the play.

It's also important to consider that plays were performed outdoors, and at midday (2:00pm) so that there was sufficient sunlight; this was before the use of deliberate lighting so everyone in the playhouse would have shared the same light. So, we have a non-descript, or neutral, stage with no focused lighting, and no purpose-built sets or costumes. Actors would have worn their own contemporary clothes with specialty pieces, such as those reserved for nobility, when needed. Henslowe's diary lists a detailed catalogue of pieces that The Admiral's Men owned and used for such purposes. This differs from our current practices, where the transformation of space and attire is chosen deliberately to suit a particular artistic vision and interpretation of a given piece of work. Without a director, there was no unifying artistic vision to adhere to. Given the volume of plays in rotation, changing the space to accommodate each one would have been prohibitive for many reasons.

Instead, Shakespeare's theatre was representative of all Elizabethan playhouses at the time, and also of their material performance conditions. For many years, until the excavation of the actual archaeological remains in 1989, the closest thing we had to piece together what the inside of an Elizabethan theatre looked like was the 1595 illustration of The Swan by Johannes DeWitt (see Figure 1.1), a Dutch tourist who visited the playhouse and documented his experience.

Open to the elements, Elizabethan playhouses were polygonal in shape: not quite round, but close to it; The Globe is believed to have been a twenty-sided polygon. At the time, playhouses featured a "neutral" platform thrust stage that featured a tiring house at the back, with two to three doors or openings, a place where the musicians would have played, the Lords' Rooms (where the wealthiest could see and be seen), and a roof that covers part of the stage. The flag, which is flying overhead, would have flown on performance days and it would have been accompanied by a trumpeted announcement close to the start of performance.

8 Excavating the foundation

FIGURE 1.1 Johannes DeWitt, illustration of The Swan, 1595

You can see from DeWitt's illustration that performances were nearly in the round, with playgoers surrounding the stage at least three-quarters of the way around. There was a yard where audience members stood on three sides of the platform stage. Known as "groundlings," they would have paid a penny: the lowest price of admission, equivalent to the price of a loaf of bread. For a penny more, there were three galleries with bench seating. Since theatre was now a capitalist venture, cushions were available for an additional penny. The "Lords' Rooms" would have been the most exclusive seats in the house, and the most expensive at six pence. Playhouses held

Shakespeare's theatrical culture **9**

about 3,000 people for a performance, and with performances six of the seven days of the week, that was a lot of theatre, and a lot of money for the shareholders.

With an assembly that reached into the thousands, crammed with mobile bodies in the pit, in the shared light of day, just off a major thoroughfare for trade (the River Thames), you can imagine that the theatre was a bustling place to be. It was far more social than what we'd expect; it more closely resembled a sporting event than today's theatre. Business was conducted; tradesmen took an afternoon break from their trades to attend (perhaps to create a marketing presence and generate more business), and overall the theatre was a rowdy and dirty place to be (remember, this was before the advent of indoor plumbing and dedicated toilets). It could also be a dangerous place: ripe with cutpurses and with so many people in such close proximity, it could be downright dangerous to your health, which is why the theatres were closed during outbreaks of the plague in order to halt the spread of disease. Not quite what you think of when we go to the theatre today, is it? You wouldn't expect the person beside you today to arrive straight from work: the butcher covered in blood, the tanner with the product of his work with animal hides, the fishmonger stinking of fish. These were very different times, indeed.

How might these circumstances have affected the performances? Companies didn't operate as they do today, actors weren't trained as they are today, plays weren't rehearsed as they are today, and theatres didn't look the way they do today. Yet today, we hardly think about this at all. As an archaeologist compiles the evidence surrounding a culture in order to study and understand it, we must begin to do the same with the evidence of Shakespeare's theatrical culture in order for us to really understand *it*.

How might it have been different for an actor in an Elizabethan playing company? I've told you about the absence of a single director, but was there a period of rehearsal? Given the fact that they were working within the confines of natural daylight and that there were performances at midday, could there have been? There certainly wasn't a period of rehearsal that would look familiar to us, but we assume that there would have been some time set aside to organize the key things that would need to happen in the performance, the tricky bits of staging, like swordplay or combat. How would the actors have kept their focus on a different play each day, especially when there could have been long periods in between the rotation of the plays? Some plays were new, some old, but the time between those older plays could have varied between just a few days to weeks or months. That is a long time to hold the framework of a performance in your head, even for the most

10 Excavating the foundation

seasoned player. There would have been an outline for each play, a "platt," which hung backstage. The players could have checked the "platt" between scenes to see what came next in the story. Over time the "platt," which contained the key details of the play and the order of the play's events, came to be known as the "plot" we recognize today.

It wasn't simply a matter of finding time for the company to rehearse daily. An actor would have needed time to learn his part, to memorize his dialogue and cues for each play. From dawn to dusk an actor would have divided his time between learning and reviewing his lines, going over the outline of the platt, and of course, the "traffic of our stage": time spent in performance. How could they have done this on a regular basis?

It would probably be safe to assume that these performances were not as polished as our performances are today. How could they have been? When we examine the parameters under which the companies worked, and the sheer volume of material they covered, it would not have been possible. The players must have needed some help recalling all of those lines, particularly with newer or lesser produced plays. Indeed, they had the support of a "book-keeper" or "book-holder," who served the company like a modern stage manager: to prompt major mishaps and keep the platt on track and the lines relatively in order.

Another thing to consider is that a resident playwright like Shakespeare would have been writing his plays with his company of players in mind. Remember that players apprenticed for particular acting "lines" within the company. That means that they were accustomed to playing a particular function in the drama, with similar types of roles. We know that Shakespeare wrote for particular players because there is evidence of changes in his writing that coincide with changes in the acting company. For many years the Lord Chamberlain's Men had a particular clown or fool named Will Kemp (sometimes known as Kempe). Kemp was known to be very physical and may have improvised a lot, much to Shakespeare's dismay if we look at Hamlet's advice to the players, which states, "let those that play your clowns speak no more than is set down for them." Kemp left the company to dance his way across England (well, from London to Norwich) over nine days and write about it in his book, *Nine Days Wonder* (1600). Kemp was replaced by another player, Robert Armin, who was known to have been much more of an intellectual than Kemp was. Armin's fools were less physical than the ones that originated during Kemp's residency. We have fools like Feste in *Twelfth Night* and the fool in *King Lear* as evidence of this shift. So, even though there were many new plays, players would have been in the practice of playing similar roles and creating familiar characters, which might have helped them to adapt readily to new scripts.

It is also important to recognize that we understand the notion of "character" differently than the Elizabethans would have. While we see "character" as the embodiment of personality traits and circumstances given to us by the playwright, the Elizabethans would have understood "character" to mean the printed marks upon the page. Upon the reading of a letter in *Hamlet* (4.7), there is an exchange between Laertes and Claudius in which Laertes asks, "Know you the hand?" and Claudius replies, "Tis Hamlets character." "Character" is also understood to mean "to write" as a form of marking, as Orlando states in *As You Like It* (3.2), "O Rosalind! These trees shall be my books / And in their barks my thoughts I'll character." Over time, we have adopted the idea that a "character" is a particular person in the fiction, but character was originally the marks by which we recognize that particular person on stage. As a result, the character on the page (the playwright's marks) has transformed literally to mean the embodiment of those marks on the stage. This is pretty amazing, when you think about it.

For all of these reasons, it is clear that Elizabethan players didn't work as we do today, and that the performance conditions in the Elizabethan theatre were simply not like ours. Elizabethan audiences did not come to the theatre with the same expectations that we do today. Most of the expectations we bring to the theatre are twentieth-century inventions, and to be blunt, they just don't serve these plays. Many of our modern practices can be traced to that other great man of the theatre, Constantin Stanislavski. Stanislavski was an actor and director at the turn of the twentieth century who transformed the way we approach performance as a result of his work at the Moscow Art Theatre. Stanislavski aimed to codify the actor's process of developing a performance, and Western acting training has been forever transformed by his teachings. Stanislavski identified and published a systematic method from which actors could work. In the West, these titles are translated as *An Actor Prepares*, *Building a Character*, and *Creating a Role*, which both indicate and perpetuate the ways in which we have adopted the terminology of earlier theatre practices.

Stanislavski was working in a theatrical paradigm that was influenced greatly by psychological realism as well as by naturalism, two forms that focused on bringing "real life" qualities to the stage. Audiences were contained to one location in the theatre with a single vantage point, and receded into anonymity with the dimming of the house lights. This paralleled developments occurring earlier in fiction, with the rise of the novel. Unlike what was happening in the Elizabethan theatre where everyone's actions were on display and the event was communal in nature, in realistic and naturalistic theatre the theatrical event could unfold on stage and the audience could

12 Excavating the foundation

watch the fiction through an imaginary (fourth) wall as though they were voyeurs peeping into an already-existing world.

The demands of realism and naturalism pressured the performance paradigm, which greatly influenced Stanislavski's work and transformed the expectations of both actors and audiences. In *An Actor Prepares* Stanislavski advocates for a continuous line of communication on stage that remains exclusively between the actors, with only indirect contact with the audience. In turn, the absence of direct contact between the actors and the audience perpetuates the voyeuristic role the audience has adopted over time. Stanislavski's teachings, theatre architecture and design, and changes in dramaturgy have all contributed to this shift towards a style of performance that separates the players from the spectators.

In Shakespeare's day, these types of expectations would have been unheard of. Elizabethan audiences knew they were watching players; there was no sense that the fiction was "real," or happening in a "real" place, but the "reality" created on stage depended fully on the audience's participation and agreement. And *this* is one of the biggest shifts for us to consider, especially since today we are accustomed to viewing the theatre from *outside* the world of the fiction as opposed to *inside* it, as an active participant. When audiences come to the theatre today, they expect the world of the play to have been considered deeply, rehearsed thoroughly, and that the play will unfold before them as a completed entity as they watch silently in the dark. The prologue to *Henry V* shows us how the expectations in the Elizabethan playhouse differ clearly from what we expect in the theatre today. Shakespeare's players depended on their audience to help tell the story—and we should be prepared to do the same.

Let's read this prologue with our attention focused on what it can tell us about Shakespeare's theatre.

Chorus

O for a Muse of fire, that would ascend

The brightest Heaven of Invention:

A Kingdom for a Stage, Princes to Act,

And Monarchs to behold the swelling Scene.

Then should the Warlike Harry, like himself,

Assume the Port of Mars, and at his heels

(Leash'd in like Hounds) should Famine, Sword and Fire

Crouch for employment. But pardon, Gentles all

Shakespeare's theatrical culture **13**

The flat unraised Spirits that hath dared,
On this unworthy Scaffold to bring forth
So great an Object. Can this Cock-Pit hold
The vasty fields of France? Or may we cram
Within this Wooden O, the very Casques
That did affright the Air at Agincourt?
O, pardon: since a crooked Figure may
Attest in little place a Million,
And let us, Ciphers to this great Accompt,
On your imaginary Forces work.
Suppose within the Girdle of these Walls
Are now confin'd two mighty Monarchies,
Whose high up-reared, and abutting Fronts,
The perilous narrow Ocean parts asunder:
Piece out our imperfections with your thoughts:
Into a thousand parts divide one Man,
And make imaginary Puissance.
Think when we talk of Horses, that you see them
Printing their proud Hoofs i' th' receiving Earth:
For 'tis your thoughts that now must deck our Kings,
Carry them here and there: jumping o'er Times;
Turning th' accomplishment of many years
Into an Hour-glass: for the which supply,
Admit me Chorus to this History;
Who Prologue-like, your humble patience pray,
Gently to hear, kindly to judge, our Play.
Exit

The Chorus lays out both the agreement and the relationship both parties must undertake in order for the event to succeed. He speaks honestly to the audience, without any pretense of a predetermined circumstance. The Chorus begs the audience's pardon (twice), entreats them to "suppose," to "piece out," to "think" and, finally, implores them to "gently . . . hear" and "kindly . . . judge, our Play." That is a lot of action required from the

14 Excavating the foundation

audience. In no way does this compare to voyeuristic viewing through an imaginary wall, does it?

We should keep in mind that when this was first performed the player entered the neutral playing space dressed in contemporary clothing, and spoke directly to his audience. In this prologue, the Chorus basically says, "O, I wish I had the greatest muse ever so I could make something really amazing happen here." What I find really interesting is that when he lays out what he'd like the muse to transform, he does it in a very deliberate way: he'd turn the stage into a kingdom, players into princes to act out the story, and monarchs to watch it all unfold. He's given the audience the most important position of status in the hierarchy: monarchs are even higher than princes, and those monarchs rule kingdoms. He's just told the audience that they are the most important component in the telling of the story. This is remarkable! He continues to outline the story he'd like to tell the audience, and then apologizes in advance for his shortcomings. He asks the audience: Can we actually do these things? Can we make this story come alive on this stage? And then he is so bold as to say "let us . . . on your imaginary forces work": let us work on your imagination! He says, "imagine this . . . " until he has to stop and be honest with his collaborators—the audience—and he is very specific with them. He instructs them to "piece out" or to make whole "our imperfections *with your thoughts*." What? The audience has to use their imaginations for the whole thing to work? They have to use their own minds to make the fiction happen. In that playhouse there is no division between the audience and the fiction, and this can be groundbreaking to your practice as a modern theatre-maker (as we'll soon examine). The Chorus even gives examples of how the audience should execute the task; the Chorus instructs them to think when we talk about something, that you can actually see it happening, because it is your thoughts that will make it so. The player essentially says to the audience, "together we can make this really cool thing happen, but if you're not on board with me then you'll just have to forgive me because this isn't really going to work, it's going to be pretty lame."

This is very different from a theatre where the actor expects the audience's quiet attention and hopes for a demonstration of their praise and gratitude at designated (appropriate) times. To a certain extent, the performance paradigm today demands that the audience behave as though they are not present at all: remain silent, unwrap your candies in advance, don't shift in your seat, silence your mobile phone (okay, even I'm completely on board with that one), and don't interrupt the actor's world (or anyone else's experience of it) by letting your presence be known. In other words: just behave as though you're not even there! I'm oversimplifying these parameters, obviously, but in truth, today's actors are more likely to be trained to disregard the audience than they are to engage them directly. This is reinforced by that twentieth-century "fourth wall" paradigm—where the audience is not supposed to be there—a paradigm that in the second half of the twentieth century was influenced greatly by film: a medium where audiences view performances only once they are completely orchestrated.

In the twenty-first century, the tradition (in the Western world) cultivates the individual over the collective. Whereas the performance paradigm in Shakespeare's theatre involved a one-room space and collective engagement, after the twentieth century, theatre was defined primarily as a two-room space: one for the performer and one for spectator. When we think about the proscenium arch stage, which has a frame around the playing space and seats for the audience in front of the stage that ripple out in rows away from that frame, we see how the event is about the individual. We have an individual (the director) who defines the production concept, an individual (the actor) who is responsible for creating a performance that is presented intact to a group of individuals (the audience) who observe the event without necessarily interacting with each other or anyone else in the room. This is slowly beginning to change, and it must change, particularly for Shakespeare.

2

EXAMINING THE GLOBE

Now that we've had a chance to look at some of the differences between theatre making during Shakespeare's time and making theatre today, let's look more specifically at Shakespeare's Globe and what we can learn from its unique properties. Throughout this chapter, I will introduce you to some key elements that help to make Shakespeare's Globe what it is: a playground for performance possibilities. I won't pretend to tell you, "this is how it was done" because we don't really know what that "how" is—at best, we can only speculate what it *might* have been. What I will do is share with you some things that I think we can take away from Shakespeare's Globe as an example of the type of space for which Shakespeare wrote, and relay that into playable possibilities that help connect you and your audiences to Shakespeare today, regardless of where you perform.

The first time I encountered Shakespeare's Globe, I was awestruck: truly awestruck. I had never seen a theatre like it. I grew up in the Boroughs of New York City, and I'd certainly seen my share of incredibly beautiful theatres on Broadway—perhaps some of the finest in the United States—theatres that typify twentieth-century theatre design. Many of these share the same properties of the twentieth-century theatres I encountered in the West End when I trained as an actor in London: incredibly beautiful spaces that were often lavish, highly ornate, and able to be transformed to accommodate the needs of a given production. That ornamentation decorated the whole of the interior in front of the footlights (where there were footlights) or draped curtains (where there were curtains). The stage space, like a cinema screen awaiting projection, was blank: devoid of decoration and naked as a blank

Examining the Globe **17**

canvas. It was as "neutral" as neutral can be, and this is pretty standard for Western theatres.

We equate this image with "theatre"; it is so common it is our default visualization. When I begin working with a group of actors I ask them to visualize themselves performing Shakespeare on stage, and to draw a picture of that visualization. They need not have any particular talent as an illustrator; stick figures are perfectly welcome. When they've finished, I ask them to share their images with the group. Inevitably, the images share this common theme: there is an actor-figure on a stage (very often with either footlights or curtains—or both!) with audience neatly lined in one central location moving away from the stage. In nearly ten years of doing this exercise there have been numerous invocations of this scene, but the only time I haven't seen this default paradigm of "theatre" is when the actor has only drawn a human figure with no context. Every time that context has been included, this is how it's looked. Right after we talk about the shared qualities present in their images, I show them a portfolio of photographs from Shakespeare's Globe.

When I first entered the Globe, even back in 1998 before the ornamentation was as extensive as it is today, I felt as though the space was an unavoidable part of the performance itself. If post-Stanislavski über-realism taught me that as an audience member I was to forget I was in a theatre and that playmaking was underway, that I was to be silent, undetectable, unaccountable, and anonymous then a completely different set of rules would have to apply at Shakespeare's Globe—and they do. Shakespeare's Globe reminds you that you are in a theatre, but that doesn't mean that you won't get completely immersed in the storytelling or feel an integral part of that world. The Globe celebrates playmaking, and the theatre confronts you with your lack of anonymity. It is extraordinary in the most literal sense of the word.

Ornamentation, meta-theatricality, and the microcosm within the macrocosm

At Shakespeare's Globe you'll notice that the stage space is decorated extensively. Due to the repertory system employed by Elizabethan theatre companies, we know that the stage space would have remained the same regardless of which play was to be performed. Aside from the Globe (and other reconstructive stages like the Blackfriars Playhouse in Stanton, Virgina and the indoor Wanamaker Playhouse in the Shakespeare's Globe complex), our stage spaces diametrically oppose this idea: they lack ornamentation so that the production design can be built into the space, and transform it accordingly. This is what we consider today as "neutral": it is impartial enough to accommodate multiple transformations.

18 Excavating the foundation

The Elizabethans would have thought of "neutral" in a very different way: the stage would have drawn the spectators' attention by signaling it was not the same as the space for audience, yet it could transform to the needs of the text purely through the audience's imagination. We think our theatre spaces are "neutral" because they are empty and therefore, are able to be filled; they would have considered theirs "neutral" because their ornamentation did not indicate a particular place. These are two very different ideas.

This ornamentation is incredibly important; aside from framing the space as a microcosm within a macrocosm (which I'll get to in just a moment) it can be seen as meta-theatrical as well as meta-historical. I consider the space meta-theatrical because, unlike modern theatres that encourage us to forget we are watching actors on stage, the Globe seems to scream, "Look! There is a stage here! It's the prettiest part of the space!" The beauty of its ornamentation helps to focus our attention there without the use of lighting design. As a result, the stage is always present in our awareness: we cannot lose sight of how special that space appears, nor how unlike the rest of the space it is. The beauty of the stage space punctuates the entire theatre; it constantly frames what happens there as part of a theatrical event.

The open air also reinforces the space's meta-theatricality. In shared daylight, the actors can see you—and you can see them. Even in the evening, you can see each other, and when you look at those actors on stage you can see other people looking at them as well. There is community instead of anonymity. As an audience member you locate yourself as part of a shared event, and this speaks to the meta-theatricality as well. I consider it meta-historical because these same differences constantly reinforce the fact that theatre design has changed from Shakespeare's time to ours.

Let's excavate further so we can get into the nitty-gritty of these differences.

As you can see from Figure 2.1, we have a platform stage that juts out, with three doorways in the upstage area, flanked by ten columns, along with the two "Pillars of Hercules" (those big columns in the downstage area). There is a second-story balcony where the Lord's rooms are, and where musicians are often positioned. Aside from the floor, the stage space is painted to resemble marble and features gold gilt. You'll notice that the space is painted with muses—in the early days before the boxes adjacent to the stage were decorated, muses decorated the posts in the audience space as well. Perhaps one of the biggest things you'll notice is that the roof over the stage is painted quite ornately with celestial, mythological, and astrological images.

Here is a closer look:

This roof is known as the Heavens (see Figure 2.2). It contains the sun, the moon, and the stars as well as representations of signs from the zodiac.

FIGURE 2.1 Stage at Shakespeare's Globe

FIGURE 2.2 Heavens at Shakespeare's Globe

20 Excavating the foundation

If you look closely, you will see a trap door where players can descend from the Heavens. We don't find this device so much in Shakespeare, but it would have been an important function for earlier plays and so it was considered a vital part of the theatre's design.

The stars come into play a lot in Shakespeare: in *Julius Caesar* (1.2) we learn that "The fault, dear Brutus, is not in the stars, / But in ourselves, that we are underlings." In the prologue to *Romeo and Juliet* we hear that "A pair of star-cross'd lovers take their life," and Beatrice explains in *Much Ado About Nothing* (2.1) that "there was a star danced, and under that was I born." The influence of the stars is great, and it lends itself to the personification of Shakespeare's world that we'll explore in the next chapter. What is unique here, and incredibly useful to us as modern practitioners, is that just as the Elizabethans stood under an open sky, the "heavens," so did the actors on stage.

In this way, the world on stage echoes the surrounding world; it is a microcosm within the macrocosm: Shakespeare's world at Shakespeare's Globe. Even further, *Hell* would have resided beneath the stage, accessible via a trap door in the stage floor. Flanked by *Heaven* and *Hell*, the world on stage was a complete representation of the world at large. This opens us up to a whole array of performance possibilities that we simply would not encounter in a blank box: we have the potential to create highly personalized connections to Shakespeare's language in ways that we wouldn't have thought of previously.

One of my favorite examples (I've used it before in my article, "Voice on the Globe Stage: An Actor's Observations, a Teacher's Recommendations") comes from *Romeo and Juliet*. Let's consider how this microcosm manifests in the "balcony scene" (2.2).

In this soliloquy Romeo says:

> It is my lady, O, it is my love!
>
> O, that she knew she were!
>
> She speaks yet she says nothing: what of that?
>
> Her eye discourses; I will answer it.
>
> I am too bold, 'tis not to me she speaks:
>
> **Two of the fairest stars in all the heaven,**
>
> Having some business, do entreat her eyes
>
> To twinkle in their spheres till they return.
>
> What if her eyes were there, they in her head?
>
> The brightness of her cheek would shame those stars,

As daylight doth a lamp; her eyes in heaven
Would through the airy region stream so bright
That birds would sing and think it were not night.
See, how she leans her cheek upon her hand!
O, that I were a glove upon that hand,
That I might touch that cheek!

Beginning with the line I've made bold, actors can begin to fall into the "trap" of the poetry: there are gorgeous metaphors that appear to Romeo, seemingly out of nowhere. I'd like to suggest that this metaphor between Juliet's eyes and the stars may not be plucked from the proverbial "thin air," which often appears to be the case in a different setting. At the Globe in Shakespeare's day and at Shakespeare's Globe today, the actor playing Romeo would have been standing directly under a blanket of stars, the painted *Heavens*. Perhaps he gets his inspiration from the visual image overhead. He sees the stars, he sees his fellow actor's eyes, and in the moment he can coin the metaphor. In some ways it is like $2 + 2 = 4$. The actor can think on his feet "I see this; I see that. What if *this* happened?" When we consider what the Globe reveals to us, there is something very concrete about the substitution that is made, and this takes the actor away from metaphorical supposition and places actual realizations that can be scaffolded into the analysis of the speech.

Outside of Shakespeare's Globe, the audience may never see the image the actor has transferred to his mind's eye, but they certainly observe the clarity behind the actor's thought process—and *this* is what empowered performance is all about. When you work in this way, you gain ownership and a deep understanding of your text and craft, while the audience observes dynamic performance choices. It's a win-win situation. Visualizing what the possibilities for performance are in the space for which Shakespeare wrote unleashes a world of possibilities in alternate spaces. I'll share my little mantra with you: "What would Burbage do?"—I should fine-tune this to "What could Burbage have done if spontaneity in performance was as prized as it is today?" but that doesn't roll off the tongue as easily, does it? (Come to think of it, given the Elizabethan repertory schedule, there may have been quite a bit more "spontaneity" than we realize, but I digress.)

I will return to this question, "What would Burbage do?" Inevitably, my mantra actually triggers a much more important question: "What creative choices can *I* make with the knowledge I have?" When I'm working my creativity is fueled by the relationship between that original space and the text; I'm empowered in the space between those two. I'm not thinking about

22 Excavating the foundation

the void of a black box. I'm not creatively inspired within Shakespeare's text by imagining performance conditions that have nothing to do with that text. I nearly always have to work under those conditions, but even when I do, I hold the possibilities the Globe offers me within.

Staging clues, staging discoveries, staging status

In addition to serving as a microcosm, the stage at Shakespeare's Globe has distinct spatial qualities that can also help to fuel your performance elsewhere. First of all, there are the two massive "Pillars of Hercules" and they are certainly problematic to work around, I won't lie. They can easily become a pseudo-Proscenium arch-like frame, which would be fine in that type of stage where the audience is only in one place, but it is a serious problem in the Elizabethan-style thrust where they block much of the audience. Given the way that the audience surrounds the action, fluidity of movement, particularly moving in and among the pillars, is a useful solution. You can think of moving between the pillars in the shape of infinity ("∞"). This kind of "sweeping" movement creates dynamic energy on stage, and allows the audience to engage with the actors by continually orienting them within different visual perspectives. Additionally, keeping the actors on a diagonal plane, rather than a horizontal one allows the audience to see more of them.

Maintaining diagonal positioning between partners also creates a greater degree of intimacy between the actors and the audience. Psychologically, the audience wants to live in the space *between* the on-stage action, and between the actors. When the actors place themselves in parallel positions to each other they close off, or narrow, the space that the audience can inhabit. Staggering creates a depth of vision that also helps to engage the body's three-dimensionality and heighten its kinesthetic awareness. Creating intimacy at a long diagonal suspends the energy between the partners and activates that "space-between"; this is true in any architectural configuration and the Globe reinforces its value.

The stage's distinctive layout invites status dynamics that can be manipulated purposely based on stage movement. To begin with, the four corners of the stage place you in the most visible positions, so moving to one of those positions can be quite powerful. However, those positions can say very different things to the audience. When you stand in the "upstage" area, near the three doorways and close to the smaller columns, you appear quite large in relation to them. As a result, these are positions of very high status, and you can incorporate moving into one of these positions as a means of raising your status. When you move into the "downstage" area, the stage proportions change drastically. The two "Pillars of Hercules" reduce your size; you appear visually smaller. This leads to a greater vulnerability, a lowering of status. You are also changing your proximity to be exposed to a larger number of audience members and this leads to gorgeous moments of intimacy and honesty in your interaction with them.

As I said earlier with regard to the Heavens, the audience (or even your fellow actors or your director) may not know the motivation, the visualization, behind your change of position on stage, but the clarity embedded in your choices speaks volumes. A downstage cross may fuel your opportunity to be intimate with your audience: to confess, to solicit, or to entreat them. An upstage cross makes you larger than you'd been; you might appear to be the biggest person on stage; from here you can demand, threaten, or proclaim.

Figure 2.3 gives an excellent glimpse of the depth perception between the up and downstage pillars, as it appears from close to the stage. Even at a distance you can see how a person's size can change drastically based on where the body is positioned on the stage—look back at the head-on image of the stage and you can visualize how this is so. This type of informed movement becomes part of the creative inspiration you have at your disposal as you work with these texts.

FIGURE 2.3 Depth of stage perspective, Shakespeare's Globe

24 Excavating the foundation

The actor/audience relationship: casting the audience

In the shared light of Shakespeare's theatre, we find shared experience. The community that develops between actor and audience—and within the audience—encourages inclusion; it expands to include the world of the play in addition to the realm of the playhouse. The audience surpasses its modern role as observer of the fiction and transforms into a *component* of that fictional world. As a component of the fictional world the audience can serve different functions, depending on the needs of the play and the needs of the actor/character. We can categorize the audience in up to three different roles: confidante, co-conspirator, or mirror.

Casting the audience: the confidante

As *confidante* the audience is privy to the character's innermost thoughts. The confidante is a supportive presence, a witness with whom the actor/character shares his/her thoughts, hopes, and fears. You'll notice that I have started using the distinction "actor/character"—now that we've established the shared experience of the one-room playhouse, we need to acknowledge that theatre-making in this paradigm includes both the playhouse and the play. So when we see the character on stage (I'll discuss this idea at length in Chapter 4) we also see the player, for we are continually located in a theatre as we see everyone that shares our experience. The audience/confidante bears witness to the machinations of the play, and is the support the actor/character needs as he/she moves through the fictional world.

The actor/character *confides* in the audience/confidante without any expectation of a reply. They may indeed receive a reply, but there is no prompt for a reply at the heart of this exchange. A thought must be shared, and the speaker needs the audience to receive it, to allow it to be spoken; they need a listener. When the audience is cast in the role of confidante, confessions—or declarations—can either come quickly, as in the case of an aside, or through a lengthy revelation, such as a soliloquy. In this case, asides can either be verbal or nonverbal, within the text or without it. Once you acknowledge that in a theatre like this the line between fiction and reality is blurred, you uncover a whole world of possibilities that promote a shared experience with everyone in the space. This shift celebrates the theatricality at play and the communal experience of all in the encounter. Consequently, this expansion helps the audience remain invested in the event and in the world of the play. When the actor/character engages with the audience/confidante there is an outlet for the character that provides a sense of release, and that relief helps to shape the fiction.

To illustrate, here is a speech from *Measure for Measure* (2.4), which exemplifies the audience-as-confidante. Just prior to this soliloquy, Isabella has visited the Deputy, Angelo, to plead for her brother's life. Her brother has been sentenced to death for fornication (evidenced by his pregnant fiancée). Angelo has given Isabella, a novice nun, an ultimatum: he will spare her brother's life if she agrees to have sex with him. Yes, the corruption and hypocrisy is deliciously ripe, and I have simplified this complex plot in order not to stray too far from my point. When Isabella threatens to expose him and his corruption, Angelo (one of the greatest "villains" Shakespeare ever wrote) tells her in no uncertain terms, "Say what you can: my false o'erweighs your true." When Angelo exits, Isabella is left alone on stage to speak this text:

Isabella

To whom should I complain? Did I tell this,

Who would believe me? O perilous mouths,

That bear in them one and the self-same tongue,

Either of condemnation or approof;

Bidding the law make court'sy to their will:

Hooking both right and wrong to the appetite,

To follow as it draws! I'll to my brother:

Though he hath fallen by prompture of the blood,

Yet hath he in him such a mind of honour.

That, had he twenty heads to tender down

On twenty bloody blocks, he'ld yield them up,

Before his sister should her body stoop

To such abhorr'd pollution.

Then, Isabel, live chaste, and, brother, die:

More than our brother is our chastity.

I'll tell him yet of Angelo's request,

And fit his mind to death, for his soul's rest.

I love this example for so many reasons: first of all, it shows us how the audience is a part of the fiction; they are witnesses to the action. When Isabella asks, "To whom should I complain?" she asks the audience because she knows that they have just played the bystanders to Angelo's corrupt demands; she is aware of their presence. Second, although Isabella asks questions of the audience, she does so in order to formulate a plan, not because she expects answers to her questions. She needs to speak in order to think, and the audience is her sounding board. Many characters in the modern theatre (starting with Anton

26 Excavating the foundation

Chekhov's work) think and *then* speak, but in Shakespeare we see characters that think *as* they speak. Isabella confesses her thoughts to the audience in order to process and devise a plan for action. We'll look more closely at line structure in Chapter 3, but if you're wondering how we can tell that Isabella needs an outlet and isn't looking for a reply, it's because her questions come in the middle of the verse line. Her next thought is already present; she isn't asking because she expects an answer. Isabella needs the release that comes from speaking to her *confidantes* because that integral exchange between her and the audience/confidante enables her to reach her conclusion, which shapes the whole rest of the play: the final two lines of text.

> I'll tell him yet of Angelo's request,
>
> And fit his mind to death, for his soul's rest.

By the end of the speech, Isabella knows that she must explain the situation to her brother, Claudio, and prepare him for death.

Casting the audience: the co-conspirator

When the audience moves beyond the role of witness and becomes embroiled in the fiction they become a *co-conspirator*. In this role, the audience is entangled in the action; the actor/character elevates the status of their relationship to include an implied response from the audience/co-conspirator in return.

As co-conspirator, the audience is embedded in the action; they are implicated in some way within the play's text. Here, the actor/character can either elicit a response from the audience, can respond to the audience's unspoken thoughts or inherent questions, or can entangle the audience into the dramatic plot. As is the case with confidantes, co-conspirators are addressed either through soliloquies or through the use of asides. Unlike confidantes, who bear witness to the intimate release of the actor/character without the expectation of an articulated response, co-conspirators are in on the action. When the audience is a co-conspirator, the character speaks as though he is in dialogue with the audience. The character may even anticipate their co-conspirator's (unspoken) response. This connection through dialogue elevates the audience from the role of spectator to a role within the world of the fiction, to the play itself.

Once the audience is entangled in the mechanics of the plot, their involvement and investment shifts. In both instances, whether an actor/character is eliciting an audience response or responding to their unspoken thoughts, the relationship between the audience and the play is energized and engaged. Let's look at two different examples where the audience plays the role of co-conspirator. In the first one we'll look at eliciting a response. This example comes from *Richard III* (1.2). Here, Richard has managed to turn Lady Anne's contempt not only to forgiveness, but to endearment, to love. The scene begins with Lady Anne following the corpse of her murdered father-in-law, King Henry VI. Still in mourning over her husband, Edward's, death, she is confronted by their murderer, Richard. She curses him, spits on him, and rails at him until he manages, quite extraordinarily, to turn all of her passion around. Richard both elicits an audience response and also implicates them as he outlines his future plans.

Richard

Was ever woman in this humour woo'd?

Was ever woman in this humour won?

I'll have her; but I will not keep her long.

What! I, that kill'd her husband and his father,

To take her in her heart's extremest hate,

With curses in her mouth, tears in her eyes,

The bleeding witness of her hatred by;

Having God, her conscience, and these bars against me,

And I nothing to back my suit at all,

But the plain devil and dissembling looks,

And yet to win her, all the world to nothing!

Ha!

Hath she forgot already that brave prince,

Edward, her lord, whom I, some three months since,

Stabb'd in my angry mood at Tewksbury?

A sweeter and a lovelier gentleman,

Framed in the prodigality of nature,

Young, valiant, wise, and, no doubt, right royal,

The spacious world cannot again afford

And will she yet debase her eyes on me,

That cropp'd the golden prime of this sweet prince,

And made her widow to a woful bed?

On me, whose all not equals Edward's moiety?

28 Excavating the foundation

> On me, that halt and am unshapen thus?
>
> My dukedom to a beggarly denier,
>
> I do mistake my person all this while:
>
> Upon my life, she finds, although I cannot,
>
> Myself to be a marvellous proper man.
>
> I'll be at charges for a looking-glass,
>
> And entertain some score or two of tailors,
>
> To study fashions to adorn my body:
>
> Since I am crept in favour with myself,
>
> Will maintain it with some little cost.
>
> But first I'll turn yon fellow in his grave;
>
> And then return lamenting to my love.
>
> Shine out, fair sun, till I have bought a glass,
>
> That I may see my shadow as I pass.

The first three lines of this speech illustrate beautifully this category of co-conspirator. When Richard asks, "Was ever woman in this humour woo'd?" he seeks confirmation from the audience. It's as though we can imagine them shouting back at him, "No way!" Richard prompts them again, "Was ever woman in this humour won?" The expectation is that his co-conspirators will reply, "Definitely not!" And then he embroils them further because he shares his plans, and in doing so, he makes the audience his accomplices because he tells them, "I'll have her; but I will not keep her long." The audience learns that he plans to kill her, too!

We'll get into this further when we're looking specifically at the textual clues that lead to empowered performance, but you may have already noticed that unlike Isabella's questions, Richard's fill the entire line of verse. This signals that he is not onto the next thought already but is poised for his co-conspirator's response. Later on in the speech, as he questions them further with another set of questions that capitalize on their parallel construction, he implores, "On me, whose all not equals Edward's moiety?" followed by "On me, that halt and am unshapen thus?" Just as in the beginning of his speech, we have a pair of lines that prompt the audience to respond with some form of, "Unbelievable!" (Which it is!)

The next example is from *The Taming of the Shrew*. In this excerpt, we have an example of inherent dialogue between the actor/character and the audience/co-conspirator. In this example we'll see how an actor/character can be one

Examining the Globe **29**

step ahead of his audience, and this text will show us how the co-conspirator is in on the action. This is different from what happens in Richard's text, which implicates the co-conspirators by making them privy to the orchestration of plot devices. In this example, the assumption is that the audience is already on board and within the world of the play beyond the role of bystander. It is as though the character is saying to his co-conspirators, "We're in this together. I know you're with me. In fact, I already know what you're thinking; I'm one step ahead of you." Let's look at *The Taming of the Shrew* (2.1).

In this scene Petruchio has just arrived at Batista's house, intent on marrying his (heretofore) un-marriable daughter, Katherine, a notorious shrew. Petruchio is both interested in the riches that will accompany Kate to the marriage as well as intrigued by the challenge of wrangling with Kate's shrewishness. He has also considered how he will reap the benefits and rewards of his success. At this point in the scene, Batista has asked Petruchio if he should send his daughter out to meet him. Petruchio replies,

Petruchio

I pray you do. I will attend her here,

And woo her with some spirit when she comes.

Say that she rail; why then I'll tell her plain

She sings as sweetly as a nightingale:

Say that she frown, I'll say she looks as clear

As morning roses newly wash'd with dew:

Say she be mute and will not speak a word;

Then I'll commend her volubility,

And say she uttereth piercing eloquence:

If she do bid me pack, I'll give her thanks,

As though she bid me stay by her a week:

If she deny to wed, I'll crave the day

When I shall ask the banns and when be married.

But here she comes; and now, Petruchio, speak.

This soliloquy also follows the classic structure of "if *this*, then *that*"—in this case, Petruchio has already worked out all of his intended responses to Katherine's shrewish behavior. The audience here is the co-conspirator because Petruchio's text illustrates how he responds to what he imagines his co-consipirators will say in order to prepare him for his impending

30 Excavating the foundation

meeting. When he begins, he tells his co-conspirators "this is what I'm going to do": "I will attend her here, / And woo her with some spirit when she comes." Because he knows that he is among his co-conspirators and that they are in on this plan with him, he is already a step ahead of their warning that Katherine will rail at him. "Say that she rail; why then I'll tell her plain / She sings as sweetly as a nightingale:"

The structure of the speech shows how Petruchio is one step ahead of his co-conspirators. Petruchio moves through the speech as though he is responding to the unspoken heckling from his audience. You can almost imagine that the groundlings at the Globe could have been shouting out to him, "She's going to rail at you!" "She's going to frown!" "She'll be mute!" "She'll tell you to pack your bags! Hit the road!" "She'll never marry you!" You can't be a step ahead of someone who isn't a part of your world, a part of your journey. Petruchio's own unspoken preemptive response is, " I know what you're going to say!" "I know what you're thinking," "yes, I know!" or "I've got it covered." The actor/character ultimately informs his audience/co-conspirators "I have got this all worked out—I'm totally in control here, and you're going to enjoy every moment." The conspiratorial relationship is deepened and the audience's investment is heightened when they are embedded so directly into the world of the play.

One of the delights that comes with casting the audience in either the role of confidante or of co-conspirator is that once they become personally involved in the world of the play and the process of playmaking, there is a brave new world of communication that becomes available and accessible. Due to the transparent nature of theatre in Shakespeare's paradigm, communication transpires on multiple levels between those who share the theatrical experience. We are empowered by the fluidity and expanse between the world of the play and the world of the spectator. As the lines blur between those two worlds, practitioners are empowered by these theatrical possibilities that enable them to engage deeply with both the text and also their audience. In turn, audience members become a greater part of the storytelling. Before I define and discuss how the audience plays the role of mirror, I'd like to expand further on another performance possibility that arises when we examine what we can learn from Shakespeare's theatre.

When the audience is integrated into the world of the play and immersed in the theatrical experience, they can become privy to new information: both textual and sub-textual. As a confidante or a co-conspirator, the audience reads the actor/character through a multi-faceted lens. Understanding this notion enables the actor to engage it purposely, and at will. Throughout Shakespeare's canon, there are characters that grapple with what I call *the mask of the divided self*: a conflict between their public and private personas.

The mask of the divided self

Shakespeare's characters often wear masks. Sometimes those masks may have outward signs—such as the masks many of Shakespeare's women wear when disguised as young boys, but often those "masks" are worn without any outward manifestation at all. The fluidity within the fiction that we can derive from Shakespeare's Globe—where everyone shares the light of day, where all can see and be seen, expands the possibilities for play. With the mask of the divided self, characters maintain two different (often conflicting) personas: the public and the private self.

The public self maintains decorum and exhibits socially acceptable behavior. Other characters within the world of the fiction interact with the public self. The private self is the raw essence of the character's needs and desires, the persona that dwells beneath the mask of public restraint. The audience witnesses both worlds: the public and the private. With a confidante or co-conspirator present, the actor/character need not struggle between those two masks in solitude. The community of confidantes and co-conspirators that surrounds them bears witness to the struggle between the public and the private: the divided self. As a result, the sense of play that arises from the need to maintain the integrity of the public mask can be mined for greater performance possibilities.

Once you are aware of the mask of the divided self you will find it throughout Shakespeare's texts. Here is an example of a character wearing a figurative mask from Act 3, scene 2 of *The Merchant of Venice*. At the beginning of the play we learn that Portia's father has died and has arranged her marriage according to an elaborate riddle involving three caskets (a gold, a silver, and a bronze). The suitor who selects correctly wins Portia's hand in marriage, and her fortune. Portia has endured an on-going parade of ill-favored suitors, each of whom has chosen incorrectly. Through the process of elimination Portia has solved the riddle, and knows which of the caskets holds her future. Bassanio, her latest suitor, is the next to choose. Portia wants him to choose correctly, yet cannot compromise the integrity of his selection because she also wants him to have chosen freely, thereby demonstrating that he truly knows her and deserves her hand in marriage. At the start of the scene, the audience knows that Portia is in love with Bassanio, and also knows which casket is the correct one.

There are many different ways to play with the mask of the divided self, and this is only one possibility for this speech—you are empowered with the tools you need to discover your own performance possibilities. Keep in mind that these private thoughts are not necessarily asides—at times they

32 Excavating the foundation

can be asides, but that is not the only way you will see the friction and the fracture between the private and the public selves. It will often manifest in a deeper understanding of what prompts the speaking of that text. I will illustrate the division between the public and the private by putting Portia's private thoughts in **bold**.

Portia

I pray you, tarry: pause a day **or two**
Before you hazard; for, in choosing wrong,
I lose your company: therefore forbear awhile.
There's something tells me, **but it is not love**,
I would not lose you; and you know yourself,
Hate counsels not in such a quality.
But lest you should not understand me well,—
And yet a maiden hath no tongue but thought,—
I would detain you here some month **or two**
Before you venture for me. I could teach you
How to choose right, **but I am then forsworn;**
So will I never be: **so may you miss me;**
But if you do, you'll make me wish a sin,
That I had been forsworn. Beshrew your eyes,
They have o'erlook'd me and divided me;
One half of me is yours, **the other half yours,**
Mine own, I would say; **but if mine, then yours,**
And so all yours. O, these naughty times
Put bars between the owners and their rights!
And so, though yours, **not yours.** Prove it so,
Let fortune go to hell for it, not I.
I speak too long; **but 'tis to peize the time,**
To eke it and to draw it out in length,
To stay you from election.

You may notice that as this speech progresses, Portia has a challenging time maintaining the decorum of her public self. She desperately loves him, and

Examining the Globe **33**

wants him to win her hand in marriage. I've said that Shakespeare's characters need to speak in order to think, and in this speech we really see how quickly Portia's thoughts are firing. She is reasoning her way into—or out of—the resolution of Bassanio's selection.

Once Portia hits on the idea that she can control the outcome, the speech transforms into a display of sport. Those thoughts and their outcomes are volleying back and forth rapidly. During the time that Shakespeare was writing, people were negotiating their way around the idea that, perhaps, they were not ruled entirely by the stars, but had their own free will, their own ability to take control of their destiny. We see this throughout Shakespeare's work, most notably in one of Shakespeare's most recognizable quotes, from *Julius Caesar*, "The fault, dear Brutus, is not in the stars, / But in ourselves that we are underlings" (1.2.140–141).

The middle section of this speech shows the negotiation between the two personas and the need to reconcile the public and the private. This is verbal and conceptual Ping-Pong. We can see her debating as though she has the stereotypical angel and devil perched on her shoulders. She reasons: "I could do *this*, but then *that* will happen":

> ~~Before you venture for me.~~ I could teach you
>
> How to choose right, (THIS!) **but I am then forsworn;** (THAT!)
>
> So will I never be: (THIS!) **so may you miss me;** (THAT!)
>
> **But if you do, you'll make me wish a sin,**
>
> **That I had been forsworn.** (THIS!) ~~Beshrew your eyes,~~

Now that you are equipped with the tools to excavate your way through the text, you can make your own choices about how you interpret the text. You could easily reason that the private thoughts should be mapped out like this:

> ~~Before you venture for me.~~ **I could teach you**
>
> **How to choose right,** but I am then forsworn;
>
> **So will I never be:** so may you miss me;
>
> **But if you do, you'll make me wish a sin,**
>
> **That I had been forsworn.** ~~Beshrew your eyes,~~

The empowering thing is that there is no ONE prescribed way of doing it. It's up to you to decide. Speak both of those choices out loud and see which one *you* find more public, and which more private. It's about *your* journey.

Casting the audience: the mirror

The final role that the audience can play is that of the *mirror*. A site for reflection, mirrors return and redirect what is before them. In a theatre like Shakespeare's Globe, where the audience is a part of the action and actors can look into their eyes, where the line between the world of the play and reality of playmaking is indistinct, the audience becomes integrated into the space between the actor/characters on stage. In Shakespeare's Globe—or in any three-quarter thrust stage—the audience has multiple vantage points, depending on their location. I've already talked about how that affects the staging dynamics, but it also affects the interaction between characters on stage. This revelation was inspired by my experience in Shakespeare's Globe, but it need not remain unique to that space.

When the audience plays the role of mirror, the actors use what I call *elliptical energy* in order to reach their partners on stage. Actors will send their energy through the audience as they continue to blur the line between the players and the spectators, and thereby continue to expand the world of the fiction. With elliptical energy, actor/characters directly address their audience/mirrors, not with the intention that their comments end there (as is the case with the Brechtian convention of "breaking the fourth wall"), but instead with the intention that the comments reflect back on stage to their fellow actors/characters. I will discuss the training sequence for elliptical energy at length in Chapter 8, but first I'd like to share how casting the audience as *mirror* will expand your possibilities for performance.

As mirror, the audience is continually drawn into the action of the play as they are lured into the interactive space between the characters on stage. The use of elliptical energy capitalizes on the fact that audience engagement is necessary in order to achieve holistic playmaking. In Chapter 1, we examined how this model of inclusive, engaged playmaking is outlined in the prologue

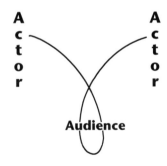

FIGURE 2.4 Illustration of elliptical energy

Examining the Globe **35**

to *Henry V*, and through elliptical energy we can explore this notion in practice. In performance, Figure 2.4 shows what using elliptical energy looks like.

When the audience is used as a mirror a sense of fluidity radiates among the participants in the space. The audience senses that the on-stage action is not a fixed entity that they merely observe. Instead, what they experience is that they are actually a part of that palpable sense of energy on stage. In this example from *Much Ado About Nothing*, the audience has already learned that "there is a kind of merry war betwixt Signor Benedick and [Beatrice]" and that "they never meet but there is a skirmish of wit between them" (1.1. 40–42). Only forty lines later, when the audience is able to witness this meeting firsthand, they are drawn into their role as mirror when the actors engage elliptical energy. You can see in the text that it is unlikely that Beatrice and Benedick are engaging each other directly throughout the beat—this would be too intimate, too confrontational, and would indicate that each one cares more than they should like to reveal. By using the audience to make their point, several tactical things happen. As they engage the audience, they engage in their foreshadowed "merry war" and the newly cast audience is drawn into their "skirmish of wit." By using the audience, they allow themselves a degree of distance to gauge their partner's response and recalibrate their line of attack. As you read this scene, envision that diagram of elliptical energy as an example of reaching the partner on stage by using the audience as a mirror.

For the purposes of illustrating the point, I will <u>underline</u> one possible performance choice, but this is not the only option for engaging elliptical energy.

Beatrice

<u>I wonder that you will still be talking, Signior</u>
<u>Benedick: nobody marks you.</u>

Benedick

<u>What, my dear Lady Disdain! are you yet living?</u>

Beatrice

<u>Is it possible disdain should die while she hath</u>
<u>such meet food to feed it as Signior Benedick?</u>
Courtesy itself must convert to disdain, if you come
in her presence.

Benedick

Then is courtesy a turncoat. <u>But it is certain I</u>
<u>am loved of all ladies,</u> only you excepted: <u>and I</u>

36 Excavating the foundation

<u>would I could find in my heart that I had not a hard</u>
<u>heart</u>; for, truly, I love none.

Beatrice

<u>A dear happiness to women</u>: they would else have
been troubled with a pernicious suitor. I thank God
and my cold blood, I am of your humour for that: <u>I</u>
<u>had rather hear my dog bark at a crow than a man</u>
<u>swear he loves me.</u>

Benedick

God keep your ladyship still in that mind! so some
gentleman or other shall 'scape a predestinate
scratched face.

Beatrice

Scratching could not make it worse, an 'twere such
a face as yours were.

Benedick

Well, you are a rare parrot-teacher.

Beatrice

A bird of my tongue is better than a beast of yours.

Benedick

I would my horse had the speed of your tongue, and
so good a continuer. But keep your way, i' God's
name; I have done.

Beatrice

You always end with a jade's trick: I know you of old.

The most important thing to keep in mind when it comes to elliptical energy—
and once you've explored it through the training and in practice you will
have this sense for yourself—is that it is always fluid and never fixed. Elliptical
energy expands your possibilities in performance rather than compartmental-
izes them. You will be connecting to your partner on stage both directly and
indirectly through your audience/mirror. You will increase your own ability to
radiate and reach your partner(s) on stage and simultaneously find greater presence both as an actor on stage and also as a character in the world of the play.

Shakespeare's social space

Another area that we can consider pertains to the social dynamics inherent in Shakespeare's playhouse. When we attend the theatre today, the social status of the audience is quite diverse. You will find patrons of all walks of life intermingled together. There can be quite wealthy patrons seated in inexpensive seats, and those with less financial means seated in the most costly ones. With discount tickets and promotional offers, there is, theoretically, virtually no separation of social classes in the theatre. One can make assumptions about patrons' status, but that is based on mere speculation and outward appearances.

At the moment, there is serious concern for the state of our audiences, and the potential elitist nature of going to the theatre. There are a host of circumstances that influence the makeup of our audience, like the quality of our education and our access to the arts. It is not my intention to diminish this incredibly important and very complicated issue, and I recognize that it is a serious problem, but I also must recognize that there are many wonderful initiatives that work to combat this—like the Globe's £5 tickets, or the Public Theatre's free "Shakespeare in the Park" in New York. My point is that in the commercial theatre—like flying on an airplane— two people seated together could have paid vastly different sums for their tickets. We can't assume anything about the social status of our audience simply by where they are positioned in the theatre. The division between social classes is not nearly as distinct as it would have been in Shakespeare's day. Today, one of the wealthiest ticketholders could choose to experience a play at Shakespeare's Globe as a groundling, and there would be no social stigma in doing so.

This would not have been the case in Shakespeare's playhouse. The lowest class of patrons, the groundlings, would have paid the lowest price for admission and stood closest to the stage. These groundlings were the working class people, the riff raff, and the commoners. Each successive gallery paid more, and was of a progressively higher status. It simply wasn't socially acceptable to comingle. This was a time when women couldn't attend the theatre unaccompanied, so the social decorum was higher than it is for us today. We can use these social dynamics to fuel our performance choices.

If we imagine what might have been possible in performance at the Globe, we have (at least) two distinct social classes in two separate locations. There are instances in Shakespeare's plays where we can use this to clarify our points and enhance our relationship to the text. Just like the example earlier

38 Excavating the foundation

from *Romeo and Juliet* that connects the textual metaphors to the microcosmic Heavens, the audience will benefit from the clarity of your choices even if they are unaware of the motivation that drives them.

Let's examine how the social dynamics of Shakespeare's playhouse can inform the text. At the top of Act 1, scene 2 of *King Lear*, Edmund enters and speaks this soliloquy. Actually, the First Folio states, "Enter Bastard," and the text is assigned to "Bast"—Edmund is essentially robbed of his humanity, his individuality, as he is reduced to his social state: a bastard. Edmund enters and speaks:

> Thou Nature art my Goddesse, to thy Law
>
> My seruices are bound, wherefore should I
>
> Stand in the plague of custome, and permit
>
> The curiosity of Nations, to depriue me?
>
> For that I am some twelue, or fourteene Moonshines
>
> Lag of a Brother? Why Bastard? Wherefore base?
>
> When my Dimensions are as well compact,
>
> My minde as generous, and my shape as true
>
> As honest Madams issue? Why brand they vs
>
> With Base? With basenes Bastardie? Base, Base?
>
> Who in the lustie stealth of Nature, take
>
> More composition, and fierce qualitie,
>
> Then doth within a dull stale tyred bed
>
> Goe to th' creating a whole tribe of Fops
>
> Got 'tweene a sleepe, and wake? Well then,
>
> Legitimate Edgar, I must haue your land,
>
> Our Fathers loue, is to the Bastard Edmond,
>
> As to th'legitimate: fine word: Legitimate.
>
> Well, my Legittimate, if this Letter speed,
>
> And my inuention thriue, Edmond the base
>
> Shall to'th'Legitimate: I grow, I prosper:
>
> Now Gods, stand vp for Bastards.

In the next chapter I will discuss the opening question that is posed in the first four lines when I address personification. Here, I'd like to focus on the

Examining the Globe **39**

two distinct social groups that are present in the speech: the bastards and the legitimates. This speech has the potential to be a real rallying cry for justice and equality. It's as much about the "haves" and the "have-nots" as it is about the circumstances of Edmund's birth and the world of the play. In Shakespeare's playhouse, we have the distinct division of those social groups in two distinct locations. The bastards certainly would have been among the groundlings, and the legitimate in the third gallery. When Edmund asks, "Why Bastard? Wherefore base?" he could be asking his fellows in the yard, or he could be asking for answers from the gallery. As he continues he provides a detailed list of all the ways he is like the "legitimate," "honest Madams issue"—here is the start of the "us" (the bastards and the groundlings) versus "them" (the legitimate). As Edmund continues, "Why brand they us with base?" and the actor can really use the dynamic of social space to illustrate the point.

As Edmund moves through the speech, he asks, "With basenes Bastardie? Base, Base?" and it is as though he is singling out his comrades in the yard, like he is gathering his army. He can see each of those members so as he refers to them he embroils them into the action of the play. And this antithetical dynamic grows even more personal between the "Legitimate Edgar" and the "Bastard Edmund." Just as he did earlier in the speech with "base and bastard," Edmund has a series of repetitive mentions of the "legitimate" that can all be directed to individuals seen in the upper gallery.

Throughout Shakespeare's work characters identify with demographics that would have been distinct when the plays were first performed and now are rather homogenized. We can use this to fuel our creative choices even if we no longer have the same dynamics readily available to us.

We have now classified several different components that are unique to Shakespeare's Globe and have surveyed areas that we will consider as we begin to build performances of our own. The possibilities we have unearthed here can be applied anywhere you are performing Shakespeare: in a theatre, in a classroom, in a pub, in a castle, in a park, or behind a microphone.

Next, we will look at the intricacies of working with Shakespeare's texts and explore how to make the verse come alive.

3

UNDERSTANDING THE TEXT

One of the biggest challenges that actors and directors face when approaching Shakespeare is finding their way into the language. If they are new to working on Shakespeare, perhaps it has to do with acquiring the tools necessary to work on heightened texts; if they already have such tools, the challenge might be in finding a way to forge a relationship with that particular text and discover what is unique about it. Essentially, we all aim to develop a profound and highly personal connection with the text that enables us to reach our audiences in a way that is meaningful and that will resonate with them. In order to do that we must become as comfortable with heightened language as we are with contemporary speech.

Some of what we will look at has to do with the way that Shakespeare uses meter because most of his texts are written in verse, or poetry. A lot of what we will examine, though, will apply to both poetry and prose. If you are not familiar with the difference between poetry and prose, don't panic; it's incredibly easy to recognize. If the first letter of each word on the line is capitalized, it's verse; it's poetry. If the lines run together like a paragraph you would read in a novel, it's prose. It's really that simple. If it's in verse then we look at what the meter is telling us, and if it's in prose then there is no meter to consider and we look at the text for other key elements we can use to activate the language.

You may hear terms like "blank verse" and "rhyming verse," and it's as easy to tell those apart as it is to tell the difference between poetry and prose. *Blank verse* is verse that doesn't follow a particular rhyming pattern, and *rhyming verse* is verse that does: the end of each verse line formulates a pattern of rhyme.

Understanding the text **41**

Verse, or poetry, is heightened language, and if the structure of that language is shaped further by the presence of a particular pattern, you can think of it as being *especially* heightened. In Shakespeare, verse is usually reserved for characters in heightened situations or for those who are of a high status. Prose is often, but not always, associated with lower-class characters, or those who have a lower status in the world of the play. There are always exceptions, of course, and these exceptions are particularly relevant to performance.

For example, at the beginning of *Twelfth Night*, Olivia is in mourning for her brother's death and although there can be a romantic notion to mourning, Olivia's existence is not particularly poetic; it is marked by the absence of life's joys. As a result, she speaks in prose even though she is a character of high status in the play. When Olivia falls in love with Cesario (who the audience knows is Viola in disguise), her language shifts to verse: she enters the world of poetry. Just imagine the performance possibilities that can arise from this kind of discovery.

In this chapter, we will look at various ways of examining Shakespeare's use of language so that you can cultivate and develop your own relationship and approach to the text, and become familiar with the tools you will need. We will start by looking at meter, and the most common variations you will need to know. I will share with you a terrific way of getting Shakespeare's *iambic pentameter* into your body so you can begin to inhabit that heightened text. Then we will begin to look at the elements that apply to all of the texts, whether they are in poetry or prose. We will look at things like punctuation, *lists and ladders*, and I'll introduce you to the technique of *telescoping*, which is a new way of focusing in on the text that helps to clarify your points and activate the language. We will also look at some of the distinctive ways that Shakespeare uses language: *alliteration* and *assonance*, *metaphors* and *similes*, and we'll look at some ways to consider the titles, names, and personifications that you will encounter when working on Shakespeare's texts. By the time you finish reading this chapter you should have a deeper understanding of how to orient yourself in the text, you will approach Shakespeare with confidence, and you'll be ready to put it all together on your feet when you come to the suggestions for practice in Part II.

Let's begin by looking at meter.

Iambic pentameter

Iambic pentameter is a form of poetry where the meter is made up of five units (penta is the prefix for the number five, hence penta-meter = meter of five), and each of those five units is iambic. An iamb is a two-syllable unit that is made up of one weak and one strong (or one "unstressed" and

42 Excavating the foundation

one "stressed") syllable in succession. So literally, you have five weak/strong units in one line.

The rhythm sounds like this:

> weak STRONG weak STRONG weak STRONG weak STRONG weak STRONG
>
> . . . and ONE . . . and TWO . . . and THREE . . . and FOUR . . . and FIVE
>
> dee DUM dee DUM dee DUM dee DUM dee DUM

A lot has been said about iambic pentameter: that it is the "heartbeat" of the verse, that it echoes our own heartbeat, that it is the vehicle for Shakespeare's heightened texts, and that it can give actors some major anxiety. The truth of it is this: it is the closest way to how we speak. That may shock you, but it's true. IT IS THE CLOSEST WAY TO HOW WE SPEAK. In fact, that is an iambic line.

> It IS the CLOSEst WAY to HOW we SPEAK.
>
> dee DUM dee DUM dee DUM dee DUM dee DUM.

See? That's not so scary, is it?

Now, clearly, I'm no "Shakespeare" (that isn't exactly the most eloquent line ever written, I'll give you that), but it does make my point, doesn't it? Iambic pentameter is closer to us than we may realize.

It is the way I speak to you right now. The rhythm is within us and we know just how familiar it can sound to us. When you begin to listen carefully, you'll see how often meter is right there, but you don't beat that meter when you speak—and nor should you when speaking Shakespeare's verse.

Now, everything I just wrote is entirely iambic. Look:

> It is the way I speak to you right now.
>
> The rhythm is within us and we know
>
> Just how familiar it can sound to us.
>
> When you begin to listen carefully,
>
> You'll see how often meter is right there,
>
> But you don't beat that meter when you speak—
>
> And nor should you when speaking Shakespeare's verse.

Understanding the text **43**

But WE don't TALK like THIS in LIFE do WE? No. No one would listen to us. We would sound like robots. We'd be devoid of all the nuances and vitality that make us human. We would never tolerate it, and audiences *certainly* won't tolerate it—nor should they. So we should know it's there, that rhythm. We should allow it to inform our connection to and our understanding of Shakespeare's verse, but we should NOT perform it outright.

Part of the reason we shouldn't perform the iambic outright is that each of those weak and strong syllables are weak or strong in relative degrees of stress. They don't exist in absolutes, but are relative to each other. Not every weak syllable is completely weak, and not every strong syllable is fully strong. Speaking with equal degrees of stress—where every unstressed and every stressed syllable vibrates and resonates from us in the same pattern over and over again creates a monotony that we can't sustain. It is a lot of work—and it doesn't help us to communicate, which is the driving force behind every word we utter.

Instead, think of those degrees like the level of volume on your electronic device. If level 1 is when you begin to hear sound and level 10 is the maximum, you have an entire range from 1–10 in which you can listen. Now, human speech is "tuned" by many more components than just volume—and we'll get to all of the other nuances shortly—but for the sake of understanding how iambic meter works for the actor let's narrow that focus and simply compare it to volume at the moment. On that scale of 1–10, not every weak syllable would be a "1" (just loud enough to be heard) and not every strong syllable a "10" (maximum volume allowed). You might have a pattern of a "4" followed by an "8," or you may have an "8" followed by a "9"—both of these are iambic. Even though the "8" might be in a stressed place in one instance and in an unstressed position in another, each of those combinations are iambic because a greater emphasis of stress follows a lesser one. This creates fully dynamic speech that is both active for the speaker and engaging to the listener. You may even want to think of the range between the less stressed syllable and the more stressed one as an even narrower scale: say, 1–5 for even greater subtlety. Of course, even using a larger scale you can envision the distance between the two parts of that iamb as narrower in scope. Perhaps the bulk of your speech falls in the range of 3–7, and you reserve the extremities on either end for major points of emphasis. It's up to you; there are multiple ways of thinking about it, provided you avoid the trap that treats your verse as diametrical to itself. It isn't one extreme or the other, but a playful dance of possibilities between everything that lies within those two opposing points.

44 Excavating the foundation

Here is another key thing to know about iambic pentameter: Shakespeare's verse is *always* iambic—unless it *isn't*. Wait, what? Shakespeare's verse is always iambic unless it isn't? What exactly does that mean? It means that you should assume that Shakespeare's verse is iambic by design, and let the verse reveal to you when it is *not* iambic. Trust Shakespeare. He will let you know—and when he *does* you can also be prepared to discover something pretty interesting going on.

When I learned about scansion and iambic pentameter I was taught that it was five measures that were weak/strong, given a list of exceptions (yes, I'll get to those) and I was sent off with a pencil and a piece of text (and then an entire play) to learn how to decipher Shakespeare's meter. I spent years agonizing over scansion, acutely aware of all of the possible deviations. Frankly, it was excruciating work. That work led to an epiphany, though, and that epiphany made my relationship with verse so much happier. Instead of laboring over every line to decipher what the meter was *supposed* to be I stopped thinking about what *I* thought it could—or should—be, and just assumed it was all standard, all regular, all "normal" iambic pentameter. I worked from the premise that if the verse line was not fully iambic, then surely Shakespeare would let it be known (and he does!).

You can skip the stress I went through and just learn from my "A-ha!" moment. Start by accepting that the verse is always iambic, and let the verse reveal when there is a deviation.

Metric deviations

Aside from sounding like a 1980s punk rock band ("the Metric Deviations"), there are some fairly regular "irregularities" that the actor will discover in Shakespeare's texts. These include both changes in the pattern of syllable stress as well as fluctuations in the length of verse lines. The most significant of these "metric deviations" are the *trochee*, the *feminine ending*, the *Alexandrine* line, the short line, and shared lines.

The trochee

In addition to having a regularly iambic pattern (weak STRONG), you will often find that Shakespeare puts a jolt into a speech by reversing that pattern (STRONG weak). So instead of having a unit that goes dee DUM, it will reveal itself as DUM dee. This pattern (STRONG weak) is known as a *trochee*. *Trochees* certainly will make themselves known to you;

Understanding the text   **45**

they energize the language and speaking them usually comes along with dynamic circumstances. You will often find that *trochees* must be spoken so: trying to force them to be iambic will go against your instincts, common sense, and flow of speech. That's the good news: they are definitely the creaky floorboards of the verse line—you can tread as lightly as you want, but you'll have to pause and pay attention once you step over it.

You'll often find *trochees* at the start of a verse line (although they do appear mid-line as well). *Trochees* are often present when you have verbs, and rhythmically they are the perfect accompaniment to those action words. The bump in rhythm spurs action; it demands attention. When you find *trochees* without a verb, it will usually illuminate a key idea (as it does with the verbs), or serve to highlight what is being said for a particular reason.

Here is a speech from the beginning of *Richard III* (1.2). Lady Anne is following the funeral procession of her father-in-law, King Henry. This is the second murder she has had to endure at the hands of Richard; the first was the untimely death of her husband, Edward. The modern actor recognizes the height of these "given circumstances" and Shakespeare helps the actor tremendously by providing a verse structure that animates performance. In this portion of the speech, Anne addresses both the body and the spirit of the dead King:

> Poor key-cold Figure of a holy King,
>
> Pale Ashes of the House of Lancaster;
>
> Thou bloodless Remnant of that Royal Blood,
>
> Be it lawful that I invocate thy Ghost,
>
> To hear the Lamentations of poor Anne,
>
> Wife to thy Edward, to thy slaughtered Son,
>
> Stabbed by the selfsame hand that made these wounds.
>
> Lo, in these windows that let forth thy life,
>
> I pour the helpless Balm of my poor eyes.
>
> O cursed be the hand that made these holes:
>
> Cursed the Heart, that had the heart to do it:
>
> Cursed the Blood, that let this Blood from hence:
>
> More direful hap betide that hated Wretch
>
> That makes us wretched by the death of thee,
>
> Than I can wish to Wolves, to Spiders, Toads,
>
> Or any creeping venom'd thing that lives.

46 Excavating the foundation

I've given you a rather long example here because I want to show you how the *trochee* not only makes itself apparent, but also helps to activate the actor in performance.

At the beginning of this passage you'll find the verse is fully iambic (there are actually four iambic lines that come before this example that I've not included, where Anne asks the attendants to put the body down). Iambic lines are usually notated with the symbol " ˘ " above the weaker syllable and " / " above the stronger one. It looks like this:

$$\breve{\ } \quad / \quad \breve{\ } \quad / \quad \breve{\ } \quad / \quad \breve{\ } \quad / \quad \breve{\ } \quad /$$

Poor KEY-cold FIGure OF a HOly KING,

Pale ASHes OF the HOUSE of LANcasTER;

Thou BLOODless REMnant OF that ROYal BLOOD,

<u>Be it</u> LAWful THAT I INvoCATE thy GHOST,★

To HEAR the LAMenTAtions OF poor ANNE,

WIFE to thy EDward, TO thy SLAUGHTered SON,★★

STABBED by the SELFsame HAND that MADE these WOUNDS.★★★

Lo, IN these WINdows THAT let FORTH thy LIFE,

I POUR the HELPless BALM of MY poor EYES.

O CURsed BE the HAND that MADE these HOLES:

CURsed the HEART, that HAD the HEART to <u>DO it</u>:★★★★

CURsed the BLOOD, that LET this BLOOD from HENCE:★★★★★

More DIREful HAP beTIDE that HATed WRETCH

That MAKES us WRETCHed BY the DEATH of THEE,

Than I can WISH to WOLVES, to SPIders, TOADS,

Or ANy CREEPing VENom'd THING that LIVES.

(★) "Be it" is a terrific example of how Shakespeare writes in the rhythm of speech: we naturally want to run "beit" together in order to get to LAWful. We wouldn't say: "Be IT lawFUL that I inVOcate THY ghost" but by linking "be" with "it," as we naturally would, it forms a perfectly iambic line: Be it LAWful THAT I INvoCATE thy GHOST.

(★★) Here is our first *trochee*! Lady Anne's widowhood demands our attention—for a multitude of reasons—and crying out the title she's been robbed of helps her to claim her space in this particular story. The title

Understanding the text 47

"WIFE" deserves far more stress than the preposition "to" that follows it, and in fact, our tendency would naturally be to say "WIFE to" rather than "wife TO." Our inherent rhythm of speaking for sense takes over: it takes work to say "wife TO" because it goes against our desire to communicate. In life we speak in order to communicate, and Shakespeare writes for the same purpose. At this point, Shakespeare gives us several key pieces of information in this *trochee*: we understand Lady Anne's familial role, we learn about her emotional response to her husband's death when she clarifies "to thy slaughtered son" after she already names Edward, and we are introduced to key pieces of exposition that help to locate us in the world of this play.

(★★★) The next *trochee* is the verb "Stabbed" and the jar in rhythm echoes the stabbing action (both physical and emotional). Again, our inherent desire to speak for sense, to affect the listener, causes us to stress the phrase in a particular way: "STABBED by" rather than "Stabbed BY." "STABBED" pulls all our energy into the story, and consequently, it thrusts us right into Lady Anne's inner life. Shakespeare wrote for actors, and this is certainly an instance where he has given the actor a means to drive the performance forward in a compelling manner.

(★★★★) Here we have another example of how a *trochee* verb evokes the same action: **CUR**sed the HEART. First, we would never say "cur**SED** the HEART"; the word is pronounced CURsed not curSED. *This* is what I mean when I say that it is always iambic unless it isn't and that Shakespeare will show us where those places are. We could sit down with our text and a pencil and mark it, " ˘ / ," but we would *NEVER* speak it that way. This is why I will introduce you in a moment to a far more effective way of exploring iambic pentameter that doesn't involve a pencil and paper. The line simply isn't iambic in that first unit: it must be a *trochee*. Second, you will notice that embracing the trochee evokes the curse itself: "**CUR**sed the HEART" is a curse; "cur**SED** the HEART" is something out of a sketch comedy routine about an actor trying to do Shakespeare.

You may also notice something else about this line: it has one of our other "metric deviations"—the *feminine ending*. I'll explore this with you in further detail when we finish looking at *trochees*, but you have already noticed that this line has an extra foot; it contains eleven syllables instead of our regular ten. How exciting!

(★★★★★) This next *trochee* "**CUR**sed the BLOOD" follows the same premise as the line before: the verb CURsed not only evokes the curse, but it rounds out a trio of curses that Lady Anne sets in motion (the first one falls in its regular iambic pattern):

48 Excavating the foundation

1. O CURsed BE the HAND
2. **CUR**sed the HEART
3. **CUR**sed the BLOOD

Later on I'm going to discuss lists and ladders and rhetorical structure, but until then you can see how Shakespeare provides the actor with language that helps to create invigorating performances. Learning how to engage these clues can empower you to develop what every actor and director longs for: strong, organic performances.

The feminine ending

When we were looking at *trochees* in the Lady Anne speech above, we discovered that one of her lines, "**CUR**sed the HEART, that HAD the HEART to <u>DO it</u>:" has eleven syllables rather than ten. This is known as a *feminine ending*, and it is one of the more common irregularities you'll find in Shakespeare's verse. When you find these longer lines, you can note that the character is in the midst of something that cannot be expressed within the regular ten-syllable verse line: he or she needs a bit more; that extra foot. Why? Could the character be experiencing something that is too full to fit the meter? The moment is surely heightened, and because Shakespeare points that out, the actor can use that information to fuel that particular moment. In the example above, Lady Anne is caught right in the middle of her trio of curses; it is quite literally the "heart" of her curse "sandwich." All you need to do is pay attention to the verse, and the deviations will make themselves known.

Before we get to the rest of the "metric deviations" I'd like to introduce you to a way to explore Shakespeare's meter that is physical and lets you investigate what is happening with the text without allowing you to manipulate it or intellectualize it. It's true that the work we do requires a great deal of intellect, but sometimes that intellect can interfere with our ability to access what Shakespeare is giving us. I believe wholeheartedly that actors should understand scansion and be able to execute the task, but I also believe that sitting studiously with a pencil and paper doesn't always affect what happens in performance.

Basketball Shakespeare, or "Shakesball"

For this exploration you will need a basketball-sized ball. It doesn't necessarily need to be a basketball, a playground ball or kickball will suffice, but it cannot be a small ball such a tennis ball or handball. I've found that

Understanding the text **49**

once you get into the rhythm of the exercise, and with text in hand, it is too difficult to maintain with smaller hand-sized balls. The point is to tap into Shakespeare's verse, not to challenge your hand-eye coordination. You will also need a copy of the text from which you are working. You can do this exercise before you begin any other work on your text. In fact, it is preferable to do so because then you won't have any preconceived ideas about where the stress lies (unless of course, you have assumed it's perfectly iambic!).

You are going to explore Shakespeare's verse by bouncing out the rhythm with the ball:

> and BOUNCE and BOUNCE and BOUNCE and BOUNCE and BOUNCE
>
> dee DUM dee DUM dee DUM dee DUM dee DUM
>
> weak STRONG weak STRONG weak STRONG weak STRONG weak STRONG
>
> and **BOUNCE** and **BOUNCE** and **BOUNCE** and **BOUNCE** and **BOUNCE**

Do that without any of Shakespeare's text for a moment.

> and **BOUNCE** and **BOUNCE** and **BOUNCE** and **BOUNCE** and **BOUNCE**

Now bounce the ball in that iambic rhythm while speaking out either "dee DUM" or "and BOUNCE" or "weak STRONG" or "and ONE"—whichever of those variations you prefer.

> and **BOUNCE** and **BOUNCE** and **BOUNCE** and **BOUNCE** and **BOUNCE**

Let's look at one of Romeo's speeches (*Romeo and Juliet* 2.2) for a moment. Read it through once out loud for sense, and then we'll begin to explore the rhythm physically, so you'll need your ball.

> But soft, what light through yonder window breaks?
>
> It is the East and Juliet is the Sun,
>
> Arise fair Sun and kill the envious Moon,
>
> Who is already sick and pale with grief,

50 Excavating the foundation

That thou her Maid art far more fair then she:

Be not her Maid since she is envious,

Her Vestal livery is but sick and green,

And none but fools do wear it, cast it off:

It is my Lady, O it is my Love,

O that she knew she were,

She speaks, yet she says nothing what of that?

Her eye discourses, I will answer it:

I am too bold 'tis not to me she speaks:

Two of the fairest stars in all the Heaven,

Having some business do entreat her eyes,

To twinkle in their Spheres till they return.

What if her eyes were there, they in her head,

The brightness of her cheek would shame those stars,

As day-light doth a Lamp, her eye in heaven,

Would through the airy Region stream so bright,

That Birds would sing, and think it were not night:

See how she leans her cheek upon her hand.

O that I were a Glove upon that hand,

That I might touch that cheek.

Read through the speech a second time and this time let's pair reading aloud and bouncing our ball:

> But SOFT, what LIGHT through YONder WINdow BREAKS?
>
> and **BOUNCE** and **BOUNCE** and **BOUNCE** and **BOUNCE** and **BOUNCE**

It's perfectly iambic, isn't it? That was easy. Let's keep going:

> It IS the EAST and JULiet IS the SUN,
>
> and **BOUNCE** and **BOUNCE** and **BOUNCE** and **BOUNCE** and **BOUNCE**

Again, it's iambic.

Understanding the text **51**

aRISE fair SUN and KILL the ENvious MOON,

Who IS alREADy SICK and PALE with GRIEF,

That THOU her MAID art FAR more FAIR then SHE:

Be NOT her MAID since SHE is ENviOUS,

Her VEStal LIVEry IS but SICK and GREEN,

And NONE but FOOLS do WEAR it, CAST it OFF:

It IS my LAdy, O it IS my LOVE,

O THAT she KNEW she WERE,

Now what happened on that last line?

and **BOUNCE** and **BOUNCE** and **BOUNCE**

It's iambic, but it's not pentameter. It's short two bounces. There are only three iambic units, instead of five. I am going to talk about short and shared lines in just a moment, but you didn't have to go out of your way to look for that irregularity—there it was! It presented itself to you because you trusted the verse to do its job and you trusted yourself to recognize when that opportunity presented itself. That's *empowerment*!

Let's keep going:

She SPEAKS, yet SHE says NOthing WHAT of THAT?

Her EYE disCOURSes, I will ANswer IT:

I AM too BOLD 'tis NOT to ME she SPEAKS:

Two OF the FAIRest STARS in ALL the HEAVen,

What is happening here? What is going on with the ball? Did you find it difficult to speak and keep to your and **BOUNCE** and **BOUNCE** and **BOUNCE** and **BOUNCE** and **BOUNCE**? The ball wants to bounce on "TWO," doesn't it? It's more work to make it bounce on "OF." The energy of the line is pulled into a *trochee*. The line wants to bounce:

TWO of the FAIRest STARS in ALL the HEAVen

You can trust yourself to listen to the verse: there is a new idea there. Perhaps that *trochee* points out how the thought rushes in to Romeo? You can make your own decision about the why that is happening and what it may mean,

52 Excavating the foundation

but you've noticed that *something* is happening there, and this is key. You didn't have to decide whether or not you thought that "two" ought to be more important than "of"; your body listened to the clues the verse provided you. What else is going on here? There is something else that your bouncing ball will illuminate.

> and **BOUNCE** and **BOUNCE** and **BOUNCE** and **BOUNCE** and **BOUNCE** <u>and</u>

Your ball is caught up in the air. It's a feminine ending. That line has an extra foot. Can you bounce it again and make "heaven" only one syllable? Does that work for you? Either way, your decisions are coming from your relationship to the text, not from your manipulation of it. Let's keep going:

> HavING some BUSIness DO enTREAT her EYES,

Now that doesn't work at the beginning, does it? We wouldn't say, "hav-ING," we would say, "HAVing." There is that *trochee*-verb combination I told you about; the action of "having" creates that syncopation in the verse that helps you to communicate. Let's see what else we can discover:

> To TWINkle IN their SPHERES till THEY reTURN.
> What IF her EYES were THERE, they IN her HEAD,

You might find here that the unit "what if" may ask you to look at it or bounce it again. Our modern speech pattern might want us to stress "what" over "if." I'll remind you that just because the energy of the new thought spurs you with the idea, "what if *this* happens?" It doesn't necessarily mean that it's a *trochee* that could be one of those higher stressed "weak" words. It could be an 8/9 pattern. Remember that you have that flexibility and elasticity in the verse. It doesn't necessarily mean that it is an 8/7 because there is energy on "What." If we lose the stress of "if," we lose the structure of the rhetoric: if (this thing) happens, then (something else) will. If we keep reading we see that we need that structure because the next few lines depend on it.

Do you also find that after the middle of the line there is a bit of break or shift in gears that also energizes the line, and may even want you to stress "THEY in" rather than "they IN"? That shift is what is known as a *caesura*. I think we can allow the *caesura* to present itself to you when it needs attention. There is no need to seek it out or you run the risk of looking for places to put it (and subsequently slowing down the verse with undue pauses).

Understanding the text **53**

A *caesura* can be a pause or break in the flow of the poetry or rhetoric. The beauty of what Shakespeare has done is point out to us when it's important to pay attention—or to honor it, if you will. Again, trust in your ability to listen, your awareness, and trust in Shakespeare's verse to let it be known.

Getting back to that midline syncopation: could that be one of your mid-line *trochees*? Does the inverted stress of "THEY in" serve your need to communicate more than "they IN"? Let's consider this: if you were sending a telegram where you had to pay by the word, or sending a "tweet" where you were limited by the number of characters, what would be the key words you would include to make your point? These are called *operative words*. Which would communicate more effectively?

"if eyes there, in head"?

or

"if eyes there, they head"?

We must remember that "there" refers to the place of the stars, and "they" are the stars, not her eyes. Would the iambic or the *trochee* best communicate the hypothesis of Juliet's eyes changing place with the stars? Would your audience understand that there are two places and two things being compared (Juliet's eyes in her head and the stars in heaven) more clearly in the first set of operatives or the second? You are empowered to make that decision; the prompt to do so isn't pulled from your own ideas about how the text *should* sound, but from what the text is asking you to notice. The decision is yours.

Let's see how the rest of the speech bounces out:

The BRIGHTness OF her CHEEK would SHAME those STARS,

As DAY-light DOTH a LAMP, her EYE in HEAVen,

Here is that extra bounce again. Is it feminine or can you *elide* it to one syllable? If you are eliding it (condensing it from two syllables to one) do you really speak it as one syllable or are you simply notating it that way? Be honest—it's easy on paper to change the scansion to suit what you think it should be, but if you can't actually speak it that way in practice, then those marks don't have any value.

Would THROUGH the AIRy REGion STREAM so BRIGHT,

That BIRDS would SING, and THINK it WERE not NIGHT:

SEE how she LEANS her CHEEK upON her HAND.

54 Excavating the foundation

Here we have one of those action *trochees*: the verb pulls all the energy out of the iambic in order to command the audience to "LOOK!." It could also certainly scan to read, "see HOW," and I think this is one of those great moments that Shakespeare gives the actor that is up for interpretation. The actor could call the audience to look at something, or could call them to look at a particular way that thing is executed. Is it "LOOK how [she does this thing]" or is it "look HOW [she does it]—is what she is doing different from the way that others do it? Is Juliet leaning in a particular way that is noteworthy or is it that everything she does is amazing and we should take notice? It works either way.

> O THAT I WERE a GLOVE upON that HAND,
>
> That I might TOUCH that CHEEK.

Notice that final line of the speech: it is short by two iambs.

Your ball has bounced up only three times. This leads me to the next thing I'd like to look at: short and shared lines.

Short and shared lines

As we saw earlier with *feminine endings*, there are times when Shakespeare gives us lines that don't fit the pentameter precisely. Working from the presumption that Shakespeare's verse is in iambic pentameter—unless it isn't—we must always look for the "isn'ts" for they hold the key to performance. These can take several forms: verse lines can either be too long, too short, or shared between two or more characters.

In this example above we see that Romeo's final line is missing two iambic units. When these variations appear we must look closely at what is happening in the surrounding verse. Our first job is to investigate whether or not the line is shared with another character.

In this instance, Romeo says,

> That I might TOUCH that CHEEK.

Here is the sequence that follows:

> *Juliet*:   Ay me.
> *Romeo*:   She speaks.

Let's look at it altogether to see whether or not that line of Romeo's is short or shared.

Understanding the text **55**

That I might TOUCH that CHEEK.

Ay ME.

She SPEAKS.

If we speak those lines together, we see that they form a line of perfect iambic pentameter.

That I might TOUCH that CHEEK. Ay ME. She SPEAKS.

and **BOUNCE** and **BOUNCE** and **BOUNCE** and **BOUNCE** and **BOUNCE**

Most modern editors will even indent the lines to give the reader a visual clue that the line is joined:

That I might TOUCH that CHEEK.

Ay ME.

She SPEAKS.

As archaeologists of performance, though, we can't rely on what an editor highlights for the purpose of reading. We must be empowered enough to be our own textual "experts." We must know what it is we seek to discover from Shakespeare about the performance possibilities in each moment.

This sequence of text indicates that these characters are synchronized with each other: the verse parallels the heightened situation between them. They share one iambic line; there are no long pauses within this exchange. The verse indicates that these units create an iambic line and demands that it is played in a particular way. If we fail to investigate this "metric deviation" further, we fail to engage the possibilities that the text lays out for us.

If you discover a line that is missing feet, the other alternative is that the line is a short line. Short lines indicate that some physical action is meant to fill the unspoken missing beats. It can indicate an exit, a false exit, or a bit of stage business.

For example, let's look at Macbeth's speech from Act 2, scene 1 when the dagger appears to him.

Is this a Dagger, which I see before me,

The Handle toward my Hand? Come, let me clutch thee

I have thee not, and yet I see thee still.

Art thou not fatal Vision, sensible

56 Excavating the foundation

> To feeling, as to sight? Or art thou but
>
> A Dagger of the Mind, a false Creation,
>
> Proceeding from the heat-oppressed Braine:
>
> I see thee yet, in form as palpable,
>
> As this which now I draw.

You may have noticed from the beginning that the first two lines have eleven feet; they have *feminine endings*, which is hardly surprising given the fact that Macbeth is seeing visions; it is indeed a heightened situation, and the meter Shakespeare provides indicates his state. What is happening in that last line? There are only six feet.

> As this which now I draw.

Many modern editors will tell you "he draws a dagger" or something to that effect. That stage direction does not appear in the First Folio; it is a modern editor's addition, taken from the inherent stage direction in the text: "this" indicates that Macbeth is speaking about a particular dagger, and "which now I draw" tells the audience what he is about to do. This is indeed fairly straightforward, but I'd like you to pay attention to those missing two units, or four feet. Shakespeare has provided four feet for the actor to execute his physical action, to do his stage business. It's almost as if the line reads:

> As THIS which NOW I DRAW. *(He DRAWS the KNIFE)*

Sometimes editors provide such clues, but we need to be the archaeologists of performance: reading the text is not the same as performing it.

The Alexandrine

In addition to short and shared lines, there is one other regular irregularity you will find in Shakespeare's text: *the Alexandrine*. An *Alexandrine* (named from the form popular in France) is a line that is made up of <u>twelve</u> beats rather than ten. Let's compare the differences.

A regular line of *iambic pentameter*:

> dee **DUM** dee **DUM** dee **DUM** dee **DUM** dee **DUM**
>
> and **BOUNCE** and **BOUNCE** and **BOUNCE** and **BOUNCE** and **BOUNCE**
>
> and **ONE** and **TWO** and **THREE** and **FOUR** and **FIVE**

Understanding the text **57**

The *feminine ending*:

> dee **DUM** dee **DUM** dee **DUM** dee **DUM** dee **DUM** <u>dee</u>
>
> and **BOUNCE** and **BOUNCE** and **BOUNCE** and **BOUNCE** and **BOUNCE** <u>and</u>
>
> and **ONE** and **TWO** and **THREE** and **FOUR** and **FIVE** <u>and</u>

The *Alexandrine*:

> dee **DUM** dee **DUM** dee **DUM** dee **DUM** dee **DUM** <u>dee **DUM**</u>
>
> and **BOUNCE** and **BOUNCE** and **BOUNCE** and **BOUNCE** and **BOUNCE** <u>and **BOUNCE**</u>
>
> and **ONE** and **TWO** and **THREE** and **FOUR** and **FIVE** <u>and **SIX**</u>

If a *feminine ending* indicates that the thought, emotion, or circumstance is too full for the regular—or expected—meter, then exceeding that regularity with another full iamb must indicate a state that is even more heightened.

In *All's Well That Ends Well*, Helena receives word that her husband Bertram, who she loves dearly, has threatened never to return home as long as she remains his wife. (This is one of those dubious situations where someone—a man—has been forced into marriage with someone else—a woman—who loves him. The complications and implications of this are the subject for another whole study, so we'll simply accept the dramaturgical scenario and explore what kind of heightened situation this creates for our love-struck heroine.)

Helena loves Bertram desperately, and she has won Bertram's hand in marriage (against his will) due to the service she has performed for the King by saving his life. She has received Bertram's letter in which he states, "Till I have no wife, I have nothing in France." He would prefer to stay at war than return safely home to his marriage. When Helena is left alone with the audience, her confidantes, she responds to Bertram's harsh words (3.2):

> *Till I have no wife I have nothing in France.*
>
> Nothing in France until he has no wife:
>
> Thou shalt have none Rossillion, none in France,
>
> Then hast thou all again: poor Lord, is't I
>
> That chase thee from thy Country, and expose
>
> Those tender limbs of thine, to the event
>
> Of the none-sparing war? And is it I,

58 Excavating the foundation

That drive thee from the sportive Court, where thou

Was't shot at with fair eyes, to be the mark

Of smoky Muskets? O you leaden messengers,

That ride upon the violent speed of fire.

Fly with false aim, move the still-piecing air

That sings with piercing, do not touch my Lord:

Who ever shoots at him, I set him there.

Let's look closely at what happens with the two last full sentences (not to be confused with two verse lines).

~~Of the none-sparing war?~~ And is it I,

That drive thee from the sportive Court, where thou

Was't shot at with fair eyes, to be the mark

Of SMOKy MUSKets? O you LEADen MESSenGERS, *(12 beats: Alexandrine!)*

That RIDE upON the VIOLent SPEED of FIre. *(11 beats: Feminine ending)*

<u>FLY with false AIM, MOVE the</u> still-PIECing AIR *(action plus mid-line trochees)*

That sings with piercing, do not touch my Lord:

Who ever shoots at him, I set him there.

If we look at those three successive lines of verse, you can see that Helena is in the midst of something incredibly heightened: she is literally trying to change the laws of physics in order to protect her loved one. Notice how intelligently she plays with her choice of words and use of imagery: "piercing" the "still-piecing" air; how she endows the atmosphere surrounding Bertram.

Her verse takes time to recover from such an extreme; once she explodes into that twelve-beat *Alexandrine* verse line, she follows with a *feminine ending*, and then a highly syncopated, *trochaic* line. Shakespeare gives the actor a major performance clue in this sequence.

Now that you know what to begin to look for, I want to empower you further. I have introduced you to the key variations you'll find when Shakespeare strays from iambic pentameter, but we haven't yet looked at what can happen when he goes for a full-on mash up and engages several of these variations simultaneously.

Understanding the text **59**

There are times when Shakespeare might give us shared short lines, or even shared *Alexandrine* lines. Let's look at examples of both of those scenarios from the same scene between Lady Anne and Richard in *Richard III*.

We looked at Lady Anne's speech from earlier in this scene. At this point, Anne is confronting Richard as the murderer of her husband and father-in-law. We have a series of shared *Alexandrine* and short lines as Anne curses Richard, and Richard responds.

Richard: Say that I slew them not. *(6 beats)*
Anne: Then say they were not slain: *(+ 6 beats = 12: a shared Alexandrine)*
 But dead they are, and devilish slave by thee.
Richard: I did not kill your husband. *(7 beats; where do the missing 3 beats go?)*
Anne: Why then he is alive. *(6 beats; where are the remaining 4 beats?)*
Richard: Nay, he is dead, and slain by Edward's hands.

This is quite a telling piece of verse: it is up to you to figure out where those missing beats go. Are they before the line or do they follow after it? The next line is also short; where do *those* missing beats go? Here, Shakespeare demands we pay attention. We never pause at random, because if we pay attention to the meter it will guide us to those moments where there are pauses, like it has here.

Later, Anne and Richard have another shared short line.

Anne: Dids't thou not kill this King? *(6 beats)*
Richard: I grant ye. *(+ 3 beats = 9 total. Where would you put the missing beat?)*

Richard later reasons with Anne that he should be thanked for sending such good men to heaven.

Richard: For he was fitter for that place then earth.
Anne: And thou unfit for any place but hell.
Richard: Yes one place else, if you will hear me name it. *(11 beats: feminine)*
Anne: Some dungeon. *(3 beats)*
Richard: Your Bed-chamber. *(4 beats)*
Anne: Ill rest betide the chamber where thou liest. *(11 beats: feminine)*

60 Excavating the foundation

> Richard: So will it Madam, till I lie with you.
> Anne: I hope so. *(3 beats)*
> Richard: I know so. But gentle Lady Anne, *(9 beats)*

What do you think is happening here? We have a long line followed by two successive short lines. Even if they are joined to a shared line, the line is still short by three beats. Afterwards, there is a long line followed by perfect iambic pentameter, and then two short lines again (which could also be combined into an *Alexandrine*). By digging into the structure of Shakespeare's verse, you have uncovered several possibilities for performance. This verse Shakespeare has given us is unusual: be curious about it. Investigate through practice what the possibilities are. This is the kind of analysis that fuels creative choices in rehearsal, rather than stifles them.

Things escalate between Anne and Richard and we have shared iambic lines comprised of several different exchanges between them as they debate.

> Richard: He lives, that loves thee better then he could. *(10 beats, fully iambic)*
> Anne: Name him. *(2 beats)*
> Richard: Plantagenet. *(4 beats)*
> Anne: Why that was he. *(4 beats; these three lines form one line of iambic pentameter).*
> Richard: The selfsame name, but one of better Nature. *(11 beats: feminine)*
> Anne: Where is he? *(3 beats)*
> Richard: Here: *Spits at him.*
> Why dost thou spit at me. *(Together this forms an iambic line, and the First Folio even provides the stage direction, although it is inherent in the text.)*

As Richard turns this contempt into a mating ritual, Shakespeare heightens the situation even further with the introduction of a rapid sequence of shared *Alexandrine* lines.

> Anne: I would I knew thy heart. *(6 beats)*
> Richard: 'Tis figured in my tongue. *(6 beats)*
> Anne: I fear me, both are false. *(6 beats)*
> Richard: Then never Man was true. *(6 beats)*
> Anne: Well, well, put up your Sword. *(6 beats)*
> Richard: Say then my Peace is made. *(6 beats)*

Understanding the text **61**

Anne:	That shalt thou know hereafter. *(7 beats, and this breaks the rhythm of the three shared Alexandrines above.)*
Richard:	But shall I live in hope. *(6 beats)*
Anne:	All men I hope live so. *(6 beats)*
Richard:	Vouchsafe to wear this Ring. *(6 beats. Are the missing 4 beats taken up with Richard putting the ring on her finger?)*
	Look how my Ring encompasseth thy Finger, *(11 beats: feminine)*
	Even so thy Breast encloseth my poor heart:

In this line, the first word "even" is elided to one syllable. Try bouncing it both ways you'll see why:

"Even SO thy BREAST enCLOSeth MY poor HEART:"

and **BOUNCE** and **BOUNCE** and **BOUNCE** and **BOUNCE** and **BOUNCE**

This works rhythmically; the alternative is impossible to speak for sense:

"eVEN so THY breast ENclosETH my POOR heart"

Speaking the verse this way is difficult to execute, and it certainly doesn't do anything to help the actor tell the story; it sounds alien and robotic. We don't have to decide whether or not things should be elided; syllables are elided when the text demands it.

We've looked so far at Shakespeare's poetic meter and the key variations that can help you create dynamic performances. If you've studied poetry you might be familiar with other terms associated with scansion and meter, such as *spondee* (two stressed syllables in succession) or *pyrrhic* (two unstressed syllables in succession). What I am going to say will shock English teachers and professors everywhere: these are totally irrelevant to performance—and I suggest you forget them immediately. Based on what I said earlier about the vocal flexibility between stressed and unstressed syllables on that numeric scale, the human voice cannot speak in equal measures of stress (or unstress) and still communicate effectively. Lady Anne says to Richard,

Blush, blush thou lump of foul Deformity:

If you were to mark your analysis with a pencil and read silently you might think the unit "Blush, blush" is *spondee*: two stressed syllables, but actually for the actor it is not. The human voice can't—or certainly *shouldn't*—speak

62 Excavating the foundation

that sequence with exactly the same weight. They can't both be a "10"; it's robotic. Plus, she's repeating herself for emphasis; the repeated command *does* have more stress. Again, the first "Blush" isn't a "0" and the second a "10"; those two could be an "8" followed by a "10" or even a "9" followed by a "10," but they can't both be identical "10"s. Try it out loud: go for it. Try to say those two words in succession with equal weight. You can't actually do it—organically, we have a vocal variation, even if it's a slight one. This is why we continue to explore the text out loud physically. Trust your instrument and the ball and you won't go wrong.

Discovering the language

Alliteration and assonance

We've been exploring the rhythm of Shakespeare's language metrically, getting that pulse within our bodies so we can sense where there are shifts in rhythm. There is another kind of rhythm in Shakespeare's language: the rhythm of repetition. Just as the meter provides us with a sense of linguistic movement, the language provides its own particular notes that help to create the symphony of Shakespeare's verse. I draw this parallel to music because it's an excellent way of thinking about how each of these components comes together to form an aural whole. For example, all waltzes follow the same beat (1–2–3, 1–2–3, 1–2–3, 1–2–3) although the composers' notes vary on top of that constant beat; the waltz follows the same rhythm even though composers arrange their notes differently. Our iambic pentameter is the beat, the rhythm underlying, but each verse line is composed of its own language on top of that structure and the way that language is composed can create a concurrent rhythm that lends itself to the text's musicality.

The presence of repeated sounds creates a musicality that helps the actor to engage and activate the language in very particular ways. As was the case with the "metric deviations," Shakespeare places these repetitive patterns in conjunction with each other as very deliberate clues that can inform the actor's practice. Once you are aware of the components to look for you have the power to use them as performance building blocks. Like archaeologists, we first excavate the structure. Once we have a clear understanding of the structure, we can imagine how that structure might be developed three-dimensionally.

Alliteration is the repetition of consonant sounds. We've been looking at the scene between Lady Anne and Richard for the metric irregularities; let's look at the beginning of Richard's speech once Anne exits for an example of alliteration (1.2). It's always important to read the text out loud—in this case especially so, because sounds don't always the match the word's spelling.

Understanding the text **63**

Was ever woman in this humor woo'd?
Was ever woman in this humor won?
I'll have her, but I will not keep her long.
What? I that kill'd her Husband, and his Father,
To take her in her hearts extremist hate,
With curses in her mouth, Tears in her eyes,
The bleeding witness of my hatred by,
Having God, her Conscience, and these bars against me,
And I, no Friends to back my suit withal,
But the plain Devil, and dissembling looks?
And yet to win her? All the world to nothing.
Hah!

Now you may have already discovered the *trochees* and *Alexandrines* here, but let's look specifically at these particular sounds: "*w*," "*t*," and "*h*."

Was ever **w**oman in <u>th</u>is **h**umor **w**oo'd?
Was ever **w**oman in <u>th</u>is **h**umor **w**on?
I'll **h**ave **h**er, but I **w**ill not keep **h**er long.
What? I <u>th</u>at kill'd **h**er **H**usband, and **h**is Fa<u>th</u>er,
To take **h**er in **h**er **h**earts extremis**t h**ate,
Wi<u>th</u> curses in **h**er mou<u>th</u>, **T**ears in **h**er eyes,
The bleeding **w**i**t**ness of my **h**a**t**red by,
Having God, **h**er Conscience, and <u>th</u>ese bars agains**t** me,
And I, no Friends to back my sui**t w**i<u>th</u>al,
But <u>th</u>e plain Devil, and dissembling looks?
And ye**t t**o **w**in **h**er? All <u>th</u>e **w**orld **t**o no<u>th</u>ing.
Hah!

Now, I've underlined the repetition of "**th**" in this speech, because this is also an unavoidable pattern. Read it through once again (out loud) and this time pay attention to those repeated sounds.

What do you discover? When we focus on the sounds "**w**," "**t**," and "**h**" we get a sense that Richard is saying to the audience "**what?**" The tip of the tongue release on "**t**" becomes a bit of a linguistic "click" of

64 Excavating the foundation

disbelief, and the "**h**" becomes **how?** In fact, just speak those three sounds in succession now:

> "**w**"
> "**t**"
> "**h**"

You *sense* the disbelief when you pay attention to that alliteration, because it *is* amazing that he's managed to pull this off. When we add the "**th**" to it, it is as though the sounds form the question: **What the hell?**

Isn't that absolutely incredible?

We also have a parallel construction in those first two lines:

> Was ever woman in this humor woo'd?
>
> Was ever woman in this humor won?

This helps to create another sense of rhythm and pulse in the language in addition to the alliteration at play.

Assonance is the repetition of vowel (and diphthong) sounds. As is the case with alliteration, assonance can provide very useful clues to help the actor imagine the three-dimensionality of the language, and it can also help to point out areas that enhance the music of what is spoken, in addition to the content. Let's return to the Helena speech we looked at earlier:

> *Till I have no wife I have nothing in France.*
>
> Nothing in France until he has no wife:
>
> Thou shalt have none Rossillion, none in France,
>
> Then hast thou all again: poor Lord, is't I
>
> That chase thee from thy Country, and expose
>
> Those tender limbs of thine, to the event
>
> Of the none-sparing war? And is it I,
>
> That drive thee from the sportive Court, where thou
>
> Was't shot at with fair eyes, to be the mark
>
> Of smoky Muskets? O you leaden messengers,
>
> That ride upon the violent speed of fire.
>
> Fly with false aim, move the still-piecing air

Understanding the text **65**

That sings with piercing, do not touch my Lord:
Who ever shoots at him, I set him there.

Let's pay attention to the diphthong sound "**I**." A *diphthong* is a blended vowel sound, like the "marriage" of two vowels, or an open sound where the shape of the mouth changes. Say it out loud:

"**I**"

Do you feel how the jaw moves and the mouth changes shape? That's a diphthong.

Let's go through and read the speech again out loud, this time paying attention to those sounds of "**I**"; remembering not to rely on the spelling of words, but on the sounds those words make.

> *Till* **I** *have no wife* **I** *have nothing in France.*
> Nothing in France until he has no wife:
> Thou shalt have none Rossillion, none in France,
> Then hast thou all again: poor Lord, is't **I**
> That chase thee from thy Country, and expose
> Those tender limbs of thine, to the event
> Of the none-sparing war? And is it **I**,
> That drive thee from the sportive Court, where thou
> Was't shot at with fair **ey**es, to be the mark
> Of smoky Muskets? O you leaden messengers,
> That ride upon the violent speed of fire.
> Fly with false aim, move the still-piecing air
> That sings with piercing, do not touch my Lord:
> Who ever shoots at him, **I** set him there.

When you read through, paying attention to that repetition, you begin to get a sense that Helena is indeed addressing the fact that "*I* am to blame [that he is in danger]." The speech says this fairly outright, but the choices Shakespeare has made in creating that vocal music enhances both the actor's playing of it as well as the language's music and rhythm.

This is another of the key components to seek out as you enter into a physical relationship with the text. Just as an archaeologist gently brushes and

66 Excavating the foundation

chips away at the surface to unearth the artifacts within a given site, we must use our own tools to reveal the foundation of Shakespeare's texts.

Punctuation

Punctuation reveals the rhythm of thought in the text. It serves to *punctuate* how expression is made, and to help clarify ideas. Punctuation can signal the end of thoughts, join thoughts together, or help to refine thoughts.

End-stops, *periods*, *question marks*, and *exclamation points* indicate the end of thoughts. It is important to consider the First Folio's punctuation when looking at how punctuation helps to shape the thoughts in a text; modern editors often increase the amount of full stops in Shakespeare's texts in order to parcel out ideas in a manageable way for readers. As practitioners, we know that reading is different from *doing*, that reading a text is a completely different process from speaking or performing it.

It is worth considering where thoughts *end* in the text. Do they end in the final position of a verse line or in the middle of the line? If they end at the end of the verse line the punctuation in the meter is orderly; the thoughts fill the line and new thoughts begin on new verse lines. That is a very different rhythm than when a thought ends mid-line and the new thought is already present within that same line of verse. If we think back to

dee DUM dee DUM dee DUM dee DUM dee DUM

we can imagine how organized a thought must be if it draws to a conclusion as the meter does, *or* how present the next thought must be in order to maintain that rhythm.

Commas are like little springboards that serve to energize the language and clarify thoughts.

In our earlier example from Macbeth's dagger speech, you can see how the comma springs you forward into the next thought:

I have thee not, *(spring!)* and yet I see thee still.

Or from Richard's speech that we looked at for *alliteration*:

I'll have her, *(spring!)* but I will not keep her long.

This begins to illustrate some of the inherent energy in the language. You want to breathe there, don't you? *Breathe!* To breathe is to inspire literally and we see the inspiration of thought in these texts. Part of the reason that

Understanding the text **67**

actors run out of breath when speaking Shakespeare is because they haven't married the inspiration of thought to the inspiration of breath. When we speak as ourselves we naturally breathe at those points, because we are forming the thoughts right at that particular moment in time. It is unusual for us to run out of breath as ourselves because our brains control both functions. Actors know exactly the words in which they will say what the *character's* thought is—the text dictates this—and so the cognitive process of formulating thought into communication doesn't function in quite the same way. Cognitively, we are recalling information that has been previously stored, not organizing the information into new thoughts. Our own thought patterns align with our own breath, but the actor must align an imposed thought process to his own breath pattern. It's complicated business when you think about it. So *breathing* with new thought is incredibly important to speaking with clarity. Creating a physical sense of this energy pulse helps you to activate the language. When you are reading aloud, give yourself a little spring when you get to those commas. Spring like a little cat. You don't need to come entirely off the floor into a leap, but that light spring will create a sense of muscle memory as you learn the text that will embed that memory in your brain in a more active way than simply reading it at a table in silence will.

Sometimes there will be multiple commas in succession, as is the case in the opening of Antony's famous speech (*Julius Caesar* 3.2):

> Friends, Romans, Countrymen, lend me your ears
>
> I come to bury Caesar, not to praise him:

You can begin to see how commas can also help to define lists: in this case the list of those in the assembly. You can also begin to sense how not all breaths are full breaths (Antony is not hyperventilating here) but the breath is light and lifts the energy; it keeps the language moving forward and towards connection, connection to the audience both on and "off" stage. Commas also help to define "ladders" (a steadily rising list of thoughts)—which we will look at in just a moment.

Commas can also help to punctuate parenthetical thoughts. When we speak, we naturally phrase our thoughts in parenthesis to create emphasis and clarity in our thoughts. These parentheses are often marked by a change in vocal rhythm, pattern, or pitch. We might say: "Can you (on your way home from work) pick up milk?" or "My friend (who has excellent taste) recommended it." Our brains organize thoughts in this way; it's ungrammatical—messy even, but very, very human.

You'll find these implied parenthesis all throughout Shakespeare's texts once you know to look for them. Here is an example from one of Launce's

68 Excavating the foundation

speeches in *The Two Gentlemen of Verona* (2.3), which we will look at in detail when we get to *colons*:

> I have receiv'd my proportion, like the prodigious son, and am going with Sir Proteus to the Imperial's Court :

The statement "like the prodigious son" is a parenthetical phrase: do you see how those commas can be replaced by parenthesis? It could have read:

> I have receiv'd my proportion (like the prodigious son) and am going with Sir Proteus to the Imperial's Court :

You'll notice that you can take the phrase out altogether and the line will still make sense:

> I have receiv'd my proportion _____ and am going with Sir Proteus to the Imperial's Court :

So you can put your own vocal parenthesis around that phrase "like the prodigious son" and this will help to clarify the text, and also help the audience to understand Launce's opinion about the lot he's been given. Even though Launce suffers from malapropism (he means to say the "prodigal" son), we understand how he feels about receiving his "proportion" (another malaprop for "portion" or "allotment"). If you run those together ("I've received *this* like *this*") you've missed an opportunity to make the speech that much more dynamic.

You may also have noticed that I used parenthetical commas when I introduced the passage. I said, "Here is an example from one of Launce's speeches, which we will look at in detail when we get to *colons*." I could have written: "Here is an example from one of Launce's speeches (which we will look at in detail when we get to *colons*)." It is right there; you just need to uncover it. That's why I talk about the *archaeology* of performance; I want you to look beyond the surface to see what you can reveal and what you can use to personalize your own connection.

Semicolons indicate a shift in thought, but not a full stop. At times, what follows the semicolon cannot stand alone as its own complete sentence, but at other times the semicolon can divide two complete sentences. You can think of a semicolon as joining two related thoughts, as if "listen" or "furthermore" sits in its place. For example, in *The Second Part of King Henry the Fourth* (2.3), Lady Percy states:

Understanding the text   **69**

There were two Honors lost; Yours and your Son's.

You have the sense that Lady Percy is saying:

There were two Honors lost; *(listen!)* Yours and your Son's.

Semicolons are found more frequently in modern editions; they do not appear with the same frequency in the First Folio. In fact, in the example above the semicolon could be replaced easily by a colon.

Colons help to clarify thoughts. Think of them as little springs that say, "I'll tell you what I mean," or "here's an example," or "I'm going to get very specific with you." Colon*s* can help to create intimacy and honesty: they help to reveal inner thoughts and clarify points in arguments. Colons can separate vows, confessions, realizations, and details from the statements they follow. Colons can help to frame the *active* moments of reflection we looked at in the previous chapter. They are the actor's best friends: they activate the language and are infinitely *playable*!

Let's return to our Helena example to see how the colons function in that speech:

> *Till I have no wife I have nothing in France.*
> Nothing in France until he has no wife: **(vows)**
> Thou shalt have none Rossillion, none in France,
> Then hast thou all again: **(realization)** poor Lord, is't I
> That chase thee from thy Country, and expose
> Those tender limbs of thine, to the event
> Of the none-sparing war? And is it I,
> That drive thee from the sportive Court, where thou
> Was't shot at with fair eyes, to be the mark
> Of smoky Muskets? O you leaden messengers,
> That ride upon the violent speed of fire.
> Fly with false aim, move the still-piecing air
> That sings with piercing, do not touch my Lord: **(confession)**
> Who ever shoots at him, I set him there.

Launce's speech from *The Two Gentlemen of Verona* (2.3) is an excellent of example of an "I'll tell you what I mean" colon. In it, Launce describes leaving his home in order to serve his master. Launce is constantly qualifying what it

70 Excavating the foundation

is that he is saying—or *trying* to say. This is one of those instances where it is particularly important to consult the First Folio. Most modern editors create complete sentences at all our lovely colons, which make the speech far tidier than it actually is. There are only two full stops in the speech: Launce just keeps going, and that information is invaluable to the actor. You'll also notice that while this speech is in prose, we can still excavate our clues to perform it.

> Nay, 'twill be this hour ere I have done weeping **:** all the kind of the Launces have this very fault **:** I have receiv'd my proportion, like the prodigious son, and am going with Sir Proteus to the Imperial's Court **:** I think Crab my dog, be the sourest natured dog that lives **:** My Mother weeping **:** my Father wailing **:** my Sister crying **:** our Maid howling **:** our Cat wringing her hands, and all our house in a great perplexity, yet did not this cruel-hearted Cur shed one tear **:** he is a stone, a very pebble stone, and has no more pity in him then a dog **:** a Jew would have wept to have seen our parting **:** why my Grandam having no eyes, look you, wept herself blind at my parting **:** nay, I'll show you the manner of it. This shoe is my father **:** no, this left shoe is my father; no, no this left shoe is my mother **:** nay, that cannot be so neither **:** yes, it is so, it is so **:** it hath the worser sole **:** this shoe with the hole in it, is my mother **:** and this my father **:** a vengeance on't, there tis **:** Now sir, this staff is my sister **:** for look you, she is as white as a lily, and as small as a wand **:** this hat is Nan our maid **:** I am the dog **:** no, the dog is himself, and I am the dog **:** oh, the dog is me, and I am myself **:** I, so, so **:** now come I to my Father; Father, your blessing **:** now should not the shoe speak a word for weeping **:** now should I kiss my Father; well, he weeps on **:** Now come I to my Mother **:** Oh that she could speak now, like a would-woman **:** well, I kiss her **:** why there tis; here's my mother's breath up and down **:** Now come I to my sister; mark you the moan she makes **:** now the dog all this while sheds not a tear **:** nor speaks a word **:** but see how I lay the dust with my tears.

There are thirty-seven colons in that speech! That is a lot of qualification; the speech is filled with clarification. For fun, read it through again and this time insert "I'll tell you what I mean," "here's an example," or "let me get specific" every time you reach a colon (you'll want to create some variety because there are so many of them in such close proximity to one another—you don't want to zone out). You'll know exactly how colons function by the end of the speech.

Lists and ladders

Throughout Shakespeare there are examples of *lists* and *ladders*, both of which help to organize thoughts and build arguments. Keep in mind that the biggest distinction between the two is that while *lists* itemize parts of a larger whole, *ladders* usually build in intensity, either to create a bigger picture of a particular event, or to make a larger point in an argument. You can visualize an image of a ladder with its rungs, and develop a vocal climb from one point to the next, with each step along the way leading to the end point.

You just read an example of this in Launce's speech. Launce begins the speech weeping, and attributes his inability to stop weeping to a family fault. Now you might think that the list is simply that: a list of who's doing what. When you take a closer look though, and examine the theme of weeping and the through-line of tears, you will realize that everything Launce says builds to the point that that his Grandmother has wept herself blind (despite having the eyes with which to do it). Then we begin to understand why Launce is having such an issue with his dog's "sour nature": it's unnatural in his world. As you read it through again, imagine that you are climbing a huge hill or scaling a mountain. You'll notice that the ladder builds until you reach that first full stop. You'll also notice that although ladders build in intensity there can be moments of pause, or perhaps poise, as you ascend. It doesn't necessarily just get louder and louder; it's subtler and more complex than that.

> Nay, 'twill be this hour ere I have done weeping **:** (») all the kind of the Launces have this very fault **:** (») I have receiv'd my proportion, like the prodigious son, and am going with Sir Proteus to the Imperial's Court **:** I think Crab my dog, be the sourest natured dog that lives **:** (») My Mother weeping **:** (») my Father wailing **:** (») my Sister crying **:** (») our Maid howling **:** (») our Cat wringing her hands, (») and all our house in a great perplexity, yet did not this cruel-hearted Cur shed one tear **:** he is a stone, (») a very pebble stone, (») and has no more pity in him then a dog **:** (») a Jew would have wept to have seen our parting **:** (») why my Grandam having no eyes, look you, wept herself blind at my parting **:** (») nay, I'll show you the manner of it.

You can see the escalation that builds to the point where Launce must then illustrate the scene.

Lists identify the components of a larger whole. Lists can classify parts of a bigger idea, or help to articulate the details of a concept. While ladders can

72 Excavating the foundation

certainly contain lists, not all lists are ladders. Some lists may follow a particular format: 1→2→3→∴ (conclusion), while others don't.

In the Lady Anne speech we looked at earlier there is a list that follows this 1→2→3→∴ format:

> More direful hap betide that hated Wretch
>
> That makes us wretched by the death of thee,
>
> Than I can wish to Wolves (1), to Spiders (2), Toads (3),
>
> ∴ Or any creeping venom'd thing that lives.

This list of creatures helps Anne (and the actor playing her) to define the larger whole. Shakespeare could have written:

> Than I can wish to venom'd things that live.

That's a perfect line of iambic pentameter, but he *didn't* write it that way. Why didn't he? Anne needs that list and because of its impact, so do we.

Lists can also have a wider reach: they aren't always as simple as the list of nouns in the above example. Lists can be implied or defined within the text. In *The Winter's Tale* (3.2) Hermione's husband Leontes accuses her of adultery and of giving birth to the progeny from that affair. He has put her on trial immediately after the birth, taken the baby and her elder child from her, wrongly accused her of infidelity, and has threatened her with death. The signposts of her list are built in pretty transparently. This speech has a double 1→2→3→∴ format; it goes all the way to 6 before it concludes.

> Sir, spare your Threats :
>
> The Bug which you would fright me with, I seek :
>
> To me can Life be no commodity;
>
> **(1)** The crown and comfort of my Life (your Favor)
>
> I do give lost, for I do feel it gone,
>
> But know not how it went. **(2)** My second joy
>
> And first Fruits of my body, from his presence
>
> I am bar'd, like one infectious. **(3)** My third comfort
>
> (Star'd most unluckily) is from my breast
>
> (The innocent milk in it most innocent mouth)

Hal'd out to murder. **(4)** My self on every Post

Proclaimed a Strumpet : **(5)** with immodest hatred

The Child-bed priviledge denied, which longs

To Women of all fashion. **(6)** Lastly, hurried

Here, to this place, i'th' open air, before

I have got strength of limit. **(∴)** Now (my Liege)

Tell me what blessings I have here alive,

That I should fear to die? Therefore proceed :

But yet hear this : mistake me not : no Life,

(I prize it not a straw) but for mine Honor,

Which I would free : if I shall be condemn'd

Upon surmizes (all proofs sleeping else,

But what your Jealousies awake) I tell you

'Tis Rigor, and not Law. Your Honors all,

I do refer me to the Oracle :

Apollo be my Judge.

In this example, you can see how Hermione's long list of wrongs detail and itemize the reasons why "life [has] no commodity," why she does not fear death.

Telescoping

There is another way to examine how the parts of an idea can come together to clarify the larger whole: *telescoping*. Telescoping is a way of focusing in on different smaller, independently contained ideas in order to reach a clearer vision at the end of a particular speech. I call this telescoping because unlike ladders, which build in intensity, telescoping focuses each part in order to better see the whole at the end. I envision the antique telescope where each section can be focused separately and bring the viewer closer to the final image. You can think of those expanding scopes where each section collapses in to the next and can be expanded outwards for a view with the greatest detail. That is what telescoping does: it brings you closer and closer to the final point. As you read through a telescoping speech, you discover how you move closer and closer towards the key point. Let's look at how it works.

This speech belongs to the Bastard in *King John* (1.1). He has just demanded that his mother, Lady Faulconbridge, reveal his paternity; she

74 Excavating the foundation

confesses that he is the son of King Richard Coeur de Lion rather than that of her husband, Sir Robert Faulconbridge. In this speech he relieves her of her guilt and defends her honor against her own shame and regret based on the argument that a woman could certainly not have resisted a King as powerful as Richard. Each component of the speech moves towards the Bastard's clarity of his vision and the point of his argument.

> Now by this light were I to get again,
> Madam I would not with a better father :
> Some sins do bear their privilege on earth,
> And so doth yours : your fault, was not your folly,
> Needs must you lay your heart at his dispose,
> Subjected tribute to commanding love,
> Against whose fury and unmatched force,
> The aweless Lion could not wage the fight,
> Nor keep his Princely heart from Richard's hand :
> He that perforce robs Lions of their hearts,
> May easily win a woman's : aye my mother,
> With all my heart I thank thee for my father :
> Who lives and dares but say, thou didst not well
> When I was got, I'll send his soul to hell.

This telescope moves towards the point made at the end of the speech:

> Who lives and dares but say, thou didst not well
> When I was got, I'll send his soul to hell.

Let's look at how he moves towards that point through the telescope:

> Now by this light were I to get again,
> Madam I would not with a better father : *(closer)*
> Some sins do bear their privilege on earth,
> And so doth yours *(closer)*: your fault, was not your folly, *(closer)*
> Needs must you lay your heart at his dispose,
> Subjected tribute to commanding love, *(closer)*

Understanding the text **75**

Against whose fury and unmatched force,

The aweless Lion could not wage the fight,

Nor keep his Princely heart from Richard's hand : *(closer)*

He that perforce robs Lions of their hearts,

May easily win a woman's *(closer)*: aye my mother,

With all my heart I thank thee for my father *(closer):*

Who lives and dares but say, thou didst not well

When I was got, I'll send his soul to hell. *(point!)*

Telescoping helps to focus his argument, and you can see that it's not necessarily a list or ladder, but it each part helps to see the whole point with greater clarity.

The first section of the telescope is the Bastard promising that if he were to be born again he wouldn't wish for a different father. Next, he makes the statement that some sins are contained to the earth; they aren't sins that are everlasting, and this is one of them. He tells his mother that her sin (or fault) was not in being foolish, but in being dutiful, and he outlines why in the next scope: as the King's subject, she needed to relinquish her love to him at his command. He focuses his reasoning further: he reminds her of the King's valorous reputation in battle, and of the legend that he raged against a lion and pulled out the beast's heart. At this locus in the scope of his argument, he moves closer to his ultimate point by drawing upon the conclusion that if Richard was capable of stealing the heart of a ferocious beast, then he could certainly steal her heart from her. This next scope is highly personal and it frames the opening of his argument: he thanks his mother for his parentage, and in that intimacy forgives her of her transgressions through the focusing of that telescope. He concludes and reaches his final point by globalizing the argument: he will fight to the death and murder anyone who condemns her actions. In fact, you may notice that the final two lines form a rhyming couplet, which would have indicated an exit to Shakespeare's audience. Perhaps this is an indication that he is to exit, but is prompted to continue:

Come Lady I will show thee to my kin,

And they shall say, when Richard me begot,

If thou hadst said him nay, it had been sin;

Who says it was, he lies, I say 'twas not.

76 Excavating the foundation

Through his telescoping the Bastard has focused and formulated his argument. You can see how each of these "scopes" build to the larger point, yet don't quite formulate a proper list or ladder. Keep this in mind and look for these when you are working on a text. I assure you that if you understand that you are focusing components of a larger whole, you will be able to use the language more actively, and be more effective in your playing. This keeps new thoughts emerging actively, and helps you to avoid the pitfall of droning on during long speeches. It also helps your audience hear the ideas come together, which makes it easier for them to engage and follow your action and the story.

Antithesis

The juxtaposition of two opposing ideas or things is known as *antithesis*. These can be in direct contrast to one another or can also create a comparison where one thing opposes another: [this] vs. [that]. We just saw examples of [this] vs. [that] in the text from *King John*. First, there was the antithesis between "fault" and "folly": the Bastard essentially tells her, "it may have been [this] but it wasn't [that]." Next, we have the antithesis between the lion and a woman. The Bastard argues that if a lion cannot resist, then how can a woman? There you also have that great example of logic and reasoning that you will find throughout Shakespeare's texts: *if* this, *then* that. It is implied in the speech from *King John*, but sometimes it is stated outright—and we saw that with the speech from Hermione:

> ~~Which I would free :~~ **if** I shall be condemn'd
> Upon surmizes (all proofs sleeping else,
> But what your Jealousies awake) **{then}** I tell you
> 'Tis Rigor, and not Law. ~~Your Honors all,~~

I'd like to look at an example of antithesis that illustrates direct contrast, and this speech from *Romeo and Juliet* (1.1) is one of my favorites for this:

> Here's much to do with hate, but more with love:
> Why then, O brawling love, O loving hate;
> O anything, of nothing first create:
> O heavy lightness, serious vanity,
> Misshapen Chaos of well-seeming forms,
> Feather of lead, bright smoke, cold fire, sick health,

Understanding the text **77**

Still-waking sleep, that is not what it is.
This love feel I, that feel no love in this.

In this speech you have the overall set up of [this] vs. [that] at play with [hate] vs. [love], but as you continue exploring it you discover these terrific direct contrasts: brawling/love, loving/hate, heavy/lightness, serious/vanity, bright/ smoke, cold/fire, sick/health, still-waking/sleep. Even though Shakespeare is giving all of these antithetical contrasts, they are interspersed with broader antithesis as well: [anything] vs. [nothing]; [misshapen chaos] vs. [well-seeming forms]; [feather] vs. [lead] (which we can also read simply as [light] vs. [heavy]); [is not] vs. [is]; [this love] vs. [no love]. Simply put, it just doesn't get much better than this! Romeo's next line is:

Dost thou not [laugh]?

There is a sense of joy in the play of that language, and the antithesis continues with Benvolio's second half of that shared line:

No Coz, I rather [weep].

If you haven't already been reading aloud, be sure to speak this one: your experience of doing so will tell you much.

Metaphors and similes

Metaphors and *similes* are an alternative form of comparison; both devices evoke imagery by relating one thing to another: one implicitly and one explicitly. With *metaphors* one thing stands in place of the other; metaphors imply that one thing actually *is* a different thing. As Stevie Wonder famously sang, "you are the apple of my eye." For example, in *The Two Gentlemen of Verona*, the ever-changing Proteus finds himself in a love triangle (or perhaps a square?) when he falls in love with Sylvia, his best friend's beloved, despite his betrothal to his previous love, Julia. In Act 2, scene 6, Proteus compares the two women using metaphors:

At first I did adore *a twinkling Star*, (Julia)
But now I worship *a celestial Sun*: (Sylvia)

Similes make an explicit comparison between two things, and use "like" or "as" to illustrate the point—"we go together like peanut butter and jelly." There are some lovely examples of both types of similes in *Twelfth Night*. In this portion, Viola attempts to persuade Orsino that women can

78 Excavating the foundation

love as men do. Let's look at this exchange between them (2.4) to see both "as" and "like" at play:

Orsino: There is no woman's sides
Can bide the beating of so strong a passion,
As love doth give my heart : no woman's heart
So big, to hold so much, they lack retention,
Alas, their love may be call'd appetite,
No motion of the Liver, but the Palate,
That suffer surfeit, cloyment, and revolt,
But mine is all ***as*** hungry as the Sea,
And can digest as much, make no compare
Between that love a woman can bear me,
And that I owe Olivia.

Viola: I but I know.

Orsino: What dost thou know?

Viola: Too well what love women to men may owe :
In faith they are as true of heart, as we.
My Father had a daughter lov'd a man
As it might be perhaps, were I a woman
I should your Lordship.

Orsino: And what's her history?

Viola: A blank my Lord : she never told her love,
But let concealment **like** a worm i'th bud
Feed on her damask cheek : she pin'd in thought,
And with a green and yellow melancholy,
She sat **like** Patience on a Monument
Smiling at grief. Was not this love indeed?
We men may say more, swear more, but indeed
Our shows are more then will : for still we prove
Much in our vows, but little in our love.

You'll notice that by the end of this speech, Viola has moved beyond similes: she makes a declaration "but indeed / Our shows *are* more than will." Of course, the audience knows that Viola is wearing a mask as Cesario; those similes help to support her façade, and the audience enjoys them all the more because they are complicit in the deception.

Titles and names

We have been looking closely at the particular and deliberate ways that Shakespeare engages with language. Let's look at an area that is often

Understanding the text **79**

overlooked: the use of titles and names. Names can reveal information about the relationship between characters, and once you are aware of some key points, a shift in name or title can help to enliven and activate both the language and the scene.

One of the first things to be aware of is that although they sound quite formal to our modern ears, the titles "thee" and "thou" are actually intimate terms. The title "you," on the other hand, is a formal address although we are accustomed to using it informally. While they may seem interchangeable at first read, the differences in formality between the two help to inform changes in status and tactics within the a speech or scene. Let's look at an example from *Henry IV, Part I* (2.3). In this scene Hotspur is about to leave, to join his conspirators in rebellion, much to the dismay of his wife, Lady Percy. She first enquires playfully where he intends to go, but as she pushes him, he pushes back with language that deliberately puts her in her place. This scene is a masterpiece of titles and names, as you will discover.

Lady Percy:	But hear you, **my Lord**.
Hotspur:	What say'st thou, **my Lady**.
Lady Percy:	What is it carries **you** away?
Hotspur:	Why, my horse (**my Love**) my horse.
Lady Percy:	Out you **mad-headed Ape**, a Weasel hath not such a deal of Spleen, as you are tossed with. In sooth I'll know your business **Harry**, that I will. I fear my Brother Mortimer doth stir about his Title, and hath sent for you to line his enterprise. But if **you** go—
Hotspur:	So far a foot, I shall be weary, **Love**.
Lady Percy:	Come, come, you **Paraquito**, answer me directly unto this question, that I shall ask. Indeed I'll break thy little finger **Harry**, if **thou** wilt not tell me true.
Hotspur:	Away, away you **trifler** : **Love**, I love **thee** not, I care not for **thee Kate** : this is no world To play with Mammets and to tilt with lips. We must have bloody Noses, and crack'd Crowns, And pass them current too. Gods me, my horse. What say'st **thou Kate**? What would'st **thou** have with me?
Lady Percy:	Do **you** not love me? Do **you** not indeed? Well, do not then. For since **you** love me not I will not love myself. Do **you** not love me? Nay, tell me if **thou** speak'st in jest or no.
Hotspur:	Come, wilt **thou** see me ride?

80 Excavating the foundation

And when I am a horseback, I will swear
I love **thee** infinitely. But hark **you Kate**,
I must not have **you** henceforth, question me,
Whether I go : nor reason whereabout.
Whether I must, I must : and to conclude,
This Evening must I leave **thee**, **gentle Kate**.
I know **you** wise, but yet no further wise
Then **Harry Percy's wife**. Constant **you** are,
But yet a **woman** : and for secrecy,
No **Lady** closer. For I well believe
Thou wilt not utter what **thou** dost not know,
And so far wilt I trust **thee**, **gentle Kate**.

Lady Percy: How so far?

Hotspur: Not an inch further. But hark **you Kate**,
Whither I go, thither shall **you** go too :
Today will I set forth, tomorrow **you**.
Will this content **you** Kate?

Lady Percy: It must of force.

You can track the relationship between these two by the flux in their address. The exchange between them begins with affectionate formality: my Lord → my Lady → you → my Love. It shifts with a change in tactic when Lady Percy begins to call names: mad-headed Ape → Harry → you → Love → Paraquito → Harry → thou; but Harry wants to put an end to this and be on his way, and he doesn't want to be questioned by his wife. The names he calls her in return may be intimate and playful (trifler → Love → thee → Kate → thou → Kate → thou) but there is a serious shift due to his content, and that is reflected in Lady Percy's reply (you → you → you → you → thou). Harry replies nicely with thou and thee, until he needs to assert himself and put her in her place, and then he returns to the formal "you." He eases things a bit with a return to "thee" only to remind her of her position in their relationship with "Harry Percy's wife" and "woman," before easing up again with "Lady," "thou," and "thee"; he ends by reminding her that he is in charge with orders and the formal "you." Metrically, Shakespeare could have interchanged many of these titles without losing the rhythm of the iambic pentameter, but he didn't and so we must consider why. It is also interesting to note that most modern editors create verse lines out of those two prosaic passages of Lady Percy's that appear in the First Folio, but you'll notice that when they do the verse is not always regular. It is possible that given the informality of her titles, that they aren't meant to be verse lines after all.

In *Othello* (3.3), Emilia has a lovely little speech about Desdemona's handkerchief, which she shares with the audience before Iago enters and she

Understanding the text **81**

relinquishes the key item. She calls object by many different names, and paying attention to those names releases the energy of the language and spurs the playing of the scene.

> Emilia: I am glad I have found this **Napkin** :
> This was her first <u>remembrance</u> from the Moore,
> My wayward Husband hath a hundred times
> Woo'd me to steal it. But she so loves the **Token**,
> (For he conjur'd her, she should ever keep it)
> That she refers it evermore about her,
> To kiss, and talk to. I'll have the work ta'en out,
> And give't Iago : what he will do with it
> Heaven knows, not I :
> I nothing, but to please his Fantasy.

When Iago enters, we discover two more names:

> Iago: How now? What do you here alone?
> Emilia: Do not you chide : I have a **thing** for you.
> Iago: You have a thing for me? It is a common thing—
> Emilia: Hah?
> Iago: To have a foolish Wife.
> Emilia: Oh, is that all? What will you give me now
> For that same **Handkerchief**.
> Iago: What Handkerchief?
> Emilia: What **Handkerchief**?
> Why that the Moore first gave to Desdemona
> That which so often you did bid me steal.

And in those shifts you can see the possibility for play. That is what being an archaeologist of performance is about: digging into the text to study it from all angles; probing the surface to brush away the generality, so that details can stand out and help you to personalize the text. You are empowered because you have uncovered things that activate the story.

Personification: casting Shakespeare's world

There is one more element that will help to empower you to create a strong relationship to the language you speak so that you develop dynamic performances of Shakespeare's texts: *personification*. In Shakespeare's texts you will find instances where Shakespeare takes concepts like Love, Nature, and

82 Excavating the foundation

Time and turns them into characters; he personifies them. These metaphysical concepts are transformed into human-like characters that become an integral part of the story; knowing this gives you the ability to transform the language into something active and further engages audiences in the story. When we looked at metaphors we looked at one of Proteus' speeches from *The Two Gentlemen of Verona*. If you are working on this speech (2.6), it's important for you to see how "Love" becomes a player in this action.

> To leave my Julia : shall I be forsworn?
>
> To love fair Sylvia : shall I be forsworn?
>
> To wrong my friend, I shall be much forsworn.
>
> And ev'n that **Power** which gave me first my oath
>
> Provokes me to this three-fold perjury.
>
> **Love** bad me swear, and **Love** bids me forswear :
>
> O sweet-suggesting **Love**, if **thou** hast sin'd,
>
> Teach me (thy tempted subject) to excuse it.
>
> At first I did adore a twinkling Star,
>
> But now I worship a celestial Sun :
>
> Un-heedful vows may heedfully be broken,
>
> And he wants wit, that wants resolved will,
>
> To learn his wit, t'exchange the bad for better;
>
> Fie, fie, unreverend tongue to call her bad,
>
> Whose sovereignty so oft thou hast preferr'd,
>
> With twenty thousand soul-confirming oaths.
>
> I cannot leave to love; and yet I do :
>
> But there I leave to love, where I should love.
>
> Julia I lose, and Valentine I lose,
>
> If I keep them, I needs must lose my self :
>
> If I lose them, thus find I by their loss,
>
> For Valentine, my self : for Julia, Sylvia.
>
> I to my self am deerer than a friend,
>
> For **Love** is still most precious in it self,
>
> And Sylvia (witness heaven that made her fair)
>
> Shows Julia by a swarthy Ethiope.

Understanding the text **83**

I will forget that Julia is alive,

Remembering that my Love to her is dead.

And Valentine I'll hold an Enemy,

Aiming at Sylvia as a sweeter friend.

I cannot now prove constant to my self,

Without some treachery us'd to Valentine.

This night he meaneth with a Corded-ladder

To climb celestial Sylvia's chamber window,

My self in counsel his competitor.

Now presently I'll give her father notice

Of their disguising and pretended flight.

Who (all enrag'd) will banish Valentine :

For Thurio he intends shall wed his daughter.

But Valentine being gone, I'll quickly cross

By some sly trick, blunt Thurio's dull proceeding.

Love lend me wings, to make my purpose swift

As **thou** hast lent me wit, to plot this drift.

In this speech you can see how **Love** is personified; it provokes, it bad and bids swearing, it is sweet-suggesting, it teaches its subjects, it is precious, it lends wings and wit; and you can see how intimately Proteus is acquainted with it, by the informal terms he is on, calling Love "thou." You'll note that Love here is also seen as the emotion or feeling in "remembering that my Love to her is dead," and perhaps that is why Proteus is so well acquainted with it: he is familiar with the personification as well what that personification imparts.

You can look for this same kind of personification in concepts like Nature and Time. Now that you are tuned in to the clues, you will find these examples as you work. In *King Lear* (1.2), the Bastard opens his soliloquy,

Thou Nature art my Goddess, to thy Law
My services are bound, wherefore should I
Stand in the plague of custom, and permit
The curiosity of Nations, to deprive me?

Right from the opening words "Thou Nature" we see that Edmund declares his allegiance, not to the sovereign Nation (the King) but to another governing

84 Excavating the foundation

body; he talks of "her" and "her Law" intimately, as seen through the use of "thou" and "thy." The Bastard is well acquainted with *this* ruler because he is bound to her by the circumstances of his birth.

Time is another friend that will appear, and you can look for where Time lends a hand beyond the examples of "first," "now," "this night," and "presently" we found in Proteus' speech above. Time serves as a great marker to help you work or telescope your way through a speech, but it also can take on qualities of personification. In *Twelfth Night* (2.2) when Viola attempts to work out the complications that arise from Malvolio's presentation of Olivia's ring, by the end of the soliloquy she enlists help from the character "Time."

> O time, thou must untangle this, not I,
>
> It is too hard a knot for me t'untie.

In these examples we can begin to see a very different way of looking at the surrounding world. Now that you are aware of the possibilities these personifications present, you can begin to use that awareness to explore the depths of these texts in your rehearsal process.

Throughout this chapter, we have looked at the various ways that Shakespeare's texts function, and considered how those elements can inspire possibilities in performance. You are equipped with the tools necessary to help you excavate a highly personalized connection to the text that will engage your audiences and the actors with which you work. The understanding you have cultivated here will inspire and inform the rest of the work you will explore in this book, in the rehearsal studio, and in the performance space.

4

CREATING CHARACTER

O learned indeed were that astronomer
That knew the stars as I his characters.

Cymbeline 3.2.27–28

Character

What does that word, *character*, mean to you? This is a book about performance so perhaps the first thought that comes to mind is a character in a play or the part an actor plays . . . the entity that is left after an actor's work. The end product, the culmination of a transformative journey between the actor's self and the work of the author: a destination point. What the audience "sees" when the actor has done the job well.

Yet this multi-faceted word means so much more than just the person in a fiction. To be a person of character is to be a person with an honored reputation, of high morality, an upstanding member of a community—someone worth vouching for. A "character witness" testifies to that reputation, and in doing so puts his or her own character on the proverbial line. We say that someone is "quite a character" when they are amusing, quirky, or odd; if there is something specifically individual about them that is worth noting. Character could be something distinguishing about a person or object, when an imperfection enhances the quality of the thing itself. A child gets a scar on his young face and outsiders assure his parents that, "it gives him character." An object worn with time—like an old house—is said to have character.

86 Excavating the foundation

The online social media phenomenon Twitter limits its user messages ("tweets") to 140 characters—in this case, letters and symbols. Due to its brevity, the ubiquitous "#" ("hashtag") has become a way to maximize the limited use of characters to direct users to a particular idea or location. In essence, the "hashtag" stands as a characterizing marker for the concept that follows; it becomes a kind of communication shorthand that is readily recognized and easily understood. The idea that character means a printed letter or symbol can be traced all the way back to the ancient Greek word for stamping tool, "kharakter."

You may be surprised to realize how close Twitter users today are to Shakespeare's audience in their understanding of character. The marks and symbols on the screen, the structure under which ideas are expressed and communicated with a larger audience is *precisely* the same meaning that would have been recognized in Shakespeare's time. In fact, the foundation of all of the meanings of character that we considered earlier relies upon this very same notion. Characters in a play or novel are recognized by the way the author wrote them, our reputations are read by our communities by the ways in which our actions are transmitted, and the highly individual nature we associate with people, places, or objects is directly linked to those marks that make them distinct.

When we think about character in terms of theatre today, we think of the three-dimensional person in the world of the play. As I mentioned earlier, Stanislavski's pivotal teaching and writing reinforce this. Stanislavski's work, translated into English as "Building a Character," tells theatre-makers that character is an object in need of construction. The building "blocks" come from the given circumstances provided by the playwright, circumstances that we interpret through the symbols—the characters—given us by the author. What Shakespeare's audience would have recognized as marks upon the page, we recognize as the embodiment of those marks upon the stage. Just as the actor's roll became the actor's *role*, character became *character*.

". . . and now is he turned orthography" (*Much Ado About Nothing 2.3.20*)

As an empowered actor—an empowered *artist* in any form: director, reader, teacher, or thinker—we can use this knowledge to further our consideration and understanding of Shakespeare's work. If the marks on the page translate into meaning for us on the stage, then surely the ways in which those marks are laid out on the page—the *orthography*—can empower us as well.

Creating character **87**

You may remember from Chapter 1 that Shakespeare's plays were popular entertainment at the time that they were performed; they were not necessarily intended for publication. Although some of the plays were published while Shakespeare was alive, the whole collection of Shakespeare's plays was not published until the printing of the First Folio in 1623, some seven years after Shakespeare's death. You may also remember that Shakespeare's audiences went to *hear* a play, not to *see* one. Shakespeare's plays continue to stand as some of the greatest written works in the English language, but unlike the playwright Ben Jonson, Shakespeare didn't necessarily have his eye on the publication "prize." Shakespeare was writing precisely for the transformative effect his words would have on the *stage*, not necessarily for their impact on the reader's *page*.

Looking back to Chapter 1, you will recall that the actors in Shakespeare's company would not have received a complete copy of a play's script; they would only have received their parts. The full script would have belonged to the company and would have been kept at the theatre. It's very likely that John Hemminge and Henry Condell, the actors from Shakespeare's company who were responsible for compiling the First Folio, used those complete copies, but it is equally possible that some of those copies were lost when the first Globe theatre burned to the ground in 1613. We simply don't know with any certainty. In many ways, it's irrelevant to our work as performers. As performers, teachers, directors, and speakers of the text, what we have to work with—the texts themselves—as they have survived, are the only things that really matter.

Having said that the texts are "the only things that really matter," I have to follow that—and quickly—by saying that not all texts are equally suitable for performance. And ay, there's the rub. You may think that *Hamlet* is, well, *Hamlet*, but one edition can be wildly different from the next. Why? Because of that little thing called character. When Laertes asks Claudius, "Know you the hand?" Claudius replies, "'Tis Hamlet's character" (4.7.45–46). Laertes illustrates that it's not just what is written down, but it is *how*—or in this case, by whom—it is written that really matters. The same is true for performance.

Some teachers will tell you that the First Folio is a venerable text that has been handed down from Shakespeare's hand and is therefore the purest text available today. Scholarship proves that there are lots of holes in that argument—most importantly that multiple compositors were responsible for laying out the print, and each of them had their own preferences and tendencies. The First Folio is venerable to actors—not necessarily because it's handed down from Shakespeare himself, but because of its relationship to character.

88 Excavating the foundation

The reason why modern texts can vary so wildly is because they are edited for readers, not for actors. Shakespeare's plays were originally scripts that were meant to be performed and experienced, not read. When you write for speaking and not for reading (and if any of you are in the habit of writing dialogue you know exactly what I'm talking about), it isn't always grammatically correct or particularly tidy. Modern editions can vary so greatly because modern editors are editing for the purposes of reading the texts, and each editor (just like each of the First Folio compositors) has his or her own views on how that text should be laid down.

If each compositor in the First Folio has his own way of laying out the text, and each modern editor has his or her own way of laying out the text, why would it matter whose version we look at? It matters because the orthography of the text in the First Folio is laid out according to the syntax and structure familiar to *its* readers, who would have been reading that text differently than we do today, readers familiar with the art of rhetoric, oratory, and argument in ways that we simply fail to recognize today. It matters—not because we think the First Folio is *exactly* as Shakespeare intended it (maybe it is; maybe it isn't)—but because those quirky, independent compositors would have been masters at laying down the texts of their time. These texts are, essentially, artifacts that are undisturbed by modern interpretation. As archaeologists of performance our job is to mine for clues and to interpret their potential meanings.

In Chapter 3 we looked at the different structural components that we will find in the text. Our job now is to look at the texts themselves, and to see how both the orthography and Shakespeare's use of language reveal character: the needs, thoughts, and desires of the fictional person.

Let's consider the Launce speech from *Two Gentlemen of Verona* that we looked at in Chapter 3. Previously, we examined how the colons help to activate the speech and how that leads to a build in the speech's intensity. We determined that Launce was seeking clarification—and indeed, his confusion is the focal point of the speech's comedic nature. The comedy builds and the performance comes alive because of the way that the characters are laid out on the page. Performance is always active because it happens in real time with the audience. A reader can put down a book and resume reading at a later time, but performance waits for no one.

Since performance is dependent on dynamic storytelling that moves the narrative forward, the actor must always be working towards active, engaged, action-based choices that transform characters into *characters*. You may recall that Launce's speech was made up of only 2 full stops and featured 37 colons. That indicates a lot of action for the actor to work

Creating character **89**

through. You probably won't be surprised to hear that the example I used came from the First Folio, which is a textual record of a performance script. I consulted three modern editions of the same speech (the Arden, the RSC, and the Bevington editions) and those editions feature between 26 and 33 full stops.

How does that change the performance? The Folio edition features a Launce whose thoughts are not well organized and who is moving towards a final point. The Launce found in the other editions is organized with many fully realized, contained, and perhaps orderly thoughts. The Launce with only two full stops needs to work towards an end—that is empowering information for the actor. The Launce with over twenty-five full thoughts must work on keeping the momentum going, on not dropping or losing the energy as each idea draws to a conclusion. It's certainly easier to *read* the editions that have those extra full stops, but the reader does not have the experience of simultaneously *reading* the actor's performance choices as he processes the text. While reading is solitary, performance is communal. Empowered actors build community; they serve as the bridge between the audience and the author. They are the interpreters and the translators of character into *character*.

Discovering "character" through character

As we mine what is on the page for clues, it is important to understand that some of these clues will be present in every edition of the text, such as alliteration, assonance, and word choice. Other discoveries will be specific to Shakespeare's earlier texts, such as the First Folio, for the reasons I outlined. The aim is to provide you with as many tools as possible that enable you to engage dynamically with the text. I like to work from the First Folio alongside another modern edition (or two or three!), not because I believe wholeheartedly in the purity of the Folio (quite the contrary) but because I want to look at that Elizabethan orthography with all of its glorious imperfections and decide for myself what moves me in performance.

Once we excavate the orthographical clues, we can begin to consider how to enter into a somatic relationship with them in order to discover and to access within us our sense of "character" in performance. When we investigate Shakespeare's texts through practice, when we rehearse, explore, probe, and test the text within our selves we create a powerful connection to those texts. Since the connection is made within us and we experience it somatically, we process it differently than we do when we work with a text intellectually sitting with pen and paper. It's the same principle we discovered with *Basketball Shakespeare* when we examined the structure of verse.

90 Excavating the foundation

Let's examine the orthography of one of Macbeth's speeches, as it appears in the First Folio, and see what we might learn about the relationship between character and *character*.

Macbeth 1.7

If it were done, when 'tis done, then 'twere well,
It were done quickly: If th'Assassination
Could trammell up the Consequence, and catch
With his surcease, Success: that but this blow
Might be the be all, and the end all. Heere,
But heere, upon this Bank and School of time,
Wee'ld iump the life to come. But in these Cases,
We still have judgement heere, that we but teach
Bloody Instructions, which being taught, return
To plague th'Inventer, This even-handed Justice
Commends th'Ingredience of our poison'd Chalice
To our own lips. Hee's heere in double trust;
First, as I am his Kinsman, and his Subject,
Strong both against the Deed: Then, as his Host,
Who should against his Murtherer shut the door,
Not bear the knife my selfe. Besides, this Duncan
Hath borne his Faculties so meek; hath bin
So cleere in his great Office, that his Virtues
Will plead like Angels, Trumpet-tongu'd against
The deep damnation of his taking off:
And Pity, like a naked New-borne-Babe,
Striding the blast, or Heavens Cherubin, hors'd
Vpon the sightless Couriers of the Air,
Shall blow the horrid deed in every eye,
That tears shall drown the wind. I have no Spur
To prick the sides of my intent, but only
Vaulting Ambition, which ore-leaps it self,
And falls on th'other.

Creating character **91**

Right from the beginning, this speech begins with what I call a "magic" word: *IF*. The word "if" is like a conjuring: it harnesses possibility and draws both the speaker and the listener into the current moment. It often sets up the premise that if "this," then "that." The linguistic structure "if/then" helps us to understand the balance and the relationship, the contingency inherent between concepts and actions. *If* we want to have dessert, *then* we need to eat our dinner. So this opening line of Macbeth's begins with this "if/then" set up; "If it were done, [. . .] then 'twere well." What is curious in this particular line's orthography is the parenthetical phrase "when 'tis done," which essentially disturbs the balance of the "if/then" argument. Many modern editions remove the punctuation there and present it as, "If it were done when 'tis done, then 'twere well," but this is a very different idea. From a performance perspective, when we enter into a somatic relationship with the text, that text is ignited by the relationship to the body, which is informed by the marks of character. If we think back to the idea that commas are springboards, then we can begin to read the text as, "If it were done (spring!) when 'tis done (spring!) then 'twere well,"—keep in mind that those moments that "spring!" are not necessarily moments of pause, so that the ideas continue to take shape actively; they don't slow down the process of making communicative sense.

In this first line, another thing to keep in mind is that second little word, "it." This is a tiny little word with a huge impact—in this case, Duncan's murder. These little words are like the Hermia of the verse line: "though [they] be but little, [they are] fierce!" (*A Midsummer Night's Dream* 3.2.325) This "it" is also in the position of stress in this iambic line, which scans:

If IT were DONE, when 'TIS done, THEN 'twere WELL,

Two other things are happening here that can inform us in performance: the progression through thought to action "if" → "when" → "then," and the stressed position in that second "little" word, "'tis."

"If it" is hypothetical; *if I won the lottery then I would take a trip around the world.* "When 'tis" is action-based; *when I receive my grant funding then I will begin the research.* We can look at Macbeth's "when 'tis" as his resolution; he's decided to take action. Macbeth realigns himself from a state of consideration to a commitment to action "If it were done," (*correction!*) "when 'tis done," (*realigned*) "then were well, / It were done quickly:" and as Macbeth moves from the first line of iambic pentameter into the second, the characters on the page reveal that he has not only moved simultaneously towards action, but he is also considering *how* that action should be

92 Excavating the foundation

executed. A lot of performance possibility hangs on that additional comma that we find in the early orthography.

As we move into the second line of text we find more orthographic clues: first, the colon, which helps to create intimacy and clarity, and then that second "magic" word, "*if.*"

> If it were done, when 'tis done, then 'twere well,
>
> It were done quickly: *(I'll tell you what I'm thinking)* If th'Assasination

Notice that capitalized word in the line: "Assassination." The "it" has been formally named, renamed, actually, and made manifest from the idea to the thing itself. Not only has Macbeth corrected and realigned himself towards action; he's moved from the abstract idea to the concrete execution of "it." Naming it formally offers a very active performance choice, which can be executed in many different ways, but we can miss that clue when we read the modern typeset, which is not capitalized.

There is another very big clue here in the orthography: the text moves from monosyllabic to polysyllabic words. Our first polysyllabic word is "quickly" with two syllables, followed by "th'Assasination," which is five syllables long—that idea is half a verse line by itself! We have these elements working in conjunction with one another, and if we're finely tuned to them they can tell us a lot about performing the speech. There are many ways that you can execute these clues, and I won't claim to prescribe that to you, but I will guide you through the evidence and it's up to you to determine how they come to life on your feet.

There is something else that you might notice through the speaking of it. These first two lines are nearly all produced with the tip of the tongue. The first sound that moves from the tip of the tongue to the back of the tongue is "quickly," which is also our first polysyllabic word. Take a moment to speak it aloud, and notice what happens. Macbeth is about to switch to more of those back of the tongue sounds "c/k" in the next line:

> Could trammell up the Consequence, and catch

The triple "c/k" sounds produce a sense that something might be caught in his throat. Notice that the word "trammel" linguistically returns to the familiar tip of the tongue—it begins and ends with the tongue pointed up towards the upper gum ridge. This dance between the tip and the back of the tongue brings us to the next capitalized word, "Consequence"—the counterpoise to "th'Assasination."

Something else is introduced in "th'Assasination": the repetition of the "s" sound, which actually begins in the first line, with the stressed word, " 'tis."

Creating character **93**

When we get to the speaking of that three-syllable word "Consequence" we begin to get a sense of the snake-like "hissing" that we associate with deception—it sounds a bit like a whisper, which supports the intimacy set up by the colon and sets us up for the clues in the fourth line of verse.

> With his surcease, Success: that but this blow

The "s" sounds in this line create friction that demands our attention. We have a triplet of words that end and begin with the same "s" sound: "his/surcease" and "surcease/Succcess."

The repetition of these adjacent sounds requires us to select the second word more deliberately so that it is "his_surcease" and not "hissurcease," which is unintelligible. We also need to observe the comma between "surcease" and "Success," which doesn't appear in many modern editions and is so informative in performance. If we look at how the ideas are shaped by the original orthography we can discover how those ideas actively emerge through the speech. Macbeth formulates, "If th'Assassination / Could trammell up the Consequence, (spring!) and catch / With his surcease, (spring!) Success:" This comma indicates that it's not necessarily the success of Duncan's death, his surcease, but it is *Macbeth's* own success that is the end of the target, the final image of the telescope. It's a different thought here: if this particular thing ("th'Assassination") could do something ("trammell up the Consequence") and through that action achieve something else ("catch With his surcease") then those combined actions all lead to a result ("Success"). That final comma "spring!" acts a bit like a question ("what?").

> If this particular thing could do something, and through that action achieve something else, then those combined actions all lead to a result—"what?" "Success."

"Success" is also our third capitalized word, which helps to shape the progression of Macbeth's thoughts: Assassination → Consequence → Success.

There is a second colon following "Success," and Macbeth is about to clarify even further.

> It were done quickly: If th'Assassination
> Could trammell up the Consequence, and catch
> With his surcease, Success: that but this blow
> Might be the be all, and the end all. Heere,

94 Excavating the foundation

With this further clarification, the orthography tells us that Macbeth is making another shift.

By examining the consonants at the beginning of the soliloquy we discovered that the speech moves from an abundance of tip of the tongue sounds to the back of the tongue, from mostly "t/d" sounds to "c/k." That shift to "c/k" is like a subconscious call, "could this work?" It's like a cat coughing up a hairball, an external manifestation of an internal desire. There is also a repetition of the "w" sound "were," "'twer well," and "were," and depending on the pronunciation, "when" can also echo this "w-w-w-w-w" as though Macbeth is considering "what is the best way to make this work?"

The vowel sounds present at the top of the speech are primarily short: the short "i" as in "if" and "it" and the short "e" as in "when" and "well." In the first line, this is most likely due to the fact that those sounds fall in the unstressed position. In the second line it falls in the stressed position, "It WERE done QUICKly," so it's possible there is slightly more length for emphasis, or not. The exception is the "er" sound in "were" and "'twer," which has the potential for length, but that potential is not fully realized. It is not until Macbeth reaches the end of the fourth line, just after that second colon, that we reach the first full, open vowel sound, which is actually a diphthong: a blend of two vowels ("blow"). The "o" in blow begins a series of vowel sounds that have potential length: the diphthong "ay" which sounds like the long "I," in "Might," and then the long "e" in "be" and "heere" that first appeared in "surcease," and the long vowel "aw" as in "all." Vowels are often associated with emotion because they are made up of an uninterrupted flow of air and sound, so they often resemble lamentations. I'm not suggesting that Macbeth is lamenting here (there is no textual evidence of that) but what I will suggest is that it's worth considering what this switch might mean—if anything.

Line four presents us with our first full stop as well, which doesn't quite reach the end of the verse line, although the line is fully iambic. That final beat is the start of a new thought, "Heere," and with that propulsion we are catapulted into the present moment. Before this moment Macbeth talks of "if" and "when" and "could"—he talks of possibility. "Heere," is a manifestation of time, it is the present, the practicality of action. It is both time and location: this very moment at this very place. Macbeth is so drawn into the immediacy of the moment that he repeats himself in what will prove to be a progression of the word "here" that will appear throughout the speech.

You may have noticed that another alliteration produces our first labial sounds in succession the repeated "b" sound: "*but* that this *blow* / Might *be* the *be* all and the end all. Heere, / *But* here, upon this *Bank* and School of time," and there is even a voiceless counterpart to "b" present

Creating character **95**

in "upon," which continues to reinforce this sound. In the next three lines this "b" sound reverberates in "But," "but," "Bloody," and "being." Move through the path of that "b" sound from start to finish, and you will discover "but" → "blow" → "be" → "be" → "But" → "but" → "Bloody" → "being." Speaking this aloud begins to connect us to all kinds of possibilities for performance.

Notice that the progression of Macbeth's language changes with regard to the deed as well: Duncan's murder begins as "it," then develops to "th'Assassination" and gets even more concrete with "blow." What might this indicate about Macbeth? How do these characters inform what happens with Macbeth's *character*? What performance clues can you grab from this change in Macbeth's language?

Let's look at how different orthography informs the meaning of the next full thought, as it appears over several lines. The Folio sets the text as:

> ~~But heere, upon this Bank and School of time,~~
> ~~Wee'ld iump the life to come.~~ But in these Cases,
> We still have judgement heere, that we but teach
> Bloody Instructions, which being taught, return
> To plague th'Inventer, This even-handed Justice
> Commends th'Ingredience of our poison'd Chalice
> To our own lips. ~~Hee's heere in double trust;~~

At the start of the thought we have a comma that springs us into the following line; the line is not *enjambed*, where the thought continues through to the next verse line. There is also a capitalized letter "C" in "Cases," which is worthy of our consideration.

> But in these Cases, *(spring! → what? What happens in these Cases?)*
> We still have judgement heere, *(spring!)* that we but teach
> Bloody Instructions, *(spring!)* which being taught, *(spring!)* return
> To plague th'Inventor, *(spring!)* This even-handed Justice

Macbeth continues the repetition of the word "heere," bringing the energy back into the present moment, and builds on the relationship inherent in education by building on the choice of "School" to include "teach" and "Instructions" and "taught" in the formulation of his argument.

Before we go any further, let's compare the orthography of these lines in three different editions of *Macbeth*: the Arden Shakespeare *Complete Works*

96 Excavating the foundation

(edited by Richard Proudfoot, Ann Thompson, and David Scott Kastan), the sixth edition of *The Complete Works of Shakespeare* (edited by David Bevington) and the Royal Shakespeare Company's *William Shakespeare: Complete Works* (edited by Jonathan Bate and Eric Rasmussen). I will underline and make bold the differences from the Folio.

The Arden Shakespeare:

> But here, upon this bank and **shoal** of time,
> We'd jump the life to come.—But in these **c**ases,
> We still have judgment here**:** that we but teach
> Bloody **i**nstructions, which**,** being taught, return
> To plague th'**i**nventor**:** this even-handed Justice
> Commends th'**i**ngredience of our poison'd **c**halice
> To our own lips. He's here in double trust**:**

The Bevington edition:

> But here, upon this bank and **shoal** of time,
> We'd jump the life to come. But in these **c**ases
> We still have judgment here, that we but teach
> Bloody **i**nstructions, which**,** being taught, return
> To plague th'**i**nventor**.** This eve**nh**anded **j**ustice
> Commends th'**i**ngredience of our poison'd **c**halice
> To our own lips. He's here in double trust**:**

The RSC edition:

> But here, upon this bank and **shoal** of time,
> We'd jump the life to come. But in these **c**ases
> We still have judgment here, that we but teach
> Bloody **i**nstructions, which**,** being taught, return
> To plague th'**i**nventor**:** this even-handed **j**ustice
> Commends th'**i**ngredience of our poison'd **c**halice
> To our own lips. He's here in double trust**:**

First, all of these editions have changed "School" to "shoal," which plays off the river imagery of "Bank." This likely draws upon its meaning as a shallow

Creating character **97**

body of water, but a shoal can also be a group of fish, also known to us as a "school." The aquatic imagery connects beautifully to the previous words "trammel" (to trap in a series of nets), and "catch"—and I imagine that this is why those editors amended it. When we look at the origins of the word "Bank," Alexander Schmidt's *Lexicon* points to an alternate potential meaning: "bench," which the RSC edition notes in its footnotes.

Second, both the Bevington and the RSC editions remove the springboard comma that follows "Cases" to create an enjambed line whose thought ends in another comma. The line is set:

> But in these cases (→)
> We still have judgment here, that we but teach

The Arden follows the Folio's springboard comma, but varies its end-thought punctuation. Where the Folio completes the phrase with a comma (as the Bevington and the RSC editions do), the Arden concludes with a semicolon.

Next, all three of these editions structure the punctuation differently than the Folio in the line that follows, and all three editions agree that the idea should appear:

> Bloody instructions, which, being taught, return

This additional comma adds a leveling moment of respite and organization in the rise to the final point. Let's apply the principle of *telescoping* to the Folio edition and see how each component that falls within the punctuation serves to clarify the argument:

> But in these Cases, *(closer)*
> We still have judgement heere, *(closer)* that we but teach
> Bloody Instructions, *(closer)* which being taught, *(closer)* return
> To plague th'Inventor, *(closer)* This even-handed Justice
> Commends th'Ingredience of our poison'd Chalice
> To our own lips. *(point!)*

In the modern editions, the additional comma that falls after "which" helps the reader to distribute the information, to parcel out the thoughts for greater understanding. When we *telescope* the verse, we apply performance principles to the text. Let's *telescope* the modern orthography and see what performance clues we can find. This time, let's use the symbol "⌒" in place of the word "*closer*" and see how we move towards the point:

98 Excavating the foundation

> But in these Cases, (&↗)
>
> We still have judgement heere, (&↗) that we but teach
>
> Bloody Instructions, (&↗) which, (&↗) being taught, (&↗) return
>
> To plague th'Inventor, (&↗) This even-handed Justice
>
> Commends th'Ingredience of our poison'd Chalice
>
> To our own lips. *(point!)*

You'll notice that the additional comma that appears after "which" does not bring us closer to the point. Expanding the thoughts from five units to six doesn't enhance the performance possibilities; it disrupts them.

Next, Macbeth shifts his deliberation from the act ("*it*" → "th'Assassination" → "blow"), to his subject, who is named only "he" at this point. Macbeth moves from reasoning his actions; he weighs and builds upon his arguments, ending in a thought that is nearly two full verse lines long: "This even-handed Justice / Commends th'Ingredience of our poison'd Chalice / To our own lips." The notion of "even-handed Justice" leads him to consider his victim: he now contemplates the range of perspectives that the personified Justice examines. The Folio sets the text as:

> ~~To our own lips.~~ Hee's heere in double trust;
>
> First, as I am his Kinsman, and his Subject,
>
> Strong both against the Deed: Then, as his Host,
>
> Who should against his Murtherer shut the door,
>
> Not bear the knife my selfe. ~~Besides, this Duncan~~

All three of the modern editions replace the semicolon ("Hee's heere in double trust;") with a colon, which makes sense to our modern sensibility; it precedes a list. There are two reasons why the compositor (or Shakespeare) set it with a semicolon rather than a colon—or the two marks may well have been somewhat interchangeable. Remember, it's not about finding an absolute answer, but about unleashing the potential performance possibilities. Perhaps it is not a colon because it precedes a trochee: the energy is syncopated with the transposition of stress to "First." That trochee jars the ear and makes it aggressive rather than intimate. It may be, however, that the colon that follows "Deed" is where the true intimacy lies. As a "Kinsman" and "Subject" Macbeth is one among many. As Duncan's "Host" he is an intimate companion. Whereas the assassination of a monarch by his subject is recognizable, murder by a trusted companion is a double betrayal; it is indeed remarkable. If we consider the implications of character on *character* we may understand more clearly how Macbeth feels about his actions

Creating character **99**

through the difference between those two units of punctuation. The colon also heightens the antithesis between "Host" and "Murderer" since the punctuation separates those two roles from the overall list.

Macbeth signposts this list, which continues into the next thought with the progression of "First" → "Then" → "Besides." His arrival at "Besides" enables him to name "Duncan." His actions have been personalized by the positioning of that colon and his title "Host," and now his victim is elevated from "He" to his given name, the familiar "Duncan."

What is curious here is that the line is set as "this Duncan." Why "this Duncan"? Are we to mistake him with another? We need "this" in order for the stress of "DUNCan" to align with the correct pronunciation, but more specifically, why "this"? Does it connect with the immediacy and temporality that has been running through the speech with the recurrence of "Heere"? It's certainly possible.

The repetition of "h" sounds continue in this passage, in "He's heere" and "Host" and through to the double set of "hath"s that follow in the next line. The continuation of that "h" is akin to Macbeth asking, "*how* can I do this?" and it can also sound like panting, depending on the actor's delivery. The play from "Hath borne" to "hath been" provides even greater clarity and specificity to Macbeth, especially when it's juxtaposed with the use of "so" in both instances: "Hath borne . . . so . . ." to "hath been so . . ."

> ~~Not bear the knife my selfe.~~ Besides, this Duncan
>
> Hath borne his Faculties so meek; hath bin
>
> So cleere in his great Office, that his Virtues
>
> Will plead like Angels, Trumpet-tongu'd against
>
> The deep damnation of his taking off:
>
> And Pity, like a naked New-borne-Babe,
>
> Striding the blast, or Heavens Cherubin, hors'd
>
> Vpon the sightless Couriers of the Air,
>
> Shall blow the horrid deed in every eye,
>
> That tears shall drown the wind. ~~I have no Spur~~

In this passage, we have another informative semicolon that is replaced with commas in the modern editions: "Besides, this Duncan / Hath borne his faculties so meek; hath been / So clear in his great Office, that his Virtues." All three modern editions set the punctuation as a comma, which creates a rising list between Duncan's faculties and his clarity of office, as opposed to joining the two separate, but related ideas.

100 Excavating the foundation

The next variation between the early and modern orthographies occurs in the description of how Duncan's virtues will plead like angels. The Folio sets the text as:

> ~~So cleere in his great Office~~, that his Virtues
> Will plead like Angels, Trumpet-tongu'd against
> The deep damnation of his taking off:

If we *telescope* the passage, we can see how the text clarifies the relationship between the images and the event.

> ~~So cleere in his great Office~~, that his Virtues
> Will plead like Angels, (☊)Trumpet-tongu'd against
> The deep damnation of his taking off:

This telescoping shows that the Angels are "trumped-tongued against the deep damnation" whereas all three modern editions place commas around "trumpet-tongued," which connects the description to the pleading, rather than the opposition. To illustrate, let's think of "trumpet-tongued" for a moment as "loud and clear," or "vehemently." With this substitution, "Trumpet-tongued against" would mean "vehemently against / The deep damnation" as opposed to "Will plead like angels, vehemently, against / The deep damnation" The latter indicates that the angels are pleading vehemently, rather than the Angels opposing vehemently the murder. This distinction is subtle, and for the purposes of reading the positions of the commas help to clarify the quality of being trumpet-tongued. The problem for the actor is that those same commas impede the clarity of the *telescope*:

> ~~So cleere in his great Office~~, that his Virtues
> Will plead like Angels, (☊)Trumpet-tongu'd, (☊) against
> The deep damnation of his taking off:

In this case, what is "Trumpet-tongu'd"?

Each of these characteristic differences, however seemingly subtle, can influence our understanding of the *character*. This very sensible comma changes the way Macbeth envisions the Heavens' reaction to his actions. Perhaps because this is related so personally to his own place in the world it precedes a colon, which enables him to become even more intimate with his audience confidantes.

The text continues:

> And Pity, like a naked New-borne-Babe,
>
> Striding the blast, or Heavens Cherubin, hors'd
>
> Vpon the sightless Couriers of the Air,
>
> Shall blow the horrid deed in every eye,
>
> That tears shall drown the wind. ~~I have no Spur~~

Of the three modern texts in our comparisons, only one retains the colon (the RSC's), the other two replace the colon with a semi-colon. Only one (the Arden) retains the capitalization of "Pity," which personifies the characteristic; the Arden did the same for "Justice" and "Cherubins." The next difference in punctuation is found in the Bevington edition, which takes the simile that compares Pity "like a naked New-borne-Babe" and expands the image to "like a naked newborn babe / Striding the blast," which changes the imagery from pity as a vulnerable newborn to a vulnerable newborn in the act of doing something fierce. These are subtle differences, but informative nonetheless.

There is some very complex imagery present in these similes and metaphors that helps us to understand how Macbeth views his actions within the balance of the world around him. He contextualizes his deed not within the predatory animal world, but within the world of heaven and nature. This may be due to the fact that kings were considered the closest beings to God and that they were chosen as God's representatives on earth, or it could be that he is balancing his actions as humans—who have the ability to reason—do.

There is another clue in this series of images to notice: the change in titles or names. In this one complete thought the natural phenomenon, "wind," is addressed and personified in three different ways. It is first referred to as "the blast," then "the sightless Curriors of the Air," and finally the wind is attributed to a form of life that can be extinguished; the wind is life that can be drowned in the water of deep sorrow. In this final image, there is also a sense that the deed will cause an imbalance in the natural world; that human action and emotion (in this case, tears) will affect the function of nature. Our contemporary experience with global warming can tell us how dangerous a prospect this is.

Macbeth's final line provides us with further insight about his complicated relationship to his deep desires.

> ~~That tears shall drown the wind.~~ I have no Spur
>
> To prick the sides of my intent, but only

102 Excavating the foundation

> Vaulting Ambition, which ore-leaps it self,
>
> And falls on th'other.

In this final thought, Macbeth shifts and sees his "intent" as a beast whose actions need prompting. Macbeth anthropomorphizes his desire quite deliberately; he doesn't say, "I have no Spur / to prick . . . my intent" but he states specifically, "I have no Spur / to prick **the sides of** my intent" and this distinction is really important. This "intent" is a three-dimensional body in motion, rather than an idea. He's gone from the imagery of babes and cherubins to beasts. Indeed, it is the beast within him that drives him forward.

The next line propels forward with a trochee: "VAULTing" followed by the capitalized "Ambition"; and the notion of *ambition* is also personified by the capitalization. The characterization of this early text indicates that this concept that drives Macbeth is its own entity, with its own name. So we have this beast that needs spurring and pricking, and this character concept that comes from a medieval morality play: "Ambition." This helps us to understand how Macbeth visualizes these forces at work.

This examination has been a close reading of how we can understand the relationship between the characters on the page and the embodied idea of those characters on the stage. What is quite wonderful is that this understanding is still open for individual interpretation; there are still as many interpretations of the nuances of meaning and the personalization of these character clues as there are individuals to interpret them. This is why I call this kind of work the *archaeology* of performance: we dig and strip away the layers that obscure the bones and foundation we study, and then we must examine and consider all of the possibilities for meaning that arise from our interpretation of what lies before us. This analysis is extra-textual; we need to examine both the text *and* its orthography to read the clues for performance, and to activate our performance choices.

PART II
Actuating practice

In the first part of this book we looked at the historical context and theoretical underpinnings that surround the Elizabethan theatre and the ways in which the replica of Shakespeare's Globe introduces new possibilities that inform and inspire how we engage with Shakespeare today. In Part II we will examine how the theoretical content from Part I informs the practical training of actors.

We will begin by "Activating the body'"(Chapter 5), which encourages whole-body engagement and heightened kinesthetic awareness in performance. "Awakening the listener" (Chapter 6) introduces a progressive series of exercises designed to bolster actors' ability to use Shakespeare's language as the main component of storytelling. "Energizing the language" (Chapter 7) helps actors forge an organic response to the text, to think actively on the line, and to coin the words for themselves.

"Expanding the fiction" (Chapter 8) introduces *Elliptical Energy Training* to address the shift from the "fourth wall" tradition of a two-room space and transforms the performance paradigm to parallel the one-room space of Shakespeare's theatre. Elliptical energy brings the audience and the actor into the same room, and incorporates them into the world of the fiction.

"Developing and playing the Shakespeare score" (Chapter 9) introduces a system of notation that helps to identify and articulate moments of theatrical practice that can be read as a musician reads a musical composition.

104 Actuating practice

Finally, "Rehearsing the part" (Chapter 10) will offer a systematic approach to rehearsing Shakespeare. I will share suggestions to help you memorize text quickly and precisely, to rehearse with a partner, and to build ensemble in the Shakespeare rehearsal.

The practice we will actuate covers a spectrum of perspectives and practitioners. When appropriate, I will speak directly to the actor; at other times I will address the group leader, teacher, or director. Some of the work is very personal and can be done independently; other portions are dependent on group dynamics. I will make suggestions about adapting larger exercises to meet the needs for solo work when it is possible to do so.

5

ACTIVATING THE BODY

One of the biggest things that we can take away from a space like Shakespeare's Globe is the heightened kinesthetic sense and proprioception it encourages in the actor. In Shakespeare's Globe, the actor is acutely aware that he is a three-dimensional being in space, that the environment surrounds him, and that the world envelops him. The space is a conduit for energy. This sense of energy is palpable; it locates and calibrates the actor's position, like a pulsing GPS pinpoint, radiating out to fill the space as it simultaneously processes the reception of energy radiating inwards. This situates the body as an epi-center in the space, which promotes poise and primes the body-instrument for engagement.

Shakespeare's Globe is unflinchingly honest—it doesn't suffer fools gladly. There is beauty in its demanding presence. It compels us to acknow-ledge the shared experience—it will rain on us; planes fly overhead, and we can look into the eyes of a stranger who is experiencing that very same moment, which will never again be exactly the same. There is something profound in that exchange. It is stirring to listen to Shakespeare's language and to consider how it was once shared among a different community, who are long dead, and who once connected to the world around them in some way through those same words. It holds the mirror up and enables us to see ourselves as a fraction of humanity in a long line of playmakers and specta-tors as we realize that one day a new generation will experience the world around them through the sharing of these same words. It makes every inch of you feel alive.

106 Actuating practice

That experience of presence and community activates the body. Imagine what it feels like to be there, inside that space. Study pictures and take a tour of the theatre, virtual or actual. Daydream about what it is like to work there. Envision the bodies that surround you. You can see them, and they can see you. They are all a part of this story. Even when you can't see them, you can sense them surrounding you. As you breathe you can feel your body expanding to reach everyone in the space. Breathe to the thatch and the wood, to the materials that once were alive and could once also breathe. You are open to the world around you—the world of the play and the world of the playhouse. The fiction and the factual, the real and the imagined: you straddle those worlds in the present.

This first series of exercises helps to stimulate the actor's sense of three-dimensionality and activates the body-instrument as a primary vehicle for storytelling. These exercises are designed to develop the actor's muscle memory and create a platform that enhances the actor's perception and reception. They are excellent ways of beginning studio practice or rehearsal, and over time their value increases exponentially.

Connecting Breath

Have the actors begin to move throughout the space. As they explore the space, and their relationship to it, encourage them to notice how their feet come in contact with the floor. Ask them to notice their backs, their bellies, and the backs of their necks. Ask the actors to observe their breath, simply, to pay attention to what is happening as they inhale and exhale. Remind them that they don't need to manipulate the breath; they don't need to elongate it or hold it, but simply to notice what is already happening within them. Ask them to pay attention to their own internal rhythms. Can they observe where they are holding tension? Is the jaw free and released? Are they holding in their bellies? Are they clenching their buttocks? Advise the actors that if they observe tension, simply note it and release it. They can synchronize the breath to encourage even deeper release, if need be. You can encourage them to allow the breath to take on a particular color as it falls into the body—they don't need to predetermine what the color is, simply allow the image to appear to them. As they breathe in this color, invite them to notice how the color fills them up. Does it reach all of their extremities? Does the color reach their fingertips? Does it fill up the whole torso? Does it reach the top of their heads? The tip of their noses? Does it reach both the back of the skull as well as the tip of the

Activating the body **107**

nose? As they exhale, can they visualize the color leaving them? Did the color change at all or did it remain the same? Give them permission to notice how connecting to their breath has affected their bodies. They are becoming more and more focused and poised, and ready to engage with one another. As they continue to move through the space, ask them to begin to notice those around them. Invite them to begin to make eye contact as they pass each other. As they make eye contact they continue to feel the breath fill them entirely, and feel their feet in contact with the floor. Encourage them not to release their previous awareness of the body, but to expand that awareness and relationship to include making eye contact with those they encounter, to layer the new task on top of the existing ones. This time, when they make eye contact with a partner they are both to stop where they are, face each other, and share an inhalation and an exhalation of breath. Once they have finished exhaling their breath, they release their connection to the partner, and continue to move throughout the space until they come in contact with the next person. They stop again, sharing an inhalation and exhalation of breath with that new partner. Have this continue until everyone in the studio has had an opportunity to connect with each other. As they gather with their partners, invite them to allow themselves to be vulnerable—to breathe that other person in, and to allow themselves to be breathed in. There is no manipulation and no judgment. If they have a response to partnering with someone, allow it to be there. Sometimes they may find joy in the exchange; that is a perfectly acceptable outcome. It is not the goal of the exercise, but if a response arises organically, allow its presence to find the release it desires. It's important to remember that although this work heightens one's awareness, focuses one's attention, and encourages one's sense of poise, it is important to respond to the body's impulses and allow the dialogue with (and within) the body to exist, even in a playful state.

Connecting Breath is a wonderful way of cultivating a physical connection to the whole body as it moves through space, and for groups to develop trust and ensemble between them. When you come together at the start of rehearsal or class and you focus the body and mind, and release tension you invite presence among the group. When you expand the body's presence to include the presence of others, it becomes a very powerful tool. In a sense the group is saying, "I acknowledge you, and I trust you to see me, to be present with me, and to share this space with me." It is a very small investment that reaps very large returns in practice.

108 Actuating practice

When you have been practicing *Connecting Breath* regularly, the ensemble becomes more finely tuned to the exercise and will respond differently to it. At this point, particularly in an acting class, I will add a variation of *Connecting Breath* that builds on the foundation that has been developed to strengthen the connection between scene partners. After moving through the sequence I outlined above, I will give the following instructions:

> Once you have had a chance to greet everyone in the room, find your way to your scene partner. Make eye contact, and share an inhalation and exhalation of breath. Stay with your partner for a moment. You are simply yourself—you are not in the fiction, you are here in this room, with this person at the present moment. Take your partner in, and allow yourself to be taken in; breathe with your partner. After enough time for a few breaths—it need not continue for too long—have the partners release from each other and continue to move throughout the space once again. This time, instruct the group that at random you will call out the direction "find." When they hear the prompt, they are to stop where they are, locate their partner kinesthetically in the room, confirm the partner's location by turning towards them, face the partner, make eye contact, and share a connecting breath with the partner with the distance and bodies between them. If they need to take a slight step aside in order to face the partner that is okay, but keep the movement to a minimum; it isn't about aligning perfectly, but about cultivating the connection with obstacles and distance between them. Have them release from their partners and continue to move throughout the space before calling "find" again, randomly. Finally, adjust the directions further: this time, when you call "find" they are to locate their partners without facing them directly, but simply by turning their heads and making eye contact. Remind them to trust the connection they have with their partner; they have been present with each other and they can trust that partners will be there to receive them and will give of themselves in return. Encourage them to take in their partners as fully as they had when squaring off with them. Continue this for several rounds so that they can refine their awareness and connection despite the obstacles. They will locate their partner, turn their heads to confirm, connect with a breath, and then release and continue walking.

Connecting Breath enables the company to tune in both to themselves as well as to each other. Once you have established that initial sense of heightened awareness of the body, and introduced the body's ability to respond

Activating the body **109**

kinesthetically, you can expand on that awareness to enhance the body-instrument's three-dimensional presence on stage. Because many actors are trained within the proscenium arch tradition, it's easy for them to lose sight of their backs and sides. It's not uncommon, particularly for young actors in training, to hear notes about the body's position in space such as "turn out" or "open up" or "don't upstage yourself"; these are all based on the premise that the audience is directly in front of that invisible fourth wall. Since there is no "wall" at Shakespeare's Globe, the body there has a much greater capacity to connect with the audience.

The next exercise deepens the awareness that's been cultivated in *Connecting Breath*, and includes the actor's sense of three-dimensionality. As *Connecting Breath* progresses to "find," the exercise expands to include the heightened proprioception of the ensemble as they radiate energy and breath throughout the whole studio. Stanislavski discusses "rays" and "irradiation," and radiating energy is one of the essential ideas of the Michael Chekhov technique. Chekhov's teaching inspires me in this next portion of the training. I recommend that you allow *Connecting Breath* to lead directly into *Radiating Box* in order to maximize the experience.

Radiating Box

As the ensemble continues to move throughout the studio space, give the directions for *Radiating Box*. Encourage the actors to continue to hold their awareness of their bodies as they listen to the next set of instructions: this will enhance their ability to maintain mindfulness as they redirect their primary focus and will prove useful to their experience.

When you have the impulse to do so, initiate the formation of a box by standing still and closing your eyes. As you stand in stillness, radiate your energy out to the group and invite them to form a box around you. The other actors receive your invitation, and when they have an impulse to join you as one of the sides of the box, they will position themselves in one of four positions: directly in front of you, behind you, or on either side of you. There is no pre-determined pattern for the box's formation; each actor joins in according to his or her own impulse at that moment, but we will limit each side of a box to only one person per side. Once in position, each side of the box radiates energy towards the actor in the center to communicate that the side of the box is complete. There is no need to wait for other sides to join—once you become a "side" of the box, you begin to radiate your energy towards the actor in the center. The center actor will continue to "listen" kinesthetically for the confirmation that the box has formed.

110 Actuating practice

When the center actor senses that he has received the energy radiating from each side and the box is complete, the actor will open his eyes to acknowledge the presence of those who surround him, and to confirm the box's completion. The box disperses when the center actor begins to move throughout the space once again. The center actor is now free to join the formation of another box, when the impulse

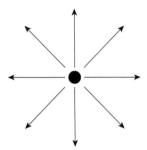

FIGURE 5.1 *Radiating Box*: initiation

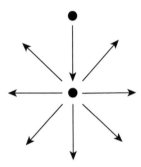

FIGURE 5.2 *Radiating Box*: formation begins

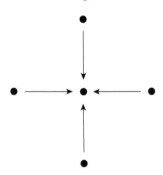

FIGURE 5.3 *Radiating Box*: formation complete

Activating the body **111**

to do so arises. Boxes will emerge spontaneously, and simultaneously. Remind the ensemble to move silently so that the center actor can rely on his proprioception and listen to the kinesthetic dialogue commencing, rather than to the shuffling of feet and movement throughout the space. Allow each member to experience initiating a box as well as forming one of the sides before you introduce any group discussion.

In addition to the benefits of heightened kinesthetic awareness and the development of radiant presence, *Radiating Box* encourages vulnerability and trust among the participants. When an actor enters into the initiation stage of the exercise, he engages in a vulnerable dialogue with his fellows. As he radiates forth his invitation to join and form a box, he simultaneously emanates his trust and vulnerability. In his initiation, he stops moving and closes his eyes. His physical position of sightless stillness among a group of sighted movers is, of itself, vulnerable physically. In addition, as he radiates his invitation he communicates essentially, "I trust that you will join me," "I trust that I am capable of receiving your energy," and "I trust that you will complete this box." Each member who follows the impulse to join the initiator as one of the box's sides is also vulnerable, and must also trust. The sides communicate, "I trust that you (the center initiator) will sense my presence"; "I trust that I will be recognized." These are very powerful exchanges. Although the primary goal of the exercise is to heighten the actor's awareness, presence, and ability to expand and radiate, the secondary outcomes of risk-taking and trust cannot be underestimated. Psychologically, this secondary mode of communication serves to empower the actor, and helps to dissipate the fear of "not being enough." When the actor can meet the demands of such highly attuned communication, it helps to build trust that he can also meet the demands of Shakespeare with comparable ease.

Like *Connecting Breath*, *Radiating Box* can be revisited regularly: the ensemble's receptivity to the radiation of energy becomes more finely tuned as the practice is cultivated. As they become more familiar with *Radiating Box* and the formation of boxes occurs with greater ease and in a shorter period of time, invite the group to play with the connections they have to one another, to expand the pliability of their kinesthetic awareness and their ability to communicate with each other non-verbally.

Radiating Box: Distance and Vertical Space

Once the actors have grown familiar with *Radiating Box*, they have explored and experienced the sensation of radiating forth and

112 Actuating practice

receiving energy; they have developed a greater sense of their three-dimensionality. To cultivate that awareness further, invite the group to segue from the basic exploration and to test the sensitivity of their awareness and connection to one another; encourage them to form boxes around the center actor at increasing distances and at differing heights. As they do this, they enhance their ability to communicate even further with the whole body: not only from their centers, but to expand the range of release and reception to include both lower and upper body, and at a varying distance: both closer and farther from the box's center. Encourage the ensemble to play: to explore how they send their energy and to allow themselves to be asymmetrical; there is no need for symmetry. This practice is more advanced: they can challenge the initiator of the box to sense the radiation of their energy at multiple levels simultaneously. What happens when one side of the box is radiating from the floor while another is quite high up? When one is rather close and another is very far? This variety really challenges the center body to listen with the whole body-instrument; it demands head-to-toe engagement. The body becomes increasingly three-dimensional in space as a result.

As we expand how responsive we are to our surroundings, we engage and activate our body-instruments, our primary means for telling the story.

When I used to work as a teaching artist I worked primarily with children ages five through ten, but on occasion I would work with very small children, sometimes as young as three or four. I would ask them, "How do we tell stories?" They would reply, "read the words on the page" or, "describe what happened" and sometimes, "act it out." I would tell them, "*Theatre* is telling stories . . . with your whole body."

One of the ways in which we do that is to pay attention to the dynamics between those bodies on stage—and when bodies are really activated, stories can be told with greater subtlety. As the body communicates nonverbally, the text is enhanced and enlivened. As the text is enlivened, the body responds even further: it's a winning cycle. The most dynamic performances tap into all available elements to create the most powerful, whole-body storytelling possible.

Status work

We can think of *status* as the relative position or standing of someone (or something) when compared to its surrounding environment. Some status positions are defined clearly for us: parent and child; boss and employee; teacher and student. It's important to remember, though, that one's status is relative to the situation. So, let's take the example of teacher and student. In that relationship, the teacher would have a higher status and the student would have the lower status. If we place that same teacher alongside the teacher's immediate supervisor, the department chairperson, that teacher's status is lowered slightly in comparison. That same teacher's status is lowered further when examined next to the headmaster or school principal, isn't it? It's a wonderfully complicated concept to consider: status is fluid and always relates to the moment of examination. Let's consider the status between teacher and student: at the outset we assume (as I did earlier) that the teacher's status is higher than the student's. While this is *usually* true, what if the moment between the teacher and student shatters our assumption? What if the student has discovered something about the teacher that the teacher would rather not be known? That student may suddenly find a raise in his or her status; the roles could be reversed and the teacher could be the individual whose status is the lower of the two. It's always possible—and always worth exploring.

It's especially necessary to consider how status affects the characters in Shakespeare's plays. The elements of status are even more pronounced than what we are accustomed to today: the nuances in status between characters of nobility help us to understand how characters are driven by their places in society. In fact, Elizabethans believed strongly that everything in the world had it's own place, that each living creature from a one-celled organism all the way up to God had a particular place, a hierarchy, in the world. This is known as the *Elizabethan Chain of Being*. This "Chain" gives us an opportunity to discover new ways of thinking about the different comparisons we encounter, the metaphors and similes Shakespeare uses—and to consider *why* he chose them.

Before we begin to delve into the nuances that surround the Chain of Being, let's first explore some basic status exercises in practice. I like to begin with a basic status exploration, one you might already be familiar with. This exercise has been done so often I've never been able to trace its origins (if you know of them, I'd love to hear from you), but it does an excellent job of laying the foundation for what will come.

Status Exploration

You will need an ordinary deck of playing cards, with the Jokers removed. Ask each actor to draw one card from the deck and to keep the results of that draw confidential. The cards are ranked from

114 Actuating practice

the lowest status (two) to the highest (Ace). Invite the actors to begin to move throughout the space and to interact with each other and the playing space, based upon the status of their card. Allow this improvisational exchange to develop and deepen so that each actor explores the nature of the card-given status, and how this status relates to the "world" of the improvisation. Observe how the status manifests in the body, how the dynamics are revealed between players, and how much more physically engaged the body becomes in the storytelling. To conclude the exploration, ask the actors to line up in the space based on where they believe they fit in the group hierarchy (be sure to designate each end of the line either low or high status).

The interesting thing about this exercise is that in all the years I've been doing it I have rarely seen the group fail to line up "correctly," according to their status. Through their interactions, they understand their hierarchy and place in the world of the improvisation. In fact, the times when there *has* been difficulty lining up, it is almost always because an actor's personal status has gotten in the way of the exploration. This can happen when an individual has a very strong sense of status—either high or low. The actor who has grown attached to his or her own personal "high status" may have difficulty relinquishing that status when issued a low-status card. As a result, the drawing of a "3" might read in the exchange as someone else's "4" or "5." On the other hand, someone with naturally lower status (what we might associate today with low self-esteem, perhaps) might have difficulty embracing fully the level of status that comes with a "9" or "10," which isn't as clearly defined as the much higher status of "royalty" card or an Ace. It's much easier for actors to fall into playing the stereotype of high status that is associated with the "royalty" cards (Jack, Queen, King) or with the Ace. The tricky part is playing higher status without the umbrella of "high status"—those "8," "9," and "10" cards are usually the hiccup in the lineup.

In Shakespeare, status is at play not only between the human characters, but also within all of the imagery that those characters employ. In the basic status exploration outlined above, the status was contained within the human world of the fiction. Within the Chain of Being there are many, many creatures that come into play. Keeping in mind that all creatures, from the most microscopic to the most majestic (the Lion, "king of the beasts") has a place within the world, we can expand our understanding of this ideology by putting it into the body in practice.

Activating the body **115**

E. M. Tillyard's book, *The Elizabethan World Picture*, has long been a classic. In it, Tillyard outlines how the Chain of Being functions: at the top of the chain is God, followed by angels, then kings (royalty are humans appointed by God) and then it breaks down into the animal world, vegetation, and so on. Tillyard also explains in great detail other things that we ought to be aware of such as how the humours function and the role that they play in the world of Shakespeare's fiction. It's a slim book, filled with information, and everyone serious about understanding Shakespeare's text ought to read it—with a discerning eye.

Here is a fun way to take those concepts that the Elizabethans would have understood, and deepen our own familiarization with them. I like to return to the status exploration, but this time putting the exchange within the Elizabethan Chain of Being. If I am working within a studio/classroom setting, I will create a deck of cards that include different "beings" mentioned throughout Shakespeare's canon. When I am rehearsing a particular play, I create a deck that includes the specific creatures mentioned in that text; this is a wonderful way of exploring the world of a given play experientially and to expand upon the intellectual understanding the ensemble develops through research and analysis.

Elizabethan Chain of Being Status

Utilizing a deck of cards that reflect the Elizabethan Chain of Being, ask each actor to draw one card, and to keep the results of that draw confidential. As with the previous status exploration, invite the actors to begin moving throughout the space, and to transition their movement from their own physicality into a manner of movement that embodies the "Being" they have drawn. Invite them to explore the shape, movement, and weight of their "Being"; invite them to release sound. Once they have entered into a physical relationship with the "Being" they have been exploring, ask them to expand their awareness and to begin to interact within the space according to what they believe their acquired status is within the Elizabethan Chain of Being. Encourage the actors to interact with the other "Beings" when it is appropriate to do so. Allow the exploration to develop long enough so that each actor embodies both the "Being" as well as the relationship to the surrounding "world." At the conclusion, ask the actors to line up according to where they believe their status falls in the Elizabethan Chain of Being.

116 Actuating practice

Due to the variety of "Beings" present within the chain, this exercise can be repeated as often as you'd like. It not only serves as an interesting warm-up to locate the actor within his own physicality, it helps the actor connect—in a very visceral way—to the imagery found in the numerous metaphors and similes within Shakespeare's work.

Earlier on, I suggested that you keep a "discerning eye" when reading Tillyard and thinking about the Chain of Being, and because I'd like you to be fully empowered, I want to share something that isn't often discussed in the studio. Among practitioners the Chain is often explained as I first did, although the status exploration I described is wholly original. While it's very possible that the "Great Chain of Being" was fully accepted by the Elizabethans, more recent scholarship challenges that idea—and *this* I'd never encountered in practice or in reading about practice before.

In Chapter 1 we looked at the differences between theatre making at the time Shakespeare was writing and theatre making today. You may recall that I talked about how theatre became a commodity for the first time, and that Shakespeare and his company became quite wealthy as a result of that commodification. As a result of his wealth, Shakespeare was able to purchase a coat of arms for his family, which celebrated this newfound wealth. This is a significant event, for Shakespeare's father, John, was reportedly involved with some shady financial deals and had previously been denied his earlier application. In fact, the motto on the Shakespeare family coat of arms is "not without right"—and you can imagine just what William Shakespeare might have been trying to say—and it might not have been his most eloquent language (if you can read between the lines). At any rate, it's a time in which people are trying to improve their status in life. A time when the son of a provincial glover can move to the big city and become one of the greatest writers ever to have lived.

Up until Shakespeare's arrival in London, the majority of plays written at that time were done by the highly educated: first by schoolmasters (see Nicholas Udall's *Ralph Roister Doister*—the first extant English comedy) and later by a group educated at Cambridge and Oxford, known as "the University Wits," which included Christopher Marlowe, Thomas Nashe, John Lyly, and Robert Greene, who infamously railed against the rise of Shakespeare's popularity, calling him an "upstart crow." So we see, just from Shakespeare's own life, that one's place in the hierarchy of society might not have been as fixed as it once was, or perhaps, not as fixed as those on the upper end of the status chain would have liked it to remain.

The Chain of Being has been seen rather recently with new possibilities: as a bit of dogma that intended to remind that rising mercantile class that

Activating the body **117**

the world ought to have been more in harmony, with each person aware of where they fall, and without the friction that comes from disrupting one's station in life. It is plausible that the "Great Chain of Being" was really an attempt to present an idealized socio-political reminder that upward mobility was not a part of "God's plan," and that individuals ought to remain satisfied with their lots in life. If so, our view that Elizabethans saw life as harmonious and hierarchical grossly oversimplifies what the Elizabethans themselves were experiencing. We need only look at Shakespeare's plays to find evidence of that, and two particular archetypal characters come to mind: the bastards and the dowry-seeking lovers.

If everyone embraced that "Great Chain" as readily as they would have us believe, we would never have a speech like Edmund's "Thou Nature art my Goddess" soliloquy (that we looked at in Chapter 2). Actually, *King Lear* would be a totally different play, wouldn't it? Edmund would say, "Bastard? Oh well, that really stinks for me"—a perfectly iambic line with a jolt of trochee to launch the point—and that would be the end of the story. It's the very fact that Edmund *won't* accept that he should be resigned to "less than" his brother that helps to make the play what it is.

The dowry-seekers that come to mind are Petruchio (*The Taming of the Shrew*) and Bassanio (*The Merchant of Venice*). They arrive in Padua and in Belmont in order to marry women who can improve their states in life, who can raise their financial status. They are not satisfied with what they have at the beginning of each play. Like Edmund, there is friction between what they have and what they want. Does that sound like any other characters that you can think of? Macbeth? Iago? Claudius? Those characters also exist in a world that is anything but an example of utopian harmony. The plays show us worlds where characters rub up against what they desire, and how that chafing spurs them to action. That friction is something that is equally worth exploring.

Here are three variations of status exercises to help explore that friction. You can present these in any order you'd like, alone or in tandem with each other. These work best when they are sprung on the group unexpectedly.

High-Status Exploration

Compile a deck of high-status cards from several regular decks of cards by removing the Kings, Queens, and Jacks. All cards should match identically as though they are from one un-manipulated deck of cards. Ask the actors to draw a card from the high-status deck, and to keep the results of that draw confidential. Invite the actors to

118 Actuating practice

begin to move through the space, and to interact with each other based upon the status assigned by their card. The participants believe they are engaged with a regular status exploration; remind them that the status ranges from "two" (lowest) to "King" (highest). Each actor will recognize his given status is high, and will expect that others will have been assigned a lower status. From this point, the exploration begins.

The High-Status Exploration gives the group an experiential understanding of a society in which all aim to be of high status. It also enables actors to experience what it is like to come up against high-status individuals when they believe themselves to be of equally high status. We find this scenario in Shakespeare's plays, and putting it into the body's experience proves quite valuable.

Middle-Status Exploration

Remove the sevens, eights, and nines from several decks of cards, and create a new deck comprised only of these middle-status cards. As before, all cards should match identically in order to conceal the manipulation of the exercise. Ask the actors to draw a card from the middle-status cards offered, and to keep the results of the draw confidential. Invite the actors to begin to move through the space, and to interact with each other based upon the status assigned by their card. The participants believe they are engaged with a regular status exploration; remind them that the status ranges from "two" (lowest) to "King" (highest). Actors will recognize their given status as somewhere in the middle, and will expect that some will have been assigned a lower while others a higher status from their own. From this point, the exploration begins.

The group will not expect to be contained only to the middle range of status and the dynamics between them will reveal nuances of status difference, even within a rather small sample assigned.

Equal-Status Exploration

From several regular decks of cards, remove only the cards with the number six and compile a new deck of cards containing all sixes. All cards should match identically in order to conceal the manipulation

Activating the body **119**

of the exercise. Ask the actors to draw a card from the equal-status cards offered, and to keep the results of the draw confidential. Invite the actors to begin to move through the space, and to interact with each other based upon the status assigned by their card. The participants believe they are engaged with a regular status exploration; remind them that the status ranges from "two" (lowest) to "King" (highest). Actors will recognize their given status as somewhere in the middle, and will expect that some will have been assigned a lower while others a higher status from their own. From this point, the exploration begins.

Even with a group assigned to equal status, natural hierarchies will be revealed. Perhaps more than any other exploration, this particular investigation enables actors to encounter their own relationship to their personal status. How one person interprets the ways in which a "six" interacts with the surrounding world is different—sometimes vastly different—from someone else's interpretation. It's incredibly useful for an actor to discover whether he has a personal tendency to play either higher or lower than what is required, or if his own personal status interferes with the character's status. Once the actor becomes aware of how status functions, he can consciously play with and manipulate the ways in which status can help to enhance the world of the play, the storytelling overall, and even the actor's relationship to the audience.

Throughout this chapter we've been looking at ways to help promote whole-body engagement in performance and activate and strengthen the kinaesthetic sense. As we aim to maximize our sense of presence, we find ourselves poised to bring that expanded awareness directly to Shakespeare's language. That activated presence radiates beyond the body instrument and roots itself into the personalized connection to what we speak.

6

AWAKENING THE LISTENER

In 1615 dramatist John Webster penned a portrait of "An excellent Actor," which was, perhaps, inspired by Richard Burbage. In it, he states, "sit in a full Theater and you will thinke you see so many lines drawne from the circumference of so many eares, whiles the *Actor* is the *Center*." Whether or not this account is a nod to Burbage, Webster's observation of the relationship between the actor and the audience is based on the paradigm of performance with which he is familiar. Webster's narrative evokes the illustration for the initiation phase of *Radiating Box*, which demonstrates how the actor sends his energy outwards in all directions as he radiates to forge a connection. What Webster describes, though, is vocal and linguistic energy; the connection resounds not only in terms of the actor's instrument, but also resonates in terms of how the language reaches the listener.

Shakespeare's audience would have gone to *hear* a play, and we are accustomed to going to *see* one. This shift in the primary mode of reception from the aural to the visual directs our attention to the next area of our training. When our audience is contained in one location, as they are within the fourth wall tradition, we grow to depend on the synthesis of the visual and the aural to communicate. We know that when one sense is compromised, the others will heighten. If you engage a group on a blindfolded trust walk, they will experience acute listening and will become attentive to the subtle changes in the air around them. Their perception of themselves, and their surroundings, changes.

Shakespeare's Globe is a twenty-sided polygon—a multidimensional space that surrounds the actor with multifaceted points of view. Unlike an end-on stage where the audience is centrally located, in this configuration

Awakening the listener **121**

the central viewpoint is constantly shifting. These variable vantage points flow together like a primitive form of stop-motion animation, with the actor—and the action—at the center. As the epicenter of that animated radius, the Globe actor can see the sea of bodies within the space, bodies whose lenses focus on the unfolding story. Since those lenses are dispersed throughout the playhouse, the actor's kinesthetic awareness prompts the need for vocal energy that radiates to reach the parameters of the space.

The performance paradigm at Shakespeare's Globe demands heightened presence in the actor. The visible surround of spectators at Shakespeare's Globe helps to galvanize the actors, who respond by returning that energy to the whole space. The transparency that accompanies daylight—and the close-as-possible replication of that lighting at dusk—calls for fully engaged storytelling from the actor. The absence of the fourth wall encourages community and inclusion, and it also affects how the actor orients himself at the center of the playmaking.

It can be quite enchanting to speak directly to someone under those circumstances, and it is especially exquisite to do so with heightened text. I know that sounds very romantic and it certainly sounds very lofty, but it is true. This truth is woven into that "magical web" that transfixes and defines how we experience performance. The inherent transparency that accompanies daylight intensifies the honesty and vulnerability of the event, and that demands a comparable degree of sincerity and clarity in the voice. When you look into the eyes of those with whom you speak—and constantly have the potential to do so—the listener is elevated and transformed by that connection, and the actor is fueled by the exchange of energy. Eye contact can be a powerful and intimate exchange, both vulnerable and aggressive. The eyes have long been known as the "windows of the soul" and, as a euphemism for female genitalia, were considered sexual in nature when these plays were first performed. That connotation is lost on us today more often than not, yet we still equate the eyes with intimacy. There is less room for pretense when you look directly into someone's eyes. In performance, direct eye contact shapes the agreement between the actor and the audience, and informs the theatrical event.

Have you ever had to look into someone's eyes and say something difficult? It is a lot harder to do than to relay the same information by phone. That phone conversation is made easier still when it's relegated to email or text message. As we get further and further from our audience, the connection diminishes between us and the body responds to these subtle changes. Both in life as well as in performance being fully present requires a greater commitment from us. If we've been trained to perform with a wall between the audience and ourselves, we will connect differently to them, and to our text.

122 Actuating practice

Take some time in your everyday life to notice how you respond—and how your instrument responds—when you engage deliberately with your listener. Take your eyes off the menu board when you order your coffee and speak directly to the barista. Notice how your voice responds to that enhanced connection. When you make eye contact, can you feel your energy radiating? When we avoid eye contact, we withhold our energy from the world around us. In our daily lives there are times when we must do that, when our safety depends on it. In performance, however, we must be willing to be at the center of those gossamer threads that emanate and connect us to the rest of the bodies that inhabit the space.

In this chapter we will explore ways to strengthen our connection to those audience members that are less accessible to us: the audience beyond our sightlines, and those who cannot rely on visual storytelling. We will exercise the "lines drawne from the circumference" between our listeners' "eares" and us. This training sequence contains three components; each section is designed to help you tap into your need to communicate and to reach your audience—in the truest sense that "audience" means "listeners." Through the series, you will develop a responsive voice that resonates and communicates from the whole body. First, we'll focus on communicating with parts of the body that can be forgotten in a fourth wall tradition. We'll explore the sensation of moving vibration through less activated parts of the body, such as the back. Then we will expand on the somatic vocabulary we developed so that we move progressively from reaching the listener with whom we are closely connected to activating the language for an audience that cannot read our facial expressions or body clues and can only rely on what they hear. Finally we'll transform the exercise once more by having each speaker connect exclusively through his own back, but this time without any physical contact with the audience. In this way, we will cultivate a new sensation of releasing and radiating energy that enhances how we engage with the language.

Blind Shakespeare

- Begin by dividing the group into pairs, designating each actor either "A" or "B."

  - As much as you are able to, do your best to partner actors with those similar in size; it will maximize their experience. This is not always possible, but it is preferable.

- Ask the actors to begin by sitting on the floor, back to back, each supporting the other. Encourage them to position

Awakening the listener **123**

themselves so that they have the most physical contact with their partner as possible.

o Have the actors begin by sitting with their bottoms as close together as possible, and rolling up through the spine, vertebrae by vertebrae in contact with their partner. Let them know that the aim is for them to have as much contact as possible, but not at the expense of holding tension in the body. The natural curve of the spine, along with the distinctiveness of each individual body means that perfect contact will not be possible. The body should not become rigid in order to increase contact, but should always remain free from tension and in a state of focused ease. The partners provide enough resistance to one another that both are relaxed and supported, but neither is pushing the other off center.

• Distribute two different descriptive texts: one to actor "A," the other to "B."

o Here are two of my favorites for this passage, but you can select any descriptive texts of similar lengths.

Text "A"

The barge she sat in, like a burnish'd throne,

Burn'd on the water: the poop was beaten gold;

Purple the sails, and so perfumed that

The winds were love-sick with them; the oars were silver,

Which to the tune of flues kept stroke, and made

The water which they beat to follow faster,

As amorous of their strokes. For her own person,

It beggar'd all description: she did lie

In her pavilion—cloth-of-gold of tissue—

O'er-picturing that Venus where we see

The fancy outwork nature: on each side of her

Stood pretty dimpled boys, like smiling Cupids,

With divers-colour'd fans, whose wind did seem

124 Actuating practice

To glow the delicate cheeks which they did cool,

And what they undid did.

(Anthony and Cleopatra 2.2)

Text "B"

There is a willow grows aslant a brook,

That shows his hoar leaves in the glassy stream;

There with fantastic garlands did she come

Of crow-flowers, nettles, daisies, and long purples

That liberal shepherds give a grosser name,

But our cold maids do dead men's fingers call them:

There, on the pendent boughs her coronet weeds

Clambering to hang, and envious sliver broke;

When down her weedy trophies and herself

Fell in the weeping brook.

(Hamlet 4.7)

- Instruct actor "A" to begin reading the text, and to focus on generating as much vocal vibration as possible through the back. The goal here is for "A" to send the vibrations through the back so that actor "B" can experience those vibrations.
- Switch partners; this time "B" will read and send vibration and "A" will receive.
- The aim here is for both actors to experience activating the back and sending and receiving vibration through the back-to-back transmission. They are creating the foundation for a different mode of communication.
- Without opening the floor to discussion yet, give the actors the next set of instructions: actor "A" will reread the text, this time focusing on both the transference of vibration as well as imparting the meaning of the text. Encourage the speakers to share both the physical and the intellectual components with their listeners so that they are communicating fully, both aurally and physically, through their backs. Actor "B" will listen to "A" and repeat, or reverberate, those images that resonate for him as a listener. Throughout the exercise, the listener will echo the speaker, and

Awakening the listener **125**

the speaker will receive those reverberations as he continues reading the passage aloud.

- o There is no predetermined number of words that ought to be repeated, nor is there a limit to the number of words per verse line. The listener will repeat what he has the strongest connection to, according to the vibration and the meaning of what is spoken.

- Both partners switch roles, with "B" speaking, and "A" listening and reverberating.
- After both speakers have had an opportunity to share their text while simultaneously getting feedback from the listener, ask the pairs to separate and to sit so that they are perpendicular to one another; have the speaker shift positions so that he is facing the ear of the listener.

- o Ask the listeners to close their eyes.
- o Instruct the speakers to reread the passage a final time, with particular emphasis on creating the images for the listeners. Some useful imagery is to "paint the picture" with the words, as though you are sitting around a campfire, telling stories.

- Once both partners have had a chance to read and respond to each other, invite them to share their experience and observations between them. After that, you can open the floor to general observations.
- After a brief discussion, give both the "A"s and "B"s a second descriptive text from which to work. Ask them to stand and walk around the space reading the text aloud once for sense. After they have completed the read-through, invite the "A"s to partner with new "B"s—this time it is not necessary for partners to be comparable in size.
- The new partners will sit perpendicular to one another, as they did in the final portion of the last exercise.

- o Ask the listeners to close their eyes.

- Instruct the speakers to read the new passage, and to evoke the imagery for the partner as fully as they can. The reader should aim to transfer the story to the listener as though they are passing a baton; the listener should be able to recall the visual images within the passage, even if he cannot recall the passage word-for-word.

126 Actuating practice

Text "A"

Now entertain conjecture of a time,
When creeping Murmur and the poring Dark
Fills the wide Vessel of the Universe.
From Camp to Camp, through the foul Womb of Night
The Hum of either Army stilly sounds;
That the fix'd Centinels almost receive
The secret Whispers of each other's Watch.
Fire answers fire, and through their paly flames
Each Battle sees the others umber'd face.
Steed threatens Steed, in high and boastfull Neighs
Piercing the Nights dull Ear: and from the Tents,
The Armorers accomplishing the Knights,
With busy Hammers closing Rivets up,
Give dreadfull note of preparation.

(Henry V, 4, prologue)

Text "B"

Suffolke first died, and York all haggled over
Comes to him, where in gore he lay insteeped,
And takes him by the Beard, kisses the gashes
That bloodily did yawn upon his face.
He cries aloud; Tarry my Cousin Suffolk,
My soul shall thine keep company to heaven:
Tarry (sweet soul) for mine, then fly a-breast:
As in this glorious and well-foughten field
We kept together in our Chivalrie.
Upon these words I came, and cheer'd him up,
He smil'd me in the face, raught me his hand,
And with a feeble gripe, says: Deere my Lord,
Commend my service to my Sovereign,
So did he turn, and over Suffolk's neck
He threw his wounded arm, and kiss'd his lips,

Awakening the listener **127**

And so espous'd to death, with blood he seal'd

A Testament of Noble-ending-love:

(Henry V 4.6)

- After listening to the passage, the listener will speak the resounding images to the reader.
- The reader and listener should switch roles and repeat the exercise with the text assigned to actor "B."
- Allow for discussion afterwards so the group can address their experiences. Some questions for discussion:

  - What did you notice about how you read the second passage?
  - What did you focus on as you tried to engage your partner?
  - Were there any particular skills or tactics you used to evoke the images and reach your partner?
  - How did you listen to the text?
  - What grabbed you about the images in the text?
  - How did you recall what you heard, and why were those passages meaningful to you?
  - Did the readers do anything specific that captured your attention and helped to communicate the text?

For the next exploration, each actor will need to have a piece of text that they have memorized and have rehearsed previously. An audition monologue or soliloquy is ideal for this; it should be something that the actor knows well and feels very comfortable with. We will build upon the foundation initiated in *Blind Shakespeare*, while introducing spatial elements.

Blindfolded Shakespeare

- Organize the space so that there are chairs positioned in a three-quarter-thrust arrangement, with a wall at the back or "upstage" position.
- Place a bandana at each chair.
- Invite the ensemble to sit in the thrust configuration.

  - Be sure that audience sits on all three sides, and fills the space.
  - If the group is small, encourage the actors to sit equally dispersed throughout the space. It is especially important to include the upstage side seats.

- While seated as audience, the actors should remain blindfolded.

128 Actuating practice

- One by one, each actor removes his blindfold and enters the playing area of the thrust space.
- The actor shares the prepared soliloquy with his blindfolded audience.
- The audience experiences what it is like to listen to a performance, and experiences each soliloquy without any visual connection.
- After each actor has had a chance to "perform," open the floor to discussion.

The series progresses with the next exercise: *Backwards Shakespeare. Backwards Shakespeare* continues to challenge the actor to work three-dimensionally, and it adds to *Blindfolded Shakespeare* the elements of radiating energy in conjunction with storytelling.

Backwards Shakespeare

- Still seated in three-quarters thrust, the audience removes their blindfolds.
- While facing "upstage" each actor performs his prepared soliloquy.
- The goal is for the actor to reach his audience by radiating his energy and vibration through his back, while simultaneously sending the text forward. He must release his energy in all directions as he engages the text vocally.

  o As was true in *Blindfolded Shakespeare*, the actor must reach an audience who cannot see him, but this time with the added layer that he himself cannot see his audience.

- After each actor has had a chance to work, open the floor up to discussion. Be sure to address the following questions:

  o Was it clear when an actor engaged and radiated through his back and activated the whole body?
  o Did you observe particular points when you felt more or less engaged? Why was that?
  o When facing upstage, were you able to locate the sense of radiation in both directions as you spoke?

There are several things to be aware of as you progress through these explorations. It is ideal to move through the progression in a single session, as each component stirs in the actor's body a deliberate response,

Awakening the listener **129**

which is expanded and developed further in the sequence that follows. In the first instance, *Blind Shakespeare* locates the three-dimensionality of the body's transference of vibration and meaning by isolating the connection through the actors' backs. Next, *Blindfolded Shakespeare* energizes and empowers the actor by exploiting the actor's creative freedom by encouraging risk-taking. The actor perceives that he is free from the audience's judgment; he is in a position of power, the blindfolded audience in a position of vulnerability. Something happens in this exchange: when the audience allows themselves to be vulnerable, the actor experiences their trust, which encourages his own vulnerability and trust in himself to communicate fully. Finally, *Backwards Shakespeare* once again reverses the relationship of vulnerability between the actor and the audience. The unfamiliarity of the spatial relationship ignites the actor's vulnerability. If the balance falters too much the actor can lose his connection to his three-dimensionality and begin to push vocally, to force the text out.

The key is to observe and learn from the times when this happens. We are retraining the habit, and it takes time for the actor-instrument to recalibrate. When you notice that an actor is losing his connection and beginning to push, it is useful to employ side-coaching from outside of the actor's sight line. Asking questions such as "what?" "how?" "who?" "where?" or "why?" is enough to prompt the actor to reconnect and to release with greater dimension and ease. A gentle reminder such as, "remember your back" and "release" or "radiate" is also useful.

In *Awakening the Listener*, we are actually locating the dynamic speaker. We've looked at the logistics of working with Shakespeare's language in Chapter 3, and through our *Blind, Blindfolded,* and *Backwards Shakespeare* (BBB) series we explored how to speak the text with an activated body: we have awakened our sensory and kinesthetic awareness. Throughout the series, *Blind, Blindfolded,* and *Backwards Shakespeare* we have heightened our awareness of how we use Shakespeare's language to reach our audiences and how we become more dynamic performers when we do. Next, we will investigate further ways in which we can expand and energize our connection to Shakespeare's texts.

7

ENERGIZING THE LANGUAGE

Energized language dances; it trips on the tongue, surprising the speaker as well as the listener. It fills the air between the mouth and the ear with suspended energy that connects to a world of ideas that pulse beneath the spoken words. It embodies *inspiration*: the breath and the thought interconnected so intimately that neither can be extracted without the unraveling the other. It is so deeply personal that no two speakers reach the moment of speech precisely in the same way. It is pure potential. And it is intoxicating.

As we immerse ourselves in Shakespeare's form, it can be challenging to find our own connection to the language, our personal need to speak only the given text, precisely the given text, and to communicate fully with it. In Chapter 3 we looked at how Shakespeare's verse is closer than we may have realized to the way we speak today. Yet, as we communicate the manner in which we progress from the origin of conceptual thought to the articulation of that thought through our syntax is not structured automatically in heightened verse. This becomes an even more cognitively complicated process when we introduce a layer of memorized text. As actors, we are empowered by our accessibility and flexibility in practice; we work diligently on recognizing and following our impulses with organic responses. We want, ultimately, to reach a point where we respond as readily within the form and structure Shakespeare provides as we do in our own lives.

One of the biggest disappointments (and where so many productions of Shakespeare can fall flat) is hearing a lot of poetry—even when spoken "well"—that lacks a personal connection to the language. If we want Shakespeare's language to pulse within us, we need to think as his

Energizing the language **131**

characters do. "Energizing the language" enables us to take ownership of the text and make it the only means in which we can communicate at that particular time. We need to discover personal connections to what we speak that originate from us. We want our thoughts to fuse with Shakespeare's text so that the *only* words that suit our expression are the ones that Shakespeare wrote. This is why I've never been a huge fan of strict paraphrasing—where you are to rewrite all of Shakespeare's lines in modern language. Of course, we absolutely must know and understand the meaning of everything we speak; of course we do. However, if we can communicate in our own tongue, we never develop within us the need for those particular words at that precise moment. We end up with our modern paraphrased response, which we then translate to our Shakespearean text. That translation process softens our impulse for organic response. It deprives us of the opportunity to *need* the words, and only the words, Shakespeare has given us. We must understand exactly what we are saying in order to root that language within us, but strict paraphrasing (like changing the word "brother" to "son of my parents") often fails to do what it intends. It brings us even further from that moment of inspiration between the impulse and the textual response. We certainly don't need to complicate that process any further.

Another reason to aim for this unity between thought and text is to support our breath capacity. Actors can find that they run out of breath when working on Shakespeare. When we looked at Shakespeare's punctuation in Chapter 3, we discovered how a character's thoughts are often longer than the way we think and write today. When we marry the inspiration of thought to the inspiration of breath we have a greater ability to synthesize Shakespeare's language and make it our own.

Have you ever noticed that we rarely run out of breath in our everyday lives? We breathe to accommodate our thoughts. When we do tend to run out of breath, it is when the thoughts are rushing in too quickly—we're in the midst of an argument, or we're incredibly excited about something. As listeners, we associate breath with thought. The next time you are in a lengthy conversation, choose a few places to breathe while the other person is speaking. I'm sure they will think you have something to say. We are so programmed as human beings to connect these two actions that simply breathing in conversation signals to the speaker that the other person wants to contribute. It's quite remarkable when you think about it.

The exercises we'll explore here are designed to forge an organic response to Shakespeare's language, to encourage thinking on the line and picking Shakespeare's words as the perfect way to make the point. We'll begin by looking at the structure of verse lines from a performance perspective.

132 Actuating practice

Just as we need to marry our breath and thought, we also need to expand the length of those thoughts without dropping the energy of the lines. Expanded thoughts will support expanded breath.

The first exercise, *Open Mic Poetry*, explores the structure of the verse line and keeps the vocal energy sustained from beginning to end. Often satirized for taking itself too seriously, open mic poetry is a post-modern form of performance art that is found in social settings like coffee houses and pubs where the microphone is literally "open" to any guest who wishes to perform poetry. We will take the premise of that post-modern performance art and apply it to Shakespeare's poetry.

Open Mic Poetry

Working with text in hand, the actor stands or sits before the ensemble audience. (The audience configuration is inconsequential as long as the "performance" and "audience" spaces are designated clearly.) The actor will speak only the first and last words of the verse line, but must communicate the essence of the speech by capturing the meaning of the entire verse line. The goal is for the audience to understand the whole of the speech through the truncated text. For example, if one were working on Hamlet's "To be or not to be . . ." speech, the beginning of the performance text would be:

TO QUESTION

WHETHER SUFFER

THE FORTUNE

OR TROUBLES

AND SLEEP

NO END

THE SHOCKS

THAT CONSUMMATION

DEVOUTLY SLEEP

For this exercise, I like the actors to be given the instructions right before the exploration. All they need to know in advance is to bring a copy of the text from which they're working, even if they already have it memorized. This encourages discoveries in practice rather than through prior analysis and embeds the sense of forward-moving energy

Energizing the language **133**

in the body. If you are an actor working solo, simply pick up your text and begin working—just resist the temptation to predetermine outcomes so that you can make discoveries along the way.

Open Mic Poetry will also help to imbue personalized meanings to the first and last words of the verse line, which creates nuanced vocal modulation. Since there is an element of performance to the exercise, the actor's intention (audience understanding) helps to keep the language active and energized rather than introspective and analytical.

Every book written on performing Shakespeare since the end of the twentieth century has been influenced in some way by the revolutionary work of Cicely Berry, and this one is certainly no exception. Berry's imprint on the way we think about performing Shakespeare permeates the entire field, and *Moving Target* is directly influenced by her work with text and resistance. *Moving Target* was prompted by many daydreams about what performing in the Globe might have been like for Shakespeare's actors.

We've already considered how different it was to perform at the time Shakespeare was writing. Today, we are used to having an attentive audience whose sole purpose for being in the theatre is to experience the play. What would it be like to perform for a group who is there to socialize or conduct business? What would it be like to vie for the audience's attention as they move about, eat, and converse? How might our performances be affected if we could see them all doing this? We have no way of knowing whether or not Shakespeare's actors were affected by the social behavior of their audiences, or how that might have manifested, but just as *Blindfolded Shakespeare* helps us to tap into the language more actively, *Moving Target* connects us to the need to communicate and capture the attention of our listeners.

Moving Target: Whole Text

Begin with the ensemble moving throughout the space. Direct their attention to their surroundings, to the other bodies in the space. When an actor has the impulse to share a piece of previously memorized text (such as a soliloquy), he will begin to share it with the ensemble as they continue to move throughout the space. The actor can speak to one person or to multiple people in the space, as the speaker desires. The speaker's goal is to capture the attention of the moving bodies in the space. The ensemble's goal is to keep moving and avert engaging with the speaker. Encourage the speaker to fight for their attention, to switch tactics, if necessary.

134 Actuating practice

Moving Target also helps to foster the synchronization between inspiration of thought and inspiration of breath. The actors discover where new thoughts arise as they fight for the audience's attention. These moments of discovery help to energize the language and enhance the actors' connection to their texts.

Moving Target: Random Text

As with the *Moving Target: Whole Text* exploration, begin with the ensemble moving throughout the space, aware of each other and their surroundings. When an actor has the impulse to share a bit of text of any length, he will begin to share it with the ensemble as they continue to move throughout the space. The actor can speak to one person or to multiple people in the space, as the speaker desires. The speaker's goal is to capture the attention of the moving bodies in the space. The ensemble's goal is to keep moving and avert engaging with the speaker. The ensemble will also be following their own individual impulses to speak. Encourage the actors to follow their impulses, to avoid predetermining when is the "right" time to speak. Remind them that there is no need to be polite; they can follow their impulses to speak even if there is another speaker at that moment. In fact, the cacophony only heightens the objectives (and obstacles) of the exercise, and helps to root the need to reach the audience even further.

Moving Target: Random Text promotes the impulse-action response and roots the actors deeply in Shakespeare's language while galvanizing the need to speak the text. While *Moving Target* connects the actor to the need to communicate, *Find It Here* channels that need toward expression. *Find It Here* gives the actor the chance to forge a personal connection to the words and images in the text by exploring what it means to coin them as the perfect instrument for expression.

In Chapter 2 we considered the ways in which Shakespeare's Globe is microcosm within a macrocosm. We examined how ideas such as metaphors and similes that can seem purely symbolic in a twentieth-century theatre are present in the Globe as tangible examples of the world in which Shakespeare's characters live. *Find It Here* enables the actor to coin images and text by taking inspiration from Shakespeare's Globe, where such examples of the Elizabethan microcosm exist. The act of coining images afresh lends a sense of spontaneity; it encourages the actor's organic connection to impulse and imparts a sense of ownership over the language spoken.

Earlier, we examined how actors' thoughts are not always synchronized with their characters. We considered how this affects the length of those thoughts, but it extends further to the thoughts themselves: how they are constructed and how they are expressed. *Find It Here* helps to bridge that gap. In *Find It Here*, actors are encouraged to discover precisely the perfect image to illustrate the character's need for expression.

Find It Here

Working with a previously prepared speech, the actor begins the speech with the intention of discovering where the images reside within the physical space. Remind the actor that there is a metaphysical space in addition to the physical one. The goal is to coin each image, selecting the precise words to capture the thought as it comes. It need not become a pantomime of the text; instead it can be useful to consider the studio space as a blank canvas upon which ideas and images can be found either in the mind's eye or in the space itself. Encourage the actor to think internally, "how can I explain this?" or "what is it I want to say?" or "oh, I have the best example!" (You can even side coach these in dialogue if the actor is too focused on the "performance" of the speech.) Encourage the actor to search and coin each image and word—the only image or word that can adequately express the thought—right at the moment of speech. As the actor searches for the discovery of "it"—the perfect expression is discovered.

In this exploration it is interesting to note the dance of thought that emerges between finding "it" externally and finding "it" internally. There is no "right" way to execute the task, but regardless of where the act of coining originates, the actor's discoveries help to imbue the text with energy and ownership.

There is no singular way to execute *Find It Here* within a given speech, but as an example, let's explore one of Berowne's speeches from *Love's Labours Lost* (3.1). I will place in bold one selection of images that can be "found" through the exploration.

O, and I forsooth in **love**,

I that have been love's **whip**?

A very **Beadle** to a **humerous sight**: A **Critic**,

Nay, a **night-watch Constable**.

136 Actuating practice

A **domineering pedant** o'er the Boy,
Then whom no **mortal** so **magnificent**.
This **wimpled, whining, purblind wayward Boy,**
This **signior Junior giant dwarf, don** Cupid,
Regent of Love-rhymes, Lord of folded arms,
Th'annointed soueraign of sighs and groans:
Liege of all loiterers and malcontents:
Dread Prince of Placcats, King of Codpieces.
Sole Emperator and **great generall**
Of trotting Parrators (O my little heart.)
And I to be a **Corporal** of his field,
And wear his colours like a **Tumblers hoop**.
What? I **love,** I **sue,** I **seek a wife,**
A woman that is like a **German Clock,**
Still a repairing: ever out of frame,
And **never going a right,** being a Watch:
But being **watched,** that it may still go right.
Nay, to be **perjured,** which is worst of all:
And among three, **to love the worst of all,**
A **whitely wanton,** with a **velvet brow**.
With two **pitch balls stuck in her face for eyes.**
I, and by heaven, one that will do the deed,
Though **Argus were her Eunuch and her guard**.
And I **to sigh for her, to watch for her,**
To pray for her, go to: it is a **plague**
That Cupid will impose for my neglect,
Of his almighty **dreadful little might**.
Well, I will **love, write, sigh, pray, sue, groan,**
Some men must love my Lady, and some **Joan**.

There are a lot of lists in this speech, and coining those images at the moment of speech, *finding it there* in the moment, helps to distinguish the need for the list, and clarify those items on it. Berowne has so many images because he's grappling to articulate and understand his circumstances.

Actors can explore *Find It Here* exclusively through the lens of possibilities found at Shakespeare's Globe. They can hold the image of the Globe in their mind's eye, and see which images connect to each of the components present at the Globe.

Examine photographs of the interior of Shakespeare's Globe and move through a guided visualization of the stage space. Begin the speech as though you are standing on stage of the Globe. Do you see the pillars? Are the heavens above? Are you standing over the trap door to hell? Can you imagine where you'd find the groundlings? Can you see the upper classes perched above? Move through the text again and allow the images and inspiration (of thought and breath simultaneously) to wash over you. Speak to those around you. Take your time; don't rush to the text until you locate it, but work honestly and with integrity. Open your imagination to the visualization as much as to the text and allow yourself to be surprised. Fight the temptation to pre-determine—and remember your back!

Open Mic Poetry, Moving Target, and *Find It Here* are all designed to encourage a personalized connection to the linguistic energy of Shakespeare's texts. Each of these explorations helps you to sweep off the surface elements of the language so that the text is rooted deeply within you. Through these explorations you gain greater ownership of the language, which enables you to respond to both the text and the dynamics of performance with greater nuance and command of the material.

8
EXPANDING THE FICTION

In Chapter 2 we examined the various ways that Shakespeare's Globe is different from the kinds of theatre spaces we've grown accustomed to in the later part of the twentieth and the early part of the twenty-first centuries. We explored how Shakespeare's theatre was a meta-theatrical microcosm within a macrocosm that placed the performers and the spectators in one room rather than in two. In Chapter 1 I introduced how the dynamics of performance shifted as the developments in realism and naturalism advanced alongside the codification of Stanislavki's system for training actors. In this chapter, I will share the sequence for *Expanding the Fiction*, which builds upon the foundation introduced in the *Activating the Body* and *Awakening the Listener* series found in Chapters 5 and 6.

When we examined the possibilities for casting the audience, we explored the pivotal ways that the audience can serve as *mirror* through the use of *elliptical energy*. Elliptical energy broadens the spectrum of the theatrical fiction by removing the fourth wall and allowing energy to move fluidly throughout the space. Within a fourth wall performance paradigm, the fiction remains intact behind the invisible fourth wall, through which the audience peers in voyeuristically to observe the fictional world.

This fourth wall paradigm is the modus operandi in Western actor training. Within the fourth wall tradition, actors send their primary energy—the subject of the actor's focus—towards the partner on stage, who exists simultaneously within the fictional world. The actor remains, however consciously or subconsciously, aware of that invisible wall's presence, and of the audience that lies beyond it. The actor is aware that he is still a performer, and that there is a still an audience watching. Even if the audience is withheld from the actor's primary energy, the actor will still emit a secondary energy that permeates the fourth wall and reaches the audience. It is the secondary energy that reminds an actor to "open out" or remain "open" to the downstage area, where the audience is contained. The theatre actor must radiate and release energy to reach the audience, unlike the film actor who works before the camera. In film, the camera comes in to the intimate space of the performance, it moves within the fictional world as though it is also within the four walls (this differs from the style of filming that happens for television, particularly for television sitcoms). To illustrate this concept, the actor's primary energy is illustrated with solid lines, the secondary energy with broken lines (see Figure 8.1).

Elliptical energy enables the fiction to expand beyond the stage; it breaks down the fourth wall so that no divide exists between the actor and the audience (see Figure 8.2). As part of the fictional world, the audience is included in the realm of primary energy. The actor's energy passes through the audience in order to reach the partner on stage. The audience serves as a conduit for that transaction. It continually locates and recalibrates the audience within the world of the fiction.

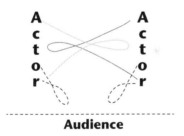

FIGURE 8.1 Primary and secondary energy in a fourth wall paradigm

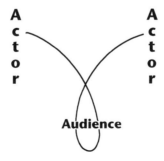

FIGURE 8.2 Illustration of elliptical energy

140 Actuating practice

Elliptical energy

With elliptical energy, the audience is like the eye of a needle; the thread is the actor's energy. In order to sew one must pass the thread through the eye of the needle, and only then can it be reinforced and anchored at its destination point: the knot. The knot is the inextricable connection between the two ends of the string—the actors. The knot's intact, reinforced, and resilient connection is dependent on that external source: the needle. Without the needle, there is no stitch. Alone, the thread is incapable of altering the fabric. The stitch binds the components together—it is the narrative that fabricates the theatrical experience. Without that connection, we are left bare indeed.

Elliptical Energy Training

The training sequence for elliptical energy has several components. I will describe them first, and discuss them afterwards. This training requires the use of mirrors. A mirrored studio is preferable, but if you are unable to access a space large enough to accommodate your group, it is also possible to do the training using large handheld mirrors (approximately 8 x 10" or A4 size). If you must use handheld mirrors, they should be large enough to accommodate the actor's image from the neck up, and include the whole face. A small compact mirror is too small to be useful. In a pinch, I have also used the strip of mirror in a theatre dressing room, but that requires the group to sit, which brings on other challenges.

I borrow from Sanford Meisner's repetition exercise as a jumpstart into this training, but my goals differ from Meisner's. If you are not familiar with Meisner's repetition exercise, Meisner developed repetition work to help actors tap into and release their impulses. He wanted to strip away the actor's desire to intellectualize, to get actors out of their heads and in touch with their organic responses. I use the repetition work in the elliptical energy sequence to help focus the exchange between the two partners in training. Meisner's training can take years to master and grasp fully. I wouldn't call this "Meisner" training, but I use repetition to engage a very different purpose altogether.

This work requires a minimum of two actors.

Elliptical Energy Training Part I

Divide your group of actors into pairs; partners can be selected at random, or you can choose to pair scene partners together to maximize and cultivate a connection between them.

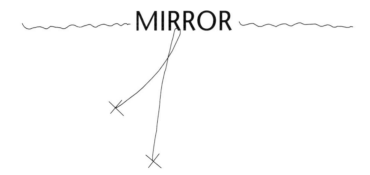

FIGURE 8.3 *Elliptical Energy Training Part I*

Each pair stands before the mirror, staggered, with some distance between the "downstage" person closest to the mirror and the mirror. The "upstage" partner should be staggered slightly behind and aside the one closer to the mirror. The partners will connect directly to one another through the image before them in the mirror (see Figure 8.3).

> Begin by observing your partner in the mirror. You are standing with your feet in contact with the floor, knees are soft, belly is free, and your breath is flowing freely. Your head is floating away from the spine.
>
> Observe your partner. Really take in your partner. See your partner fully. What do you notice? When you have the impulse to do so, begin by stating an observation about your partner. The observation should be concrete and factual rather than subjective or abstract. Allow that observation to come from this moment; the past is past. When you are ready, share your observation. Allow it to be simple and factual: "You're wearing a blue shirt" or "Your hair is pulled back." Each partner will repeat the observation. It is okay for the partner that is observed to change the pronoun in the statement.
>
> > "You're wearing a blue shirt."
> > "I'm wearing a blue shirt."
> > "You're wearing a blue shirt."
> > "I'm wearing a blue shirt."
> > "You're wearing a blue shirt."

142 Actuating practice

> "I'm wearing a blue shirt."
>
> "You're wearing a blue shirt."

Continue with this dialogue; don't look to change for the sake of change. Allow new things to come to you with the repetition, and see what you discover. Be present with it, and remain connected to your partner. You will eventually discover something with your partner, for example:

> "You're wearing a <u>blue</u> shirt."
>
> "I'm wearing a <u>blue</u> shirt."
>
> "You're wearing a <u>blue</u> shirt."

Which may eventually lead to:

> "You're wearing a blue <u>shirt.</u>"
>
> "I'm wearing a blue <u>shirt.</u>"
>
> "You're wearing a blue <u>shirt.</u>"

Remain focused on your partner. The impulse to change will eventually emerge. You may have the impulse to continue:

> "You're wearing a blue <u>shirt.</u>"
>
> "I'm wearing a blue <u>shirt.</u>"
>
> "You're wearing a blue <u>shirt.</u>"
>
> "You're wearing blue <u>jeans.</u>"
>
> "I'm wearing blue <u>jeans.</u>"
>
> "You're wearing blue <u>jeans.</u>"
>
> "I'm wearing blue <u>jeans.</u>"
>
> "You're wearing blue <u>jeans.</u>"
>
> "I'm wearing blue <u>jeans.</u>"
>
> "You're wearing blue <u>jeans.</u>"

The key is not to manipulate, not to change for the sake of being clever or to drive the exercise, but if you are feeling impatient, notice your impatience and allow that to inform your repetition. Stay connected

Expanding the fiction **143**

to your partner in the mirror. Continue to observe your partner. You can eventually branch out and make broader observations that relate to your partner in this given moment.

> "You're wearing blue jeans."
>
> "I'm wearing blue jeans."
>
> "You're wearing blue jeans."
>
> "I'm wearing. Blue. Jeans."
>
> "You're wearing BLUE jeans." (laughs)
>
> "You just laughed."
>
> "I just laughed."
>
> "You just laughed."
>
> "I just laughed."
>
> "You think it's funny."
>
> "I think it's funny."
>
> "You think it's funny."
>
> "I do think it's funny."
>
> "You do think it's funny."

And so on. Allow this to continue for some time, until the observations have had a chance to shift, and each partner has had the opportunity to follow new impulses. The partners should be observing and connecting freely with one another, comfortably settled into the exercise before the next phase is introduced.

Elliptical Energy Training Part II

Maintaining the same position as Part I, you will now follow an internal impulse when it arises—to share with your partner a piece of Shakespeare's text. So you are observing your partner and following your impulse to state your observation(s), and you are also allowing the impulse to come from within to respond to the stimulus you receive from your partner with a piece of Shakespeare's text. In turn, the partner may respond with text as well, or may return to the repetition as the impulse suits. If the partner responds with an observation and not

144 Actuating practice

with a piece of text, the partner will want to invite the impulse to share and follow it when it presents itself. The segue between the repetition and Shakespeare will look like this:

"You have brown hair."

"I have brown hair."

"You have brown hair."

"I have brown hair."

"You have brown hair."

"I have brown hair."

(impulse)   Do not think so, you shall not find it so

And Heaven forgive them, that so much have sway'd

Your Majesty's good thoughts away from me:

I will redeem all this on Percy's head,

And in the closing of some glorious day,

Be bold to tell you, that I am your Son,

At this point the partner can either respond with an observation or be inspired to respond with a piece of text. All the while, the partners maintain their connection to one another in the mirror. The response that includes text may look like this:

Partner A: I will redeem all this on Percy's head,
And in the closing of some glorious day,
Be bold to tell you, that I am your Son,

Partner B: This is the air; that is the glorious sun;
This pearl she gave me, I do feel't and see't;
And though 'tis wonder that enwraps me thus,
Yet 'tis not madness. Where's Antonio, then?
I could not find him at the Elephant:
Yet there he was; and there I found this credit,
That he did range the town to seek me out.

The partner may continue to respond with another piece of text or may return to the repetition, based on the impulse.

Partner A: You surprised yourself
Partner B: I surprised myself
Partner A: You surprised yourself
Partner B: I surprised myself
Partner A: You surprised yourself
Partner B: I DID surprise myself!

As the exchange continues, the partner may have the impulse to respond with another piece of text:

Partner B: I could not find him at the Elephant:
Yet there he was; and there I found this credit,
That he did range the town to seek me out.
Partner A: Out damned spot: out I say. One: Two: Why
Then 'tis time to doo't: Hell is murky. Fie, my Lord, fie,
A Soldier and affear'd? What need we fear?

Allow the partners to continue, as time permits, so they experience sharing both their own observations and Shakespeare's texts as they maintain their connection in the mirror. If a piece of text ends and the partner does not have an immediate response, encourage them to remain connected to each other and to observe the silence until a new impulse emerges.

When the group has developed a comfortable relationship to the repetition and response and the secondary level that includes memorized text, they are ready to move on to Part III. You will know that they are comfortable when the ease with which they address each other in the mirror is equivalent to face-to-face interaction. You will sense the relaxation and ease set in; they will be "working" less and connecting more, their interactions will grow more playful and organic.

Elliptical Energy Training Part III

At this stage, the partners will move from the mirror and stand before a blank wall.

As they did before the mirror, each pair stands before the wall, staggered, with some distance between the "downstage" person and the wall. The "upstage" partner should be staggered slightly behind and aside the other partner.

146 Actuating practice

Standing before the wall, you will follow the impulse to share a piece of Shakespeare's text with your partner by bouncing it off the wall to reach him. Just as you used the mirror, you will connect with your partner by sending the energy forward. This is like playing a game of pool or snooker: you direct the energy at one place (the cue ball) with the intention of creating a response somewhere else (sending a different ball to a particular pocket). You will each take turns sharing a piece of text with your partner using the wall to reach him. In your mind's eye, hold the connection you have already established with your partner by using the mirror and aim for the same ease of connection.

Allow the partners to share their texts in dialogue a few times before moving on to the next phase. Don't rush through this portion; allow enough time for the partners to experience more than one exchange.

It is useful for the partners to each share a larger piece of text, such as a monologue or soliloquy. Unlike *Backwards Shakespeare*, which requires the actor to send their energy through their backs, the purpose here is for the actor to reflect the text off the wall to reach the partner, as they did with the mirror.

Elliptical Energy Training Part IV

Part IV begins the final sequence in the elliptical energy training—it introduces the use of the audience. You can choose to have the audience either sit or stand for this portion. I prefer to have the audience sit because it parallels the relationship most actors and audiences are familiar with. Since we are training, it is useful not to introduce too many variables at once. The sequence will work and remain effective if your audience is standing, though most performance conditions will feature a seated audience.

Gather the group in one central location, facing the playing space. For this exploration, only one pair of actors will be able to work at a time; the rest will serve as the audience. Each pair will enter the playing space and resume the same configuration as before, with one partner slightly aside and behind the other. Both face the audience, with some distance between the audience and them.

As your feet come in contact with the floor and your breath falls in and out begin to observe your partner. Listen to your partner. Observe him with your whole being, with all of your awareness. Even if you

Expanding the fiction **147**

are in front of your partner you can trust yourself to observe. You do not need to see your partner in order to observe him. Don't rush. When you are ready, begin the repetition by sharing an observation about your partner. You will continue with your repetition until you have the impulse to segue into Shakespeare's text. It can be whatever piece of text you are compelled to share; it doesn't matter what it is, allow the moment of impulse to reveal the text that you will speak. Trust yourself and trust your partner. When you speak to your partner, either with the repetition work or with Shakespeare's text, you will engage your partner through the audience before you. You will send your energy through the audience in order to reach your partner in the exploration. The audience is now your mirror.

When one partner segues into text, the other partner can respond either by returning to observation and repetition, or by replying with his own piece of text. Throughout this exploration you use the audience to reach your partner, sending the energy through them to engage and affect your partner.

Allow each group to explore how to engage the audience through the use of elliptical energy before you move on.

Elliptical Energy Training Part V

Once the group has had a chance to explore how to engage their partners through the use of elliptical energy, you can offer this variation, which will draw upon some of the earlier three-dimensional training used in *Activating the Body* to conclude the cycle of physical work.

Re-configure the group into a thrust configuration, with the audience on three sides of the actors. The actors will resume the position of one slightly aside and behind the other.

Observe your audience as well as your partner. Notice that your audience now surrounds you on three sides. Observe them even if you do not see them. Be sure to include and reach all of those with whom you share the space. You radiate and receive from your partner and the audience, and use the audience to connect to your partner through the use of elliptical energy. Share a piece of text with your partner and the audience through elliptical energy. The partner will respond with his own text using the audience and elliptical energy to reply.

148 Actuating practice

Elliptical Energy Training Part V: variations

Once you've reached the final stage of the elliptical energy training, there are a few variations that can help to deepen your relationship to and understanding of elliptical energy in practice.

- If you have had a break between your Part IV and Part V explorations, reintroduce the repetition work as a warm-up to the text portion of the exploration.
- Increase the distance between the partners in the exploration; play with the proxemics to test the flexibility between the partners and the audience.
- If you are working on a particular scene in class or in rehearsal, allow the scene partners to investigate their scene through the exploration.
- If the actors are already comfortable with and accustomed to the use of elliptical energy, expand the exploration: allow them to improvise movement or explore existing blocking while engaging their partners through the use of the audience.
- Add additional actors to the exploration for an even greater challenge. How do the dynamics change when you have groups of three, four, five (or more) working at once?
- Assemble the group in the round and explore elliptical energy three-dimensionally.

There are many ways to implement the use of elliptical energy both in training and in performance. Before I talk further about elliptical energy in performance, I'd like to share some thoughts about the training, some things to keep in mind as you investigate and pursue it.

Elliptical Energy Training: observations

At the beginning of the training sequence, it will take some time for the actors to adjust. Particularly if they have no previous experience with Meisner's repetition (and they certainly don't need any previous experience with Meisner to explore elliptical energy) they can grow impatient with the monotony of the repetition. Remind them to stay present with the partner; if they are feeling impatient, let the impatience inform the impulse.

Repetition is used because it gives the actors an opportunity to work as themselves, to use their own texts to connect with their partners. The repetition is dependent on the immediate relationship between the partners. The observation and repetition provides a framework for the dialogue to

Expanding the fiction **149**

begin so that the partners need not worry about shaping the exchange between them; they can focus exclusively on their connection through the use of the mirror. This is vital: it enables the actors to have a spontaneous reaction between them while they cultivate their connection in the absence of face-to-face interaction.

The majority of actor training in the Western world depends on the direct connection between actors in the fiction. This first part of the training expands upon that direct connection through the use of the mirror, which serves as a portal for the explicit link between the actors. Through the training, they discover how they can create intimacy through an alternate form of interaction. Once they are comfortable as themselves, they will build upon that comfort and add memorized text. This progression parallels the actor's work.

In the beginning it is important that the partners commit to each other with enough vocal energy to be heard. The intimacy of the mirror can sometimes encourage (falsely) a greater sense of intimacy between the partners than is actually the case; the partners need to be able to hear each other with some distance between them. If the partners are not fully committed to the volume necessary for their partner to receive their repetition, the intention can fall back into the speaker and become too small or internalized. The actors should remember that their goal is always to affect their partners, which is the hallmark of powerful performances.

It is also common in the beginning for actors to become self-conscious at times when they observe themselves in the mirror. This is usually because they have lost or lessened their focus on their partner. When their focus strays, it introduces an opportunity for their attentiveness to redirect inwards; they become aware—or are reminded—of how they look in the mirror. This is easily remedied by recommitting the focus to the partner. It is a bit like meditating: when the mind wanders you commit to redirecting it. The same is true with the use of the mirror. When the actor becomes aware of his own image in the mirror, it is a signal to focus more attention on the partner. This can provide an unexpected opportunity for the actor to consider how strongly he remains focused on the partner.

It is important for the actors to remain committed to observing their partners and to connecting with them. As they observe, they should remain in the present moment; they need to let go of previous observations, of ideas that are imbedded in memory or that generate from themselves rather than their partners. This can become a form of manipulation; it robs them of the opportunity to be fully present and in the moment. They may not be aware that they are hanging on to old observations or that they've pre-planned

150 Actuating practice

what they will say; it can simply be that they are keen to be in control of the unknown in the exploration. As technology informs our ability to get the information we need in an instant, it can be increasingly challenging to linger in the unknown.

The use of the mirror enables the actors to maintain their direct connection to each other; it redefines the parameters of their relationship. When we expand the fiction, we depend on the redefinition of those parameters. The middle sequence strips them of the newfound comfort the mirror offers. The wall is cold and unresponsive. The wall lacks the simplicity and ease that the pair has cultivated through their explorations before the mirror. The wall demands a greater athleticism; the actors must propel their energy with enough force to bounce off the wall and continue on the path to the partner. As a result, the actors may find that they begin to push vocally, or energetically. There is a greater sense of force necessary to reach the partner when using the wall. If they stay there long enough, the actors may even grow frustrated with their experience and with their expended efforts.

This work before the wall is necessary because the wall's inability to conduce the actors' energy promotes the use of the audience as conduit. The sense of frustration and effort that marks the actors' struggle for connection dissipates when the exercise moves to the final stage, before the audience. When the actors begin their work before the audience, they rediscover the ease with which they connected before the mirror. The living, breathing audience members reflect and release the actors' energy in ways that the wall does not. While it may be tempting to skip the wall and go straight from the mirror to the audience, the wall serves an important psychological step. The mirror enabled the actors to look directly at each other. The wall does not radiate as the human body does, it demands propulsion of energy that is unnecessary, even abrasive, between people. Elliptical energy expands the world of the fiction to include all of the bodies in the space. The audience becomes a natural extension of the actors' communication when they are introduced after the wall.

When working with the audience, it is useful to keep the following distinction in mind: that the actors are including the audience in their exploration rather than performing for them. The audience is no longer an "audience," they have become part of the exploration. As the actors stand before the observers, they themselves observe the other. This loop of observation becomes like an Escher print—the source of observation changes depending on the perspective with which you look. For the partner closest to the spectators, in the downstage position, he must trust that the upstage partner is still there. The downstage actor engages his ability

Expanding the fiction **151**

to radiate energy to find the partner. That partner also must trust his own ability to observe without a line of vision. Both partners must trust that the impulse to share will come; it is important not to begin simply out of a desire to "save" each other from the potentially uncomfortable situation of waiting for an impulse while standing before a group. This level of trust is complex; it's built upon the foundation of the earlier training and the progression within the sequence.

At some point in the sequence, it is useful for both partners to switch positions so that each one has an opportunity to experience the exploration from each location and each perspective. The experience is different for both the downstage partner as well as for the upstage counterpart. Training from multiple vantage points enables the actors to embody the technique with even greater ownership.

Elliptical energy in performance

Performance is always in real time; it's never fixed. Unlike the experience of reading plays, performance is not internalized, not a solitary endeavor. Performance is fluid. Elliptical energy is also fluid. Most often it is used *indirectly*—where the actors move seamlessly between addressing each other directly and addressing each other through the use of the audience. This creates a loop that constantly engages the audience and roots them in the theatrical experience; they are an integral part of the fiction, not just witnesses to it.

Used either directly or indirectly, elliptical energy draws the audience into the world of the play, into the playmaking, and defines the theatrical experience. It shapes the relationship between the actors and the audience, and it cultivates inclusion and investment—it embodies the *Chorus'* requests in the prologue to *Henry V*: to piece out our imperfections and to think; to create the world together in order to *share* the story.

The training sequence uses direct elliptical energy, which can be implemented on stage for a highly stylized effect. With direct elliptical energy, the actors only connect to one another through the audience. The actors don't have any face-to-face interaction at all. This can help alleviate complications that arise from staging in a particular configuration or within the demands of a given set, or the direct use of elliptical energy can be implemented to explore new modes of performance. Once actors are comfortable with the use of direct elliptical energy, it becomes part of the repertoire of the actor's skill set.

As the fictional spectrum broadens through the use of elliptical energy, so do the possibilities in performance. When staging Shakespeare's plays, we

152 Actuating practice

have a whole host of opportunities to expand the fiction: from casting the role(s) the audience plays to embodying the dynamics of the playhouse for which Shakespeare wrote, we can activate and enliven the stories in ways that enhance their meaning for today's audiences. Both actors and audiences are aware of the heightened circumstances surrounding the plays, particularly in performance. When we celebrate how community is forged through sharing these circumstances, it enriches the experience for us all.

I like to describe the relationship between two actors as elastic, like a rubber band. The bond remains intact even if there are times when the connection is very slack and barely discernable and other times when it is stretched taut. The elasticity between two engaged, dynamic bodies is alive with potential. The audience wants to exist within that realm of potential, to experience the palpable exchange as the narrative unfolds. Elliptical energy helps to locate them in the field of that potential—they become part of the band that binds the actors together. By sharing the fiction, they are able to experience those things that bring forth catharsis; it enables them to see the world differently for a brief moment of time. Elliptical energy helps to position them even closer to that world, and as it does so, it helps to define the event itself.

9

DEVELOPING AND PLAYING THE SHAKESPEARE SCORE

In Chapters 3 and 4 we looked closely at how various elements of Shakespeare's texts help to fuel our performance choices. We also explored how the text and its orthography provide us with the foundation, the spine, of what supports our practice. The stronger that foundation is, the greater flexibility we have in performance.

A musical score holds all of the necessary marks for a musician to perform a piece of music. The composer provides the notes; the conductor identifies phrasing, and the musician includes further marks that indicate ideas or reminders of how to execute the task of playing the instrument. A music historian can read a score and understand what a particular performance could have sounded like, and scholars believe that some of our most famous pieces of music were performed differently during the time they were written than they are today. This is related to the interpretation of those musical scores.

Actors can also create scores that diagram how they navigate through performances of Shakespeare's texts. This is useful for many reasons: it helps to identify key elements in the texts, it creates a visual means to navigate through all of those elements, and it provides a record of how a particular performance developed. Shakespeare's texts are very complex; creating a system of notation to read those elements helps actors to include all of the components they've explored throughout their creative process. It also serves as a visual prompt that can fuel creative exploration in the rehearsal studio and in performance.

The Shakespeare score is comprised of several components: the structure of the verse, the development of thoughts, the use of language, the dynamics of orthography, and the process of balance—the ways in which ideas are formulated and considered. Each of these areas help to contribute to how we can embody the foundation that we find on the page and create vibrant performances on stage.

154 Actuating practice

The process of creating a score is a creative practice in itself. While the finished score provides a record of the detailed analysis and performance choices of that role, the act of formulating a score illuminates elements inherent in the text that can otherwise be overlooked. This synergy between excavating and notating properties in the text helps to spark creative impulses and facilitates connections that make the text your own.

Scores are visual maps to performance. When I create a score, I act as though I am embarking on an art project. I gather up a variety of colored pencils, highlighters, and pens in a variety of colors and lines. I have also used a giant box of crayons, but I have found that crayons don't allow for the same degree of transparency as the pencils and highlighters do, and I don't love the waxy residue they leave on the page. You'll find the system you like best, but highlighters and pencils are my favorite instruments. I prefer to use color: it makes each element stand out from the page.

You can choose to use complementary colors or color families to distinguish one element from another. For example, you might choose a range of oranges to denote vowels, and a range of reds to denote diphthongs. Or, you may assign one color family to short vowels and another to long vowels or diphthongs. Consonants can be noted in blues or greens. Thematic ideas can be brought to the forefront with a particular color highlighter. Repetition can be highlighted in its own way. You can layer each of these elements into one final, rainbow-colored text that is a work of art. That artistic vision of your performance transforms the text on the page, and that transformation affects your relationship to that text on stage. This process fosters your embodiment of Shakespeare's text, and makes it easy to refresh that text at a later time.

In the next section, I will offer suggestions for how you can create a system of notation for scoring the text. The key is to remain systematic in your approach so that the marks are read easily and understood equally. The process of creating a score also helps you to understand and learn the text. It serves as a bridge between textual analysis and practice, and creates a record of your performance. The aim here is to highlight those elements to bring to the forefront. It's entirely up to you how you will create and execute scores of your own.

The structure of the verse

One of the first things to examine and notate will be the structure of the language. Is it prose or poetry? Are there any shifts from one form to another? Are there any of the "regular irregularities" present?

Developing and playing the Shakespeare score **155**

There are two crucial symbols that notate if the text is not a regular line of iambic pentameter. If the line is a feminine ending, you will mark the line's end with the symbol: ♀.

> To be, or not to be, that is the Question: ♀
>
> Whether tis Nobler in the mind to suffer ♀
>
> The Slings and Arrows of outrageous Fortune, ♀
>
> Or to take Arms against a Sea of Troubles, ♀
>
> And by opposing end them: to die, to sleep.
>
> (*Hamlet 3.1*)

If the line is an Alexandrine, you will mark the line's end with the symbol (A). A circled "(A)" is even better. This circled "A" is similar to the universal copyright symbol (©).

> I loose your company; therefore forbear a while, (A)
> (*The Merchant of Venice 3.2*)

Or

> A thousand times more fair, ten thousand times
>
> More rich, that only to stand high in your account, (A)
> (*The Merchant of Venice 3.2*)

These two different notations for feminine endings (♀) and Alexandrines (A) provide a quick, visual reference of the metrical irregularities present in that verse line.

If your line is not a regular line of iambic pentameter, but is short, you will notate the number of beats it contains in parenthesis. Here are two examples from *The Two Gentlemen of Verona* (5.4).

> How? Let me see. (4)

Or

> I gave this unto Julia. (7)★

★This could be (8) if "*Julia*" is pronounced as three syllables. I recommend keeping the two-syllable pronunciation here because at this moment in the play Julia, who has been disguised as a boy, is about to reveal

156 Actuating practice

herself to Proteus in the next two lines of dialogue. After her revelation, Proteus replies,

> How? Julia? (4)

The shift in his pronunciation of her name from two syllables to three helps to reveal his sense of wonder about Julia's revelation and transformation.

I also like to draw a bubble [⊂⊃] alongside the notation to give a visual prompt that the line is short and there is something happening that fills the missing feet.

> How? Julia? (4) ⊂⊃

If the business that completes the line is an exit, you can note that instead [**EXIT**].

In Chapter 3 we looked at shared lines and how those inform performance. Shared lines are notated with wavy brackets: [}]. You can extend the bracket for the length of all the short lines that comprise a full line. This provides a visual cue for the connectedness of the characters through their respective dialogue.

Julia:	Will ye be gone?	(4)
Lucetta:	That you may ruminate.	(6)

When the text shifts from prose to verse (or vice-versa), it can be marked with a circled "P" for prose or "V" for verse at the moment of change.

In this example from *The Two Gentlemen of Verona* (1.1), the text shifts from verse to prose for a brief moment before returning to verse.

Speed:	Sir Proteus, save you. Saw you my master?
Proteus:	But now he parted hence to embark for Milan.
Speed:	Twenty to one, then, he is shipped already,
	And I have played the sheep in losing him.
Proteus:	Indeed, a sheep doth very often stray,
	An if the shepard be awhile away.
Speed:	You conclude that my master is a shepherd then, and I a sheep? (P)
Proteus:	I do.
Speed:	Why then, my horns are his horns, whether I wake or sleep.
Proteus:	A silly answer, and fitting well a sheep. (V)
Speed:	This proves me still a sheep. (6) ⊂⊃

Developing and playing the Shakespeare score **157**

Proteus:	True, and thy master a shepherd. (7) ⊂⊃
Speed:	Nay, that I can deny by a circumstance.
Proteus:	It shall go hard but I'll prove it by another. (A)
Speed:	The shepherd seeks the sheep, and not the sheep the shepherd; but I seek my master, and my master seeks not me. Therefore I am no sheep. (P)
Proteus:	The sheep for fodder follow the shepherd, the shepherd for food follows not the sheep; thou for wages followest my master, thy master for wages follows not thee. Therefore thou art a sheep.
Speed:	Such another proof will make me cry 'baa'. (V)

While it's true that the orthography of the verse is such that it reflects a visual difference from the orthography of prose, the notation helps to reveal the shifts in character and the status play between Proteus and Speed. *That's* what the notation identifies: the deliberate shift in the use of the language for a desired effect.

Each of these notations helps to articulate the structure of the text. Once the structure is notated, we can mark the key features of how the thoughts are developed within that given structure.

The development of thoughts

As we continue to score our text, we will introduce new visual cues to the existing marks that serve to punctuate the vital elements that shape performance. Among other things, this can help to illustrate key elements such as *telescoping* and *lists and ladders*.

The enjambed line (a verse line with no punctuation at the end) can be notated with an extended arrow symbol, to indicate that the energy and thought continue [→].

> I pray you tarry, pause a day or two
>
> Before you hazard, for in choosing wrong →
>
> I lose your company; therefore forbear a while, (A)
>
> > (*The Merchant of Venice 3.2*)

The ends of lines—full stops—are notated with either a colored underline or by highlighting the final three words. Full stops would be periods, question marks or exclamation points. In this chapter, full stops are identified with a <u>bold underline</u>.

158 Actuating practice

> I would detain you here some month or two →
>
> Before you <u>venture for me</u>, I could teach you →
>
> > (*The Merchant of Venice 3.2*)

This helps you to visualize the journey and the length of the thoughts present. Next, highlight all the colons in one color for quick visualization.

> Nay, 'twill be this hour ere I have done weeping **:** all the kind of the Launces have this very fault **:** I have receiv'd my proportion, like the prodigious son, and am going with Sir Proteus to the Imperial's Court **:** I think Crab my dog, be the sourest natured dog that lives **:** My Mother weeping **:** my Father wailing **:** my Sister crying **:** our Maid howling **:** our Cat wringing her hands, and all our house in a great perplexity, yet did not this cruel-hearted Cur shed one tear **:** he is a stone, a very pebble stone, and has no more pity in him then a dog **:** a Jew would have wept to have seen our parting **:** why my Grandam having no eyes, look you, wept herself blind at my parting **:** nay, I'll show you the <u>manner of it</u>.
>
> > (*The Two Gentlemen of Verona 2.3*)

For lists and ladders, add circled numbers to each component, and draw your conclusion clearly with the symbol [∴].

> ①Friends, ②Romans, ③Countrymen, ∴ lend me your ears →
>
> I come to bury Caesar, not to praise him **:**
>
> The evil that men do, lives after them,
>
> The good is oft interred with their bones,
>
> So let it <u>be with Casesar,</u> ~~The Noble Brutus,~~
>
> > (*Julius Caesar 3.2*)

Highlighting or circling repeated words or ideas tracks the journey and development of that thought. The repetition can be quite close together or it can evolve over a longer series of thoughts, an entire speech, or in dialogue between characters. You can also connect these repeated ideas by drawing lines between them. I've highlighted the repetition in these passages by making bold the repeated text.

Here are two examples from Leontes in *The Winter's Tale* (1.2):

> Go **play** (Boy) **play :** thy Mother **plays**, and I →
>
> **Play** too: but so disgrac'd a part, whose issue → ♀
>
> Will hiss me to my Grave **:** Comtempt and Clamor → ♀

Developing and playing the Shakespeare score **159**

Will <u>be my Knell</u>, Go **play** (Boy) **play**, there have been → ♀
(Or I am much deceiv'd) Cuckolds ere now,

Or

<u>Is whispering</u> **nothing**?
Is leaning <u>Cheek to Cheek?</u> Is meeting Noses
Kissing <u>with inside Lip?</u> Stopping the Career
Of Laughter, <u>with a sigh?</u> (a Note infallible
Of breaking Honesty) horsing <u>foot on foot?</u>
<u>Skulking in Corners?</u> Wishing <u>Clocks more swift?</u>
<u>Hours, Minutes? Noon, Midnight?</u> And all Eyes
Blind with the Pin and Web, but theirs; theirs only,
That would <u>unseen be wicked? Is this</u> **nothing**?
Why then the World, and all that's in't, is **nothing**,
The covering Sky is **nothing**, Bohemia **nothing**,
My Wife is **nothing**, nor **Nothing** have these **Nothings**,
If <u>this be</u> **nothing**.

It is also worth noting how the list of verbs builds in this speech. Leontes has a long list: *whispering* → *leaning* → *meeting* → *kissing* → *stopping* → *horsing* → *skulking* → *wishing*. Outlining the list like this reveals the bookends of the "w" sound at the beginning and end of the progression.

It is possible for the repetition to be shared between characters, and that is useful to see mapped out. This example reveals the connection between Bassanio and Portia in *The Merchant of Venice* (3.2). Read it through first, before we highlight the repetition; there are several concepts that repeat. Some concepts and words repeat directly, others are indirect forms of repetition.

Portia: To stay you from election.
Bassanio: Let me choose,
            For as I am, I live upon the rack.
Portia: Upon the rack Bassanio, then confess
            What treason there is mingled with your love.
Bassanio: None but that ugly treason of mistrust.
            Which makes me fear the enjoying of my love :
            There may as well be amity and life,
            'Tween snow and fire, as treason and my love.

160 Actuating practice

Portia: I, but I fear you speak upon the rack,
             Where men enforced doth speak any thing.
Bassanio: Promise me life, and I'll confess the truth.
Portia: Well then, confess and live.
Bassanio: Confess and love
             Had been the very sum of my confession :
             O happy torment, when my torturer
             Doth teach me answers for deliverance:
             But let me to my fortune and the caskets.

For clarity, each repeated concept would be assigned it's own highlighted color. Here, I have used different fonts and underlines to illuminate the different repetitions throughout the text.

Portia: To stay you from **election**. (7) ⎤
Bassanio: Let me <u>choose</u>, (3)   ⎦
             For as I am, I live upon the rack.
Portia: Upon the rack Bassanio, then **confess** →
             What treason there is mingled with your <u>love</u>.
Bassanio: None but that ugly treason of mistrust.
             Which makes me fear the enjoying of my <u>love</u> :
             There may as well be amity and life,
             'Tween snow and fire, as treason and my <u>love</u>.
Portia: I, but I fear you **speak** upon the rack,
             Where men <u>enforced</u> doth **speak** any thing.
Bassanio: Promise me life, and I'll **confess** the truth.
Portia: Well then, **confess** and *live*.   (6) ⎤
Bassanio: **Confess** and <u>love</u> →   (4)   ⎦
             Had been the very sum of my **confession** : ♀
             O happy <u>torment</u>, when my <u>torturer</u> →
             Doth teach me **answers** for deliverance:
             But let me to my fortune and the caskets. ♀

This section of the score reveals more of the shape within the linguistic structure; it illuminates the ways that *character* drives the thoughts and actions of these *characters*.

The dynamics of orthography

Next, we'll highlight the alliteration of the text. If there are multiple sounds that repeat, you can vary the notation using multiple colors for even greater

Developing and playing the Shakespeare score **161**

clarity. Keep in mind that there are voiced and voiceless counterparts that relate to one another as well. For extra clarity, write the alliteration that has been highlighted after the unit of text. The alliteration in this text is underlined in bold.

> Oh yet, for God's sake, go **n**ot to these **W**ars;
>
> The Time **w**as (Father) **wh**e**n** you broke your **w**ord,   (w/wh)
>
> **Wh**e**n** you **w**ere more e**n**deer'd to it, the**n** **n**ow,
>
> **Wh**e**n** your ow**n** Percy **wh**e**n** my heart-deere Harry, ♀ (n)
>
> Threw ma**n**y a **N**orth**w**ard look, to see his Father → ♀
>
> Bring up his Powers **:** but he <u>did long in vain</u>.
>
> (*Henry IV, Part 2, 2.3*)

Then, highlight the assonance in the speech. Trust what speaking the text reveals to you. Remember not to rely solely on the textual spelling; in the English language, that orthography is unreliable. Instead, focus on the repetition you feel and sense; repeated sounds can emerge in many different forms of spelling. Include vowels, diphthongs, and triphthongs.

> I pr<u>ay</u> y<u>ou</u> tarry, pause a d<u>ay</u> **or** t<u>wo</u> →   (ay, oo, or)
>
> Bef**or**e y<u>ou</u> hazard, **for** in ch<u>oo</u>sing wrong   (or, oo)
>
> I l<u>o</u>se y**our** company; theref**ore** f**or**bear a while, (A)   (oo, or)
>
> (*The Merchant of Venice 3.2*)

You can choose to include repeated sounds when they recur throughout the speech as well; they resonate between lines to create an overall aural shape to the speech. For example, we can expand our examination to include the sound "I" as the speech progresses.

> **I** pr<u>ay</u> y<u>ou</u> tarry, pause a d<u>ay</u> **or** t<u>wo</u> →   (ay, oo, or)
>
> Bef**or**e y<u>ou</u> hazard, **for** in ch<u>oo</u>sing wrong   (or, oo)
>
> **I** l<u>o</u>se y**our** company; theref**ore** f**or**bear a wh**I**le, (A)   (oo, or)

When a sound repeats in rapid succession, you'll want to separate the sounds for clarity. Choose to give comparable weight to each component of the repetition with the "slash" notation, [/]. This both helps the listener hear and understand the language clearly, and gives you the opportunity to let the orthography inform your performance.

162 Actuating practice

For example,

> When you were more endeer'd to it, then / now,

This mark of separation helps to prevent "thennow" from happening. Also, in separating the two "n" sounds, the essence of time—in this case, "Time" personified in the narrative—is heightened.

> Thy counsel / lad smells of no cowardice.
>
> > *(Titus Andronicus 2.1)*
>
> Bidding the law make / curtsy to their will
>
> > *(Measure for Measure 2.4)*
>
> Is Brutus / sick? And is it Physical
>
> > *(Julius Caesar 2.1)*

As you continue to look at the orthography, seek out places where you can find even greater clarity. In Chapter 3 we looked at parenthetical thoughts. Are there any parenthesis you can mark to clarify the text's meaning? Mark those with bold parenthesis [( )]. Here is a text that includes embedded parenthetical thoughts. Separating those out will help to create a dynamic vocal framework that enhances your performance.

> My Lord, I would I might entreat your Honor
> To scan this thing no farther : Leave it to time,
> Although tis fit that Cassio have his Place;
> For sure he fills it up with great Ability;
> Yet, if you please, to him off a-while :
> You shall by that perceive him and his means :
>
> > *(Othello 3.3)*

The fourth line of this speech could be a parenthetical thought.

> Although tis fit that Cassio have his Place;
> (For sure he fills it up with great Ability;)
> Yet, if you please, to him off a-while :

Here is another example to examine:

> And that thou mayst perceive my fear of this,
> Knowing that tender youth is soon suggested,

Developing and playing the Shakespeare score **163**

I nightly lodge her in an upper Tower,

The key whereof myself have ever kept :

And thence she cannot be convey'd away.

(The Two Gentlemen of Verona 3.1)

The second line can be framed with parenthesis:

And that thou mayst perceive my fear of this,

(Knowing that tender youth is soon suggested,)

I nightly lodge her in an upper Tower,

The key whereof myself have ever kept :

And thence she cannot be convey'd away.

The capitalized words that appear in the First Folio often help to highlight operative words that move the actor through the speech. Highlight these heightened words with a dotted underline.

Chorus

O for a Muse of fire, that would ascend

The brightest Heaven of Invention:

A Kingdom for a Stage, Princes to Act,

And Monarchs to behold the swelling Scene.

Then should the Warlike Harry, like himself,

Assume the Port of Mars, and at his heels

(Leash'd in like Hounds) should Famine, Sword and Fire

Crouch for employment. But pardon, Gentles all

The flat unraised Spirits that hath dared,

On this unworthy Scaffold to bring forth

So great an Object. Can this Cock-Pit hold

The vasty fields of France? Or may we cram

Within this Wooden O, the very Casques

That did affright the Air at Agincourt?

O, pardon: since a crooked Figure may

Attest in little place a Million,

And let us, Ciphers to this great Accompt,

On your imaginary Forces work.

164 Actuating practice

> Suppose within the Girdle of these Walls
> Are now confin'd two mighty Monarchies,
> Whose high up-reared, and abutting Fronts,
> The perilous narrow Ocean parts asunder:
> Piece out our imperfections with your thoughts:
> Into a thousand parts divide one Man,
> And make imaginary Puissance.
> Think when we talk of Horses, that you see them
> Printing their proud Hoofs i' th' receiving Earth:
> For 'tis your thoughts that now must deck our Kings,
> Carry them here and there: jumping o'er Times;
> Turning th' accomplishment of many years
> Into an Hour-glass: for the which supply,
> Admit me Chorus to this History;
> Who Prologue-like, your humble patience pray,
> Gently to hear, kindly to judge, our Play.
>
> *(Henry V, Prologue)*

Underlining these capitalized words can be particularly helpful when you are working with a modern text; it enables you to utilize the orthography of the Folio in conjunction with whatever text you work from.

The process of balance

Balance is all about the equilibrium between two separate, but related, forces. Shakespeare's texts demand that we consider the poise between ideas, the opposition in the apposition. Next, we'll identify these moments in our scores: the "this vs. that." It not only helps to clarify the text; it also helps the actor to think on the text, to actively move through the ideas in order to arrive at a destination point. These balances and oppositions, usually in the form of antithesis, are notated with circles or brackets around each idea and lines connect them. At the end of each line, write out the apposition for further clarity.

Here is an example from *Measure for Measure* (2.2), as Angelo weighs the circumstances of his actions.

Developing and playing the Shakespeare score **165**

What's this? What's this? Is this her fault, or mine?

The Temptor, or the Tempted, who sins most? Ha?

Not she: nor doth she tempt: but it is I,

That, lying by the Violet in the Sun,

Do as the Carrion does, not as the flower,

Corrupt with virtuous season: Can it be,

That Modesty may more betray our Sense

Then woman's lightness? Having waste ground enough,

Shall we desire to raze the Sanctuary

And pitch our evils there? Oh fie, fie, fie:

What dost thou? Or what art thou Angelo?

Dost thou desire her foully, for those things

That make her good? Oh, let her brother live:

Thieves for their robbery have authority,

When Judges steal themselves: what do I love her,

That I desire to hear her speak again?

And feast upon her eyes? What is't I dream on?

Oh cunning enemy, that to catch a Saint,

With Saints dost bait thy hook: most dangerous

Is that temptation, that doth goad us on

To sin, in loving virtue: never could the Strumpet

With all her double vigor, Art, and Nature

Once stir my temper: but this virtuous Maid

Subdues me quite: Ever till now

When men were fond, I smiled, and wondered how.

Below, I have highlighted in bold those concepts and objects that oppose one another:

What's this? What's this? Is this **her** fault, or **mine**? [her vs. mine]

The **Temptor**, or the **Tempted**, who sins most? Ha? [Temptor vs. Tempted]

166 Actuating practice

Not **she**: nor doth she tempt: but it is **I**, [she vs. I]

That, lying by the Violet in the Sun,

Do as the **Carrion** does, not as the **flower**, [Carrion vs. flower]

Corrupt with virtuous season: Can it be,

That **Modesty** may more betray our **Sense** [Modesty vs. Sense]

Then woman's lightness? Having waste ground enough,

Shall we desire to **raze** the **Sanctuary** [raze vs. pitch]

And **pitch** our **evils** there? Oh fie, fie, fie: [Sanctuary vs. evils]

What **dost thou**? Or what **art thou** Angelo? [dost thou vs. art thou]

Dost thou desire her **foully**, for those things

That make her **good**? Oh, let her brother live: [foully vs. good]

Thieves for their robbery have **authority**, [Thieves vs. authority]

When Judges steal themselves: what do I **love** her,

That I **desire** to hear her speak again? [love vs. desire]

And feast upon her eyes? What is't I dream on?

Oh cunning **enemy**, that to catch a **Saint**, [enemy vs. Saint]

With **Saints** dost bait thy hook: most dangerous

Is that **temptation**, that doth goad us on [Saints vs. temptation]

To **sin**, in loving **virtue**: never could the **Strumpet** [sin vs. virture]

With all her double vigor, Art, and Nature

Once **stir** my temper: but this virtuous **Maid** [Strumpet vs. Maid]

Developing and playing the Shakespeare score **167**

Subdues me quite: Ever till now	[stir vs. Subdues]
When **men** were fond, **I** smiled, and wondered how.	[men vs. I]

The process of balancing and examining the antithesis and apposition is one of the keys to understanding Angelo's need—and why he must speak this speech.

Let's return to the scene from *Richard III* (1.2) that we considered in Chapter 3 to examine how this apposition can be shared between characters. Read it through once for sense, and then examine the notated copy that follows. To illustrate, the antithetical thoughts are highlighted.

Richard: Lady, you know no Rules of Charity,
Which renders good for bad, Blessings for Curses.
Anne: Villain, thou know'st nor law of God nor Man,
No Beast so fierce, but knows some touch of pity.
Richard: But I know none, and therefore am no Beast.
Anne: O wonderful, when devils tell the truth!
Richard: More wonderful, when Angels are so angry:
Vouchsafe (divine perfection of a Woman)
Of these supposed Crimes, to give me leave
By circumstance, but to acquit my self.
Anne: Vouchsafe (defus'd infection of man)
Of these known evils, but to give me leave
By circumstance, to curse thy cursed Self.

A notated score that highlights antithesis will look like this:

Richard:	**Lady, *you know*** no Rules of Charity,	[**Lady** vs. **Villain**] [you know vs. thou know'st]
	Which renders **good** for **bad**, **Blessings** for **Curses.**	[good vs. bad] [Blessings vs. Curses]
Anne:	**Villain,** *thou know'st* nor law of **God** nor **Man,**	[God vs. Man]
	No Beast so **fierce**, but knows some touch of **pity**.	[fierce vs. pity]
Richard:	But I know none, and therefore am no Beast.	
Anne:	O wonderful, when **devils** tell the truth!	[devils vs. Angels]

168 Actuating practice

Richard:	More wonderful, when **Angels** are so angry:
	Vouchsafe (divine perfection of a Woman)
	[divine perfection . . . vs. defus'd infection . . .]

Of these supposed Crimes, to give me leave   [supposed vs. known]

By circumstance, but **to acquit** my self.   [to acquit vs. to curse]

Anne:	Vouchsafe (defus'd infection of man)
	Of these known evils, but to give me leave
	By circumstance, **to curse** thy cursed Self.

The Shakespeare Score

When we put all of these elements together, we have notated and analyzed our text. We have explored Shakespeare's language in a variety of ways: somatically, intellectually, and experientially. Even the physical act of marking the text and creating the score by hand affects our brains and the ways in which we process information. All of these interactions with the text lead us to embodied performance.

Let's work systematically through the elements that comprise *The Shakespeare Score*. We will layer each component and culminate in a fully realized score. We will note:

- ☑ Verse: feminine endings ♀, Alexandrines (A); short ⊂⊃ / shared lines }; switches from verse (V) to prose (P)
- ☑ Line energy: enjambed lines ; colons (:) ; lists and ladders
- ☑ Repetition; related words and ideas
- ☑ Alliteration (consonants)
- ☑ Assonance (vowels/diphthongs)
- ☑ Textual clarity: parenthetical thoughts; capitalized words, line endings
- ☑ Antithesis/apposition

Let's examine a score for Mark Antony's speech addressing the people of Rome in *Julius Caesar* (3.2).

Friends, Romans, Countrymen, lend me your ears

I come to bury Caesar, not to praise him :

The evil that men do, lives after them,

The good is oft interred with their bones,
So let it be with Caesar. The Noble Brutus,
Hath told you Caesar was Ambitious
If it were so, it was a grievious Fault,
And grieviously hath Caesar answer'd it.
Heere, under leave of Brutus, and the rest
(For Brutus is an Honorable man,
So are they all; all Honorable men)
Come I to speak in Caesar's Funeral.
He was my Friend, faithful, and just to me;
But Brutus says, he was Ambitious,
And Brutus is an Honorable man.
He hath brought many Captives home to Rome,
Whose Ransoms, did the general Coffers fill :
Did this in Caesar seem Ambitious?
When that the poor have cried, Caesar hath wept :
Ambition should be made of sterner stuff,
Yet Brutus says, he was Ambitious :
And Brutus is an Honorable man.
You all did see, that on the Lupercall,
I thrice presented him a Kingly Crown,
Which he did thrice refuse. Was this Ambition?
Yet Brutus says, he was Ambitious :
And sure he is an Honorable man.
I speak not to disprove what Brutus spoke,
But heere I am to speak what I do know;
You all did love him once, not without cause,
What cause with-holds you then to mourn for him?
O judgement! Thou are fled to brutish Beasts,
And Men have lost their Reason. Bear with me,
My heart is in the Coffin there with Caesar,
And I must pause, till it come back to me.

170 Actuating practice

First, we will note the metrical irregularities (feminine endings and Alexandrines, short and/or shared lines) and any changes between verse and prose that appear in the text:

Friends, Romans, Countrymen, lend me your ears
I come to bury Caesar, not to praise him : ♀
The evil that men do, lives after them,
The good is oft interred with their bones,
So let it be with Caesar. The Noble Brutus, ♀
Hath told you Caesar was Ambitious
If it were so, it was a grievious Fault,
And grieviously hath Caesar answer'd it.
Heere, under leave of Brutus, and the rest
(For Brutus is an Honorable man,
So are they all; all Honorable men)
Come I to speak in Caesar's Funeral.
He was my Friend, faithful, and just to me;
But Brutus says, he was Ambitious,
And Brutus is an Honorable man.
He hath brought many Captives home to Rome,
Whose Ransoms, did the general Coffers fill :
Did this in Caesar seem Ambitious?
When that the poor have cried, Caesar hath wept :
Ambition should be made of sterner stuff,
Yet Brutus says, he was Ambitious :
And Brutus is an Honorable man.
You all did see, that on the Lupercall,
I thrice presented him a Kingly Crown,
Which he did thrice refuse. Was this Ambition? ♀
Yet Brutus says, he was Ambitious :
And sure he is an Honorable man.
I speak not to disprove what Brutus spoke,
But heere I am to speak what I do know;
You all did love him once, not without cause,

Developing and playing the Shakespeare score **171**

What cause with-holds you then to mourn for him?

O judgement! Thou are fled to brutish Beasts,

And Men have lost their Reason. Bear with me,

My heart is in the Coffin there with Caesar, ♀

And I must pause, till it come back to me.

This text features four feminine endings (♀). It has no Alexandrines, short, or shared lines. You will notice that some lines feature expanded pronunciation to fill the verse line. In the line, "But Brutus says, he was Ambitious," the word "Ambitious" is expanded to four syllables: AMbiTIous.

Second, we will note enjambed lines, colons, lists and ladders:

①Friends, ②Romans, ③Countrymen, ∴lend me your ears →

I come to bury Caesar, not to praise him ;

The evil that men do, lives after them,

The good is oft interred with their bones,

So let it be with Caesar. The Noble Brutus,

Hath told you Caesar was Ambitious →

If it were so, it was a grievious Fault,

And grieviously hath Caesar answer'd it.

Heere, under leave of Brutus, and the rest →

(For Brutus is an Honorable man,

So are they all; all Honorable men)

Come I to speak in Caesar's Funeral.

He was my Friend, faithful, and just to me;

But Brutus says, he was Ambitious,

And Brutus is an Honorable man.

He hath brought many Captives home to Rome,

Whose Ransoms, did the general Coffers fill ;

Did this in Caesar seem Ambitious?

When that the poor have cried, Caesar hath wept ;

Ambition should be made of sterner stuff,

Yet Brutus says, he was Ambitious ;

And Brutus is an Honorable man.

172 Actuating practice

> You all did see, that on the Lupercall,
>
> I thrice presented him a Kingly Crown,
>
> Which he did thrice refuse. Was this Ambition?
>
> Yet Brutus says, he was Ambitious :
>
> And sure he is an Honorable man.
>
> I speak not to disprove what Brutus spoke,
>
> But heere I am to speak what I do know;
>
> You all did love him once, not without cause,
>
> What cause with-holds you then to mourn for him?
>
> O judgement! Thou are fled to brutish Beasts,
>
> And Men have lost their Reason. Bear with me,
>
> My heart is in the Coffin there with Caesar,
>
> And I must pause, till it come back to me.

Next, we will highlight the repetition:

> Friends, Romans, Countrymen, lend me your ears
>
> I come to **bury** Caesar, not to **praise** him :
>
> The evil that men do, lives after them,
>
> The **good** is oft **interred** with their **bones**,
>
> So let it be with Caesar. The Noble Brutus,
>
> Hath told you *Caesar was Ambitious*
>
> If it were so, it was a grievious Fault,
>
> And grieviously hath Caesar answer'd it.
>
> Heere, under leave of Brutus, and the rest
>
> (For Brutus is an Honorable man,
>
> So are they all; all Honorable men)
>
> Come I to speak in Caesar's **Funeral**.
>
> He was my Friend, **faithful**, and **just** to me;
>
> But Brutus says, *he was Ambitious,*
>
> And Brutus is an Honorable man.
>
> He hath brought many Captives home to Rome,
>
> Whose Ransoms, did the general Coffers fill :

Developing and playing the Shakespeare score **173**

Did this in *__Caesar__ seem Ambitious*?

When that the poor have <u>cried</u>, <u>Caesar</u> hath **wept** :

Ambition should be made of sterner stuff,

Yet <u>Brutus</u> SayS, *__he__ was Ambitious :*

And <u>Brutus</u> is an Honorable man.

You all did see, that on the Lupercall,

I <u>thrice</u> presented <u>him</u> a Kingly Crown,

Which <u>he</u> did <u>thrice</u> refuse. Was this *Ambition*?

Yet <u>Brutus</u> SayS, *__he__ was Ambitious :*

And sure <u>he</u> is an Honorable man.

I speak not to disprove what <u>Brutus</u> spoke,

But heere I am to speak what I do know;

You all did love <u>him</u> once, not without <u>cause</u>,

What <u>cause</u> with-holds you then to **mourn** for <u>him</u>?

O judgement! Thou are fled to brutish Beasts,

And Men have lost their Reason. Bear with me,

My heart is in the **Coffin** there with <u>Caesar</u>,

And I must pause, till it <u>come back</u> to me.

Through this examination, the repetition of both "Caesar" and "Brutus" is prevalent throughout. To illustrate, I have double-underlined "Caesar" and those words associated with him. "Brutus" has a single underline. The theme of burial and mourning is in non-italicized bold text. The concepts related to "Ambition" are featured in italicized bold. There is a repetition related to the word, "come"; this has a dotted underline. The theme of virtue that emerges through the words "praise," "good," "faithful," and "just" are featured in a different font, as is "wept," which is evidence of Caesar's empathy. There are instances where there are repeated words in close proximity to each other, such as "grievious" and "grieviously" or related words such as "Captives" and "Ransoms." I have marked these with a wavy underline. If I were working in color, I would give each individual group it's own identifying color to distinguish them even further. The concept of listening and speaking is woven throughout this speech. I have noted this relationship with a different font as well.

Next, we will examine the alliteration and consonant pairs (voiced/voiceless counterparts):

174 Actuating practice

Friends, Romans, Countrymen, lend me your ears	z; n; m
I come to bury *C*aesar, not to praise him :	b/p; s
The evil that men do, lives after them,	**v/f** ; z; m; th
The good is oft interred with / their bones,	th; **v/f**; n
So let it be with *C*aesar. The Noble Brutus,	s; b/p; th
Hath told you *C*aesar was Ambitious	z/s
If it were so, it was a grievious Fault,	**v/f**; s
And grieviously hath *C*aesar answer'd it.	n; s
Heere, under leave of Brutus, and the rest	**v/f**; n; s
(For Brutus is an Honorable man,	n
So are they all; all Honorable men)	n
Come I to speak in *C*aesar's Funeral.	**c/k**; s
He was my Friend, faithful, and just to me;	**v/f** z/s; m
But Brutus / says, he was Ambitious,	b/p; s; z
And Brutus is an Honorable man.	n
He hath brought many Captives home to Rome,	b/p ; **c/k**; z; m;
Whose Ransoms, did the general Coffers fill :	z
Did this in Caesar seem Ambitious?	s
When that the poor have Cried, *C*aesar hath wept :	b/p
Ambition should be made of sterner stuff,	s; **v/f**
Yet Brutus / says, he was Ambitious :	s; z
And Brutus is an Honorable man.	n
You all did see, that on the Lupercall,	b/p; th; **c/k**
I thrice presented him a Kingly Crown,	th; **c/k**
Which he did thrice refuse. Was this Ambition?	th; s
Yet Brutus / says, he was Ambitious :	b/p; s
And sure he is an Honorable man.	n
I speak not to disprove what Brutus / spoke,	b/p; s; **c/k**
But heere I am to speak what I do know;	b/p; **c/k**; n
You all did love him once, not without Cause,	**c/k**

Developing and playing the Shakespeare score   **175**

What Cauſe with-holdſ you **then** to mourn **f**or him?   **c/k**; **z**; **th**;
n; m

O judgement! **Th**ou are **f**led to brutish Beaſtſ,b/p ;ſ
And **M**en ha**v**e loſt **th**eir Reaſon. Bear with me,   **v/f**; m; **th**
My heart iſ in **th**e **C**offin **th**ere with *C*aeſar,   **c/k**; **th**
And I muſt pauſe, till it come bac**k** to me.   b/p; m

Then, we will focus on the assonance in the speech:

Fri<u>e</u>nds, R**o**mans, Countrym<u>e</u>n, l<u>e</u>nd me your ears →   <u>e</u> as in "let";
o

I come to b<u>u</u>ry Caesar, not to praise h**i**m :   *I*; <u>e</u>; **i** as in
"if"

The evil that m<u>e</u>n do, l**i**ves after th<u>e</u>m,   <u>e</u>; **i**
The good **i**s oft int<u>e</u>rr<u>e</u>d with their b**o**nes,   **i**; <u>e</u>; **o**
So l<u>e</u>t **i**t be w**i**th Caesar. The N**o**ble Brutus,   **i**; **o**
Hath t**o**ld you Caesar was Ambitious   **o**
If **i**t were s**o**, **i**t was a grievious Fault,   **i** ; **o**
And grieviously hath Caesar answer'd **i**t.   **i**
Heere, under leave of Brutus, and the r<u>e</u>st   <u>e</u>
(For Brutus **i**s an Honorable man,   **i**
So are they all; all Honorable m<u>e</u>n)   **o**; <u>e</u>
Come *I* to speak **i**n Caesar's Funeral.   *I*; **i**
He was m**y** Fri<u>e</u>nd, faithful, and just to me;   **i**; <u>e</u>
But Brutus says, he was Amb**i**tious,   **i**
And Brutus **i**s an Honorable man.   **i**
He hath brought many Capti**v**es h**o**me to R**o**me,   **i**; **o**
Whose Ransoms, d**i**d the g<u>e</u>neral Coffers f**i**ll :   **i**; <u>e</u>
D**i**d th**i**s **i**n Caesar seem Amb**i**tious?   **i**
Wh<u>e</u>n that the poor have cr*I*ed, Caesar hath w<u>e</u>pt :   <u>e</u>; *I*
Amb**i**tion should be made of sterner stuff,   **i**
Y<u>e</u>t Brutus says, he was Amb**i**tious :   <u>e</u> ; **i**
And Brutuſ **i**s an Honorable man.   **i**

176 Actuating practice

You all did see, that on the Lupercall,	i
I thr*I*ce pres<u>e</u>nted him a Kingly Crown,	*I*; <u>e</u>
Which he did thr*I*ce refuse. Was thi*s* Ambition?	i; *I*
Y<u>e</u>t Brutus says, he was Ambitious :	<u>e</u> ; i
And sure he is an Honorable man.	i
I speak not to disprove what Brutus sp**o**ke,	*I*; i; **o**
But heere *I* am to speak what *I* do kn**ow**;	*I*; **o**
You all did love him once, not without cause,	i
What cause with-h**o**lds you th<u>e</u>n to mourn for him?	i; **o**; <u>e</u>
O judgem<u>e</u>nt! Thou are fl<u>e</u>d to brutish Beasts,	**o**; <u>e</u>
And M<u>e</u>n have lost their Reason. Bear with me,	<u>e</u> ; i
M*Y* heart is in the Coffin there with Caesar,	*I*; i
And *I* must pause, till it come back to me.	*I*; i

When you highlight the assonance, you will notice the repetition of the sounds "e" as in "let," the long (diphthong) "O," the long (diphthong) "I," and the short "i" as in "if." You could also choose include the vowel sound "oo" that appears in the name, "Brutus." To keep it manageable in this case, I have not highlighted that sound, since we have already highlighted the repetition of the name, "Brutus." Aside from the occasional "to," "you", and the word "brutish"—clearly a play on the name "Brutus"—the "oo" sound mainly occurs in the repetition of the name, "Brutus." The same is true for the long "e" sound in "C<u>ae</u>sar," "me," "be," and "grievious." Since "Caesar" resounds in the repetition of the name (and to keep this typeset score manageable) I have not highlighted that sound, although we certainly could. If I were making a colored score, I might break down the assonance into multiple scores: one exploration for those sounds produced with rounded lips, another score that highlights the sounds produced with the lips slightly smiling (or, even those sounds produced in the front of the mouth followed by those sounds produced in the back of the mouth). You have a lot of flexibility when you are scoring your text by hand. You can even use vellum or tracing paper to see how various components of the score can be brought to the foreground at different times.

This next set of notations focuses on the parenthetical thoughts, capitalized words, and line endings:

Friends, <u>Romans</u>, <u>Countrymen</u>, lend me your ears	[or: <u>Friends</u>]
I come to bury Caesar, not to praise him :	

The evil that men do, lives after them,

The good is oft interred with their bones,

So let it be with Caesar. The Noble Brutus,   [or: Noble Brutus]

Hath told you Caesar was Ambitious

If it were so, it was a grievious Fault,

And grieviously hath Caesar answer'd it.

Heere, under leave of Brutus, and the rest

(For Brutus is an Honorable man,

So are they all; all Honorable men)

Come I to speak in Caesar's Funeral.   [or: Caesar's Funeral]

He was my Friend, faithful, and just to me;

But Brutus says, he was Ambitious,

And Brutus is an Honorable man.

He hath brought many Captives home to Rome,   [or: Rome]

Whose Ransoms, did the general Coffers fill :

Did this in Caesar seem Ambitious?

When that the poor have cried, Caesar hath wept :

Ambition should be made of sterner stuff,

Yet Brutus says, he was Ambitious :

And Brutus is an Honorable man.

You all did see, that on the Lupercall,

I thrice presented him a Kingly Crown,

Which he did thrice refuse. Was this Ambition?

Yet Brutus says, he was Ambitious :

And sure he is an Honorable man.

I speak not to disprove what Brutus spoke,

But heere I am to speak what I do know;

You all did love him once, not without cause,

What cause with-holds you then to mourn for him?

O judgement! Thou are fled to brutish Beasts,

And Men have lost their Reason. Bear with me,

178 Actuating practice

> My heart is in the Coffin there with Caesar,
>
> And I must pause, till it come back to me.

In this notation, you can see how there are certainly some areas that are up to your own personal interpretation. While I normally wouldn't highlight or underline the first word in a verse line or a proper name, you can see how sometimes those first words or proper names help to facilitate the progression of an idea. There are no hard and fast rules, so feel free to select whatever brings you closer to the text.

The line endings are noted with a thick underline. You can see here how using a highlighter or a colored pencil would enable you to mark simultaneously a variety of elements in one word, phrase, or line. There are no additional parenthetical notations needed to enhance the clarity of this text.

Finally, we will notate the antithesis, and any appostion:

> Friends, Romans, Countrymen, lend me your ears
>
> I come **to bury** Caesar, not **to praise** him :   [to bury vs. to praise]
>
> The **evil** that men do, **lives** after them,   [evil vs. good] or:
>
> [the evil vs. the good]
>
> The **good** is oft interred with their bones,   [lives vs. interred]
>
> So let it be with Caesar. The Noble Brutus,   [Brutus vs. Caesar]
>
> Hath told you Caesar was **Ambitious**   [Ambitious   vs.
> Honorable]
>
> If it were so, it was a grievious Fault,
>
> And grieviously hath Caesar answer'd it.
>
> Heere, under leave of Brutus, and the rest
>
> (For Brutus is an **Honorable** man,
>
> So are they all; all Honorable men)
>
> **Come I to speak** in Caesar's Funeral.   [Come I to speak vs. But
> Brutus says]
>
> He was my Friend, **faithful, and just** to me;
>
>   [faithful,   and   just   vs.
> Ambitious]
>
> **But Brutus says**, he was **Ambitious**,
>
> And Brutus is an Honorable man.

Developing and playing the Shakespeare score **179**

He hath brought many Captives home to Rome,

Whose Ransoms, did the general Coffers fill :

Did this in Caesar seem Ambitious?

When that the **poor** have cried, **Caesar** hath **wept** : [poor vs. Caesar]

Ambition should be made of **sterner stuff**, [wept vs. sterner stuff]

Yet Brutus says, he was Ambitious :

And Brutus is an Honorable man.

You all did see, that on the Lupercall,

I **thrice presented** him a Kingly Crown, [thrice presented vs. thrice refuse]

Which he did **thrice refuse**. Was this Ambition?

Yet Brutus says, he was Ambitious :

And **sure** he is an Honorable man. [sure vs. disprove]

I speak not to **disprove** what **Brutus spoke**, [I speak vs. Brutus spoke]

But **heere** I am to speak what I do know; [heere vs. there]

You all did {**love**} him once, not without cause, [{love} vs. {mourn}]

What cause with-holds you then to {**mourn**} for him?

O judgement! Thou are fled to brutish **Beasts**, [Beasts vs. Men]

And **Men** have lost their Reason. Bear with me,

My heart is in the Coffin **there** with Caesar,

And I must pause, till it come back to me.

As we excavate the text in search of the ideas that both oppose and appose each other, we encounter a range of possibilities that are up for our interpretation. For example, we have a sense that there is opposition between loving and a lack of mourning, even if "love" and "mourn" are not true antitheses of each other. There is inherently an opposition between "once" and "then" (which is related in time to the present, to "now") although the terms themselves aren't necessarily direct opposites, nor do they stand out as antithetical to each other. "Fled" and "lost" are another pairing that heightens the friction between what "is" and what "should be" in the Marc Antony's world. One

180 Actuating practice

could argue that "My heart" opposes "Caesar"—which stands essentially for "Caesar's heart," or "my beating heart" versus "Caesar's still one." There is even material to be mined in the friction between "Coffin" and "come back."

This is the archaeology of performance: the constant sifting through material for clues and meaning, the possibility at each brush stroke to discover what might unlock the world.

When you have moved through all of these elements in your score, you can put them all together to have a global view of what you've discovered. Below, you can see what it looks like when all of our components are featured together:

①**Fri**e**nd**s, ②**R**o**Man**s, ③**C**ountry**Me**n, ∴**le**nd **M**e your ear**s**
→(①→②→③→∴.)

	Z; e as in "let"; n; m
I **C**o**M**e t.o. b**u**ry. *C*ae**S**ar, **n**ot t.o. prai**S**e hi**M** ; ♀	m; b/p ;ℰ; e; i as in "if";
	[to b**u**ry. vs. to prai**se**]
The **e**v**il** **th**at **Me**n do, **liv**es a**f**ter **th**e**m**, [evil vs. go**od**]	**v/f** ; e;. z; m; **th**;
The **go**od i**s** o**f**t **int**e**rr**ed with / **th**eir b**one**s, **int**e**rr**ed]	i; **th**; [lives vs.
*S*o l**e**t it be with *C*ae**S**ar. **Th**e **N**o**b**le B**rutu**s, ♀	i;ℰ; b; **o**; **th**; [B**rut**us vs. C**ae**sar]
Hath **t**o**l**d you *C*ae**S**ar wa**s** **A**m**bitiou**s →	Z / ℰ [Ambitious vs. Honorable]
If it were ℰℴ, it wa**s** a grie**v**iou**s** **F**ault,	i; **v/f**;ℰ; If /**th**en
And grie**v**iou**s**ly h**a**th *C*ae**S**ar an**s**we**r**'d it.	n; ℰ
Heere, under lea**v**e o**f** Brutu**s**, and **the** r**e**ℰt	**v/f**; n; ℰ
(**F**or Brutu**s** i**s** an H**o**n**o**ra**b**le **M**an,	n
*S*o are **th**ey all; all Honorable **M**e**n**)	n
Co**M**e *I* to ℰpea**k** in *C*ae**S**ar'S **F**uneral.	**C** /**k**;ℰ
He wa**s** **M**y **Fri**e**n**d, **faith**ful, and ju**s**t to **M**e;	**v/f**; z/ℰ; **m**;
	[faithful, and just vs.**A**mbitious]

Developing and playing the Shakespeare score **181**

But Brutus / says, he was **Ambitious**,	b; s; z
And Brutus is an Honorable man.	n
He hath brought many Captives home to Rome,	b/p ; c/k; z; m; o
Whose Ransoms, did the general Coffers fill ;	z; i; c/k; v/f
Did this in **Caesar seem Ambitious?**	i; s [was vs. seem]
When that the poor have Cried, Caesar hath wept ;	b/p [poor vs. Caesar]; [wept vs. sterner stuff]
Ambition should be made of **s**terner **s**tu**ff**,	m; s; f
Yet Brutus / says, he was **Ambitious** ;	s; z
And Brutus is an Honorable man.	n
You all did see, that on the Lupercall,	b/p; th; c/k
I thrice presented him a **K**ingly Crown,	*I*; th; c/k
	[thrice presented vs. thrice refuse]
Which he did thrice refuse. Was this **Ambition?** ♀	i; s
Yet Brutus / says, he was **Ambitious** ;	b/p; s
And sure he is an Honorable man. disprove]	n; [sure vs. disprove]
I speak not to disprove what Brutus / spoke, spoke]	[I speak vs. Brutus spoke]
	b/p; s; c/k
But heere *I* am to speak what *I* do **know**;	b/p; *I*; c/k; n
	[heere vs. there]
You all did {love} him once, not without Cause, {mourn}]	c/k; [{love} vs. {mourn}]
What Cause with-holds you then to {mourn} for him? e; n; m	c/k; z; i; th; o;
O judgement! **Th**ou are **f**led to	

182 Actuating practice

brutish Bea__sts__,	b/p; __e__; __s__; [Bea__sts__ vs. M__en__]
And M__en__ ha**v**e lo__st their Reason.__	
Bear **with** me,	**v/f**; m; **th**
M*y* heart i__s__ **in the** Coffin	
__there__ **with** *C*ae__s__ar, ⊂⊃	*I*; **c/k**; i; **th**
And *I* mu__st__ pau__s__e, till it come __back to me.__	b/p; **i;** m

By the time you have explored all of the elements that go into the Shakespeare score, you will be intimately familiar with your text and ready to play. You will have fostered a deep and personal connection to Shakespeare's language and to the *character* you have—through this process—unearthed.

10

REHEARSING THE PART

The second part of this book has been devoted to training and to putting Shakespeare's texts into practice. We have explored ways to activate the body, to awaken the listener, to energize Shakespeare's language, to expand the world of the fiction, and to develop and play the Shakespeare "score." In this final chapter, we will consider ways to rehearse and to spark connections within the ensemble. These suggestions will heighten the actor's focus, commitment to risk, and their sense of vulnerability, as well as forging a connection between the self, the text, and the ensemble.

In the last chapter we focused on creating a system for notating Shakespeare's texts. We applied what we learned in Chapter 4 about the dynamics of the text's orthography to the practice of preparing for performance. Next, we'll focus on ways to learn those texts through a different type of close examination of the text's *characters*.

Memorizing Shakespeare

This technique is something that will help you to memorize Shakespeare's text quickly and precisely. It was born out of sheer desperation. Years ago I had an opportunity to replace an actor as Juliet, which was an absolute dream. What wasn't particularly dreamy was the fact that the production was opening in two weeks, and I'd never played the part before. (Yes, indeed, it was a potential nightmare.) I needed to learn the text very quickly and very precisely if I was to have any time to explore in rehearsal. I think

184 Actuating practice

this strategy saved me, and the actors I've shared it with have all found it as effective as I have.

When you are memorizing with the text in front of you, do you find that you're always *sure* that you know it, and then you're up on your feet and the lines escape you? Do you find it difficult to prompt yourself when you are testing whether or not you are actually off book? When you prompt yourself, you have the book in front of you and so, of course, you can quickly deceive yourself into believing you really do know the text. This method will enable you to know—in an instant—whether or not you really are word perfect, and it's impossible to "cheat" because the prompts actually prompt you without giving you the whole answer. It's one of the greatest tools I've ever worked with, and I don't think I will ever go back to memorizing without it. In fact, the prompt works so well that I can pick up a piece of text several years after working on it, and within minutes, I am able to trigger my memory of that text. If I ever need to refresh a part, I go back to my prompts and in a very short time I can refresh all I need to know. I am continually amazed by it and I hope you'll find it as useful a tool as I do. Here's how it's done:

Prompt cards for a single piece of text (a soliloquy, a sonnet, or any large, uninterrupted chunk of text)

Get a stack of lined index cards. On the lined side of the cards, write out each line of verse as a complete verse line until you've written the whole speech.

On the opposite side of the card, write out only the first letter of each word in the verse line.

Study the full line of text, and when you need to test how well you have memorized it, prompt yourself with the initials-only side of the index card. You can even incorporate the initials-only side into your memorization process by studying the full line and then reinforcing it with the initials. When you go back and forth between the two sides of your card in this way, you really imbed the initial prompts into your memorization process, and as a result, you are likely to learn your material even faster.

I also like to include the punctuation marks along with the initials on my card, because it helps to retain the overall shape of the speech.

Be sure to number your cards (I number mine in the upper right hand corner); they can easily jumble in your bag or find themselves out of order and you don't want to learn them incorrectly.

TABLE 10.1 Initials-only index card

Y	S	M,	L	B,	W	I	S
S	A	I	A:	T	F	M	A
I	W	N	B	A	I	M	W
T	W	M	M	B;	Y,	F	Y

TABLE 10.2 Full-text index card

You	See	Me,	Lord	Bassanio,	Where	I	Stand
Such	As	I	Am:	Though	For	Myself	Alone
I	Would	Not	Be	Ambitious	In	My	Wish
To	Wish	Myself	Much	Better;	Yet,	For	You

In addition, when you create the cards, the act of writing also fuels your familiarity with the text. Scientists have shown that the motor skills involved with handwriting are connected to the portion of our brains associated with learning and memory, a process that is very different from what happens when we type on a keyboard. Mine don't tend to look quite as neat as those shown above. Those shown in Figure 10.1 are a bit more accurate:

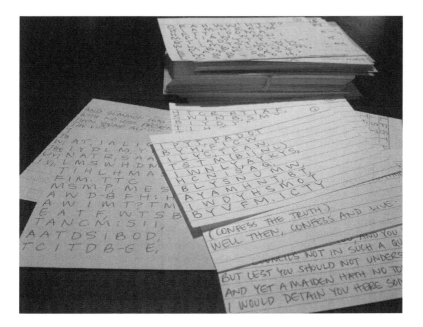

FIGURE 10.1 Prompt cards

186 Actuating practice

Personally, I like the rustic feel of my handwritten cards—I feel as though I own that text afterwards, like I've made it my own.

Prompt cards for dialogue

When memorizing dialogue, I follow the same instructions as I do for single chunks of text, except that I include the cue for my lines, usually the final double-iambic unit of the line (or as close as possible to it) in parenthesis:

TABLE 10.3 Initials-only index card for dialogue

(your	name	I	hear)					
W	H	Y	H,	B	S	H	O	H:
T	C	M	K	T	D	T	O	M.
(thee	for	my	wife)					

TABLE 10.4 Full-text index card for dialogue

(your	name	I	hear)				
Well	Have	You	Heard,	But	Something	Hard Of	Hearing:
They	Call	Me	Katherine	That	Do	Talk Of	Me.
(thee	for	my	wife)				

Carry these with you and look at them randomly throughout the day, even when you don't have dedicated time to sit down and study them; those few minutes while you're waiting for the barista to make your coffee or while you are out running errands can make a big difference.

Mental athletes (yes, there are such a thing!) use the ancient technique of "memory palaces" or the method of Loci—a means for placing each item along a journey that can be visualized: a journey such as moving through your home. You can combine these techniques and visualize your prompt letters in particular places. I know that I can visualize very easily how to travel certain routes near where I live, and I have to confess that if I had to map them out properly for you to follow, I wouldn't know the actual names of half the roads, yet I don't get lost driving them. In fact, I can still visualize my way around places I lived years ago. Can you? Can you visualize your childhood home or the home of a loved one that you haven't seen in some time? It can be any place you remember well, or it can even be a place that is entirely fictitious, as long as you have a strong image of it. Set aside some time to visualize the text imposed on that familiar memory and see if the method proves useful to you.

Learning text with a partner

The Rolling Line

This is an exercise for partners that you can use for either larger or smaller chunks of text.

Two partners sit in chairs across from one another, with the selected text in front of them. One partner will be "A," the other "B." Let "A" be the partner who speaks first. Partner "A" will look down at the text, gather the first line, make eye contact with the partner ('B'), and speak the line. Partner "B" will receive the line and repeat it back to "A" as a question. For example:

A: But soft, what light through yonder window breaks?
B (asks): But soft, what light through yonder window breaks?

"A" confirms the line, then gathers the next line from the page and then delivers that next line to the partner.

A: But soft, what light through yonder window breaks?
   It is the East, and Juliet is the Sun,

"B" returns the newly spoken line in the form of a question.

B: It is the East, and Juliet is the Sun?

"A" confirms the spoken line, gathers the next line, and continues:

A: It is the East, and Juliet is the Sun,
   Arise fair Sun and kill the envious Moon,

B: Arise fair Sun and kill the envious Moon?
A: Arise fair Sun and kill the envious Moon,
   Who is already sick and pale with grief,

B: Who is already sick and pale with grief?
A: Who is already sick and pale with grief,
   That thou her Maid art far more fair than she

Continue until the end of the speech, or unit of dialogue.

188 Actuating practice

The Stacked Line

This variation of *The Rolling Line* is based on expansive breath work. With expansive breath work, you build your breath capacity by replenishing and expanding the inhalation of breath to match a rising number you count aloud. Beginning with 1, then 1-2, 1-2-3, 1-2-3-4, 1-2-3-4-5, 1-2-3-4-5-6, 1-2-3-4-5-6-7 and so on until you reach your maximum length that you can sustain on that single breath, say 25 or 30 or more. The key with breath work is to keep the ease and control, to avoid either expelling the air too quickly, taking in too much, or squeezing the air out at the end. Over time you train your breath capacity to expand. This is also known as "stacking the breath". *The Stacked Line* applies the same principle to memorization. Instead of building the length of breath, you build upon the foundation of the lines that make up a given speech.

The Stacked Line (solo work)

With a copy of the text in hand, gather the line, and then begin to speak the first line of text. When you reach the end of each line, gather the next line, but return to the first line before moving on, following the pattern: (line) 1, (lines) 1 and 2, (lines) 1 and 2 and 3, etc.

Prince:	Do not think so, you shall not find it so:
Start:	Do not think so, you shall not find it so:
Add:	And Heaven forgive them, that so much have sway'd
Start:	Do not think so, you shall not find it so: And Heaven forgive them, that so much have sway'd
Add:	Your Majesty's good thoughts away from me:
Start:	Do not think so, you shall not find it so: And Heaven forgive them, that so much have sway'd Your Majesty's good thoughts away from me:
Add:	I will redeem all this on Percy's head,
Start:	Do not think so, you shall not find it so: And Heaven forgive them, that so much have sway'd Your Majesty's good thoughts away from me: I will redeem all this on Percy's head,
Add:	And in the closing of some glorious day,
Start:	Do not think so, you shall not find it so: And Heaven forgive them, that so much have sway'd

Rehearsing the part **189**

>   Your Majesty's good thoughts away from me:
>   I will redeem all this on Percy's head,
>   And in the closing of some glorious day,
> Add: Be bold to tell you, that I am your Son,

This line stack creates within you a swelling sense of build as the ideas emerge that helps you to recall the text and to understand how the thoughts feed into each other and drive towards a point.

The Stacked Line (solo work, variation)

In this variation, which is inspired by Patsy Rodenburg, Cicely Berry, and Peter Brook, you can build the line one word upon the other so that each word is connected to the surrounding ideas and the expansion of breath. This can be done while sitting or standing, or while lying in constructive rest: with your head and neck supported by a book so that your spine is in alignment, your knees are bent, and point up towards the sky, and your feet are flat on the floor so that the pelvis is supported).

Begin with the first word, and stack each word in the line as you work towards the line's end:

> Do
> Do not
> Do not think
> Do not think so
> Do not think so you
> Do not think so you shall
> Do not think so you shall not
> Do not think so you shall not find
> Do not think so you shall not find it
> Do not think so, you shall not find it so:

The Stacked Line (partner work)

In the partner variation of this exercise, the partner side-coaches, or "heckles," prompts at the speaker that help to engage the next line. They offer retorts such as, "so?" "what?" "yeah?" "tell me more," etc. These can be spontaneous responses to the text; they do not need to be pre-organized or planned. It is more important to prompt the speaker

190 Actuating practice

to continue with greater clarity than to pre-arrange a perfectly logical or accurate piece of dramaturgy. For example:

A: Do not think so, you shall not find it so:
B: No?
A: Do not think so, you shall not find it so:
    And Heaven forgive them, that so much have sway'd
B: What?
A: Do not think so, you shall not find it so:
    And Heaven forgive them, that so much have sway'd
    Your Majesty's good thoughts away from me:
B: Really?
A: Do not think so, you shall not find it so:
    And Heaven forgive them, that so much have sway'd
    Your Majesty's good thoughts away from me:
    I will redeem all this on Percy's head,
    And in the closing of some glorious day,
B: Yes, then what?
A: Do not think so, you shall not find it so:
    And Heaven forgive them, that so much have sway'd
    Your Majesty's good thoughts away from me:
    I will redeem all this on Percy's head,
    And in the closing of some glorious day,
    Be bold to tell you, that I am your Son,

This partner engagement really activates the speaker and forges a strong connection to the text and to the need to get the point across. It heightens the actor's objectives.

Basketball Partner Pass

This exercise helps to keep the energy lifted and moving, particularly at the ends of the lines. It is suitable for any length of text, from short exchanges of dialogue to longer passages. It builds upon *Basketball Shakespeare*.

Two partners stand at a distance from one another, facing each other. Actor "A" speaks the text while bouncing the ball. At the end of the verse line, the actor quickly passes the ball to the partner, Actor "B." If "A's" text continues, "B" quickly returns the ball to "A" and "A" begins immediately to bounce the ball and speak the next line of text before passing the ball again.

Rehearsing the part **191**

For example:

A (bounces the ball):
Do not think so, you shall not find it so: (passes the ball with energy)
B catches and returns the ball immediately
A (catches the ball, and begins bouncing): And Heaven forgive them, that so much have sway'd (passes the ball with energy)
B catches and returns the ball immediately
A (catches the ball, and begins bouncing): Your Majesty's good thoughts away from me: (passes the ball)

In dialogue the exercise looks like this:

A (bounces the ball):
Stay, though thou kill me, Sweet Demetrius (passes the ball with energy)
B (catches the ball, and begins bouncing):
I charge thee hence, and do not haunt me thus (passes the ball with energy)
A (catches the ball, and begins bouncing):
O wilt thou darkling leave me? Do not so. (passes the ball with energy)
B (catches the ball, and begins bouncing):
Stay on thy peril, I alone will go. (passes the ball with energy)
A (catches the ball, and begins bouncing):
O I am out of breath, in this fond chase, (passes the ball . . .)

Each time the ball is passed, it should be passed with great energy and purpose; do not allow the energy to lag or drop in between. It ought not to become casual, but should remain energized and purposeful, full of sport. It should be more aerobic than contemplative. It works best if the actor knows the lines so that the energy can continue to move forward. If the lines are shaky, the actor will be more focused on recalling the lines than on keeping the energy moving forward.

Ensemble work

Many of the exercises in this book foster a sense of ensemble in the studio. These are a few of my favorite ensemble-building explorations that are particularly suited for working with heightened text, but don't appear elsewhere in this volume. At the end of the chapter I will list exercises suitable for solo, group, or classroom exploration.

192 Actuating practice

Shakespeare was influenced greatly by the *commedia dell'arte*. One of the things I love most is to shake the group of any tendency to be precious with the text, to fall into patterns of heightened speech that lack connection. I aim to create a sense of play and vulnerability that demands the trust and respect of those involved. Depending on the circumstances, class, or play, certain explorations may be better suited than others—these appear in no particular order.

Listening and storytelling

Iambic Storytelling

Gather the group into a circle, standing with a comfortable distance from shoulder to shoulder. They need not be touching, but should be close enough to sense the flow of energy coming from those next to them. The group will tell a story—in iambic pentameter—that they devise on the spot. It should have a beginning, a middle, and an end. Each person will speak one line of verse, passing the story around the circle. Storytellers will not be able to pre-plan their contributions; they must listen to how the story evolves and plunge in from there. There are two variations: you can tell any story that emerges from the group, or you can tell the story of a particular play you are exploring. Just begin with a line of iambic pentameter, one that invites the person next to you to join your story is ideal.

For example:

One day from school I came home and I found

The door ajar and no one was at home

My Mom should have been there and yet was not

Where was she? I wondered and then I found

A note that told me to go round the back

In the backyard they all yelled out "Surprise!"

A party formed right there and then I cried.

I cried from shock and awe and then I saw

My Dad who I have missed and have not seen

Since he was gone, I felt as though I'd dreamed

I saw him there, but there he was and then

He picked me up and hugged me tight so hard

Rehearsing the part **193**

> I could not breathe, but wished right from the start
> He'd never let me go, my Dad's the best
> He always finds a way to make my day
> I never thought he'd be here yet he was
> So soon I was completely o'er the moon.

It's okay if the lines of iambic pentameter are simple; they don't need to be perfectly written or flawless; it's more important to be flexible and willing to be "wrong"—to leap in and create spontaneously. This exercise serves double duty: it immerses the group in the energy of the iambic pentameter, and it encourages spontaneity. It encourages spontaneous verse, and when you think in verse on the spot, it embeds a sense of verse ownership in the speaker, a heightened connection between thought and speech.

There are several ways to tailor this to a particular play. The group can tell the story of the whole play, an act, a scene, or even an event.

Here is an example of the story of Romeo and Juliet:

> Well once upon a time there was a girl
> Whose parents threw a party and who came
> The boy from enemies in a disguise
> She'd no idea that he was Montague
> Yet Montague he was and so it goes
> That Juliet would love him all the same
> In secret they would wed and then some strife
> Would fall upon the families; Tybalt dies
> And Romeo is banished from this place
> Poor Juliet is forced to wed Paris
> Which she just cannot do and to the Priest
> To Friar Lawrence she goes for some help
> Who gives her poison to escape this truth
> And so her family thinks that she has died
> She's buried in the tomb with all the bones
> And Friar sends a letter to her love
> No letter was received and Romeo hears

194 Actuating practice

> The news of Juliet's death and so he goes
> Into the tomb to die right there with her
> He doesn't know she'll wake, and wake she shall
> Right after he is dead and then her woe
> Will lead her to despair and take her life.

Depending on the group, you may want to start with some basic listening and responding skills before you reach iambic pentameter—these are good for all kinds of groups, from beginning to advanced, from newer to established ensembles. To warm up, here are a few suggestions from the existing repertoire of theatre games:

Counting

I first discovered this exercise while working with the education practitioners from the Royal Shakespeare Company; I believe it originated with Peter Brook.

> While in a circle, have the group turn so that their backs are facing the inner most part of the circle (this can be done either while sitting or standing). They must count to twenty as a group, but only one person may count at a time; if more than one person counts simultaneously, the group must return to the start and begin again with "one." The group must count randomly, with each person contributing at least once, and not passing the numbers along in the order of the circle.

Volleying (via Mallory Catlett)

Using the basketball (or any larger sized ball) the group must work together to volley the ball _fifty_ times without letting the ball fall to the ground. The group can be in any configuration; they are not confined to a circle. The group must adhere to the following rules:

- Each time contact is made with the ball, the person who volleys the ball calls out the number (from 1–50).
- The ball must remain in motion; it cannot be held.
- Each person must make contact with the ball at least once.
- There should be no talking whatsoever, except for the calling out of numbers.
- The group must not discuss strategies, but may lead by example through their actions.

Group Storytelling (via Viola Spolin)

Similar to *Iambic Storytelling*, with the following adjustments to make up for the lack structure in the verse:

- Assemble the group in one central location so you can select storytellers randomly by gesturing to them when it is their turn (the leader will "conduct" the story as a conductor would a piece of music).
- Each time you select a storyteller, they should continue the story immediately on the heels of the last speaker.
- Each person will carry the story forward until they are stopped by the story "conductor."
- The story should have a beginning, a middle, and an end.

One-Word Storytelling (via Rose Burnett Bonczek and David Storck)

Both the *Group Storytelling* and *One-Word Storytelling* can be done in a circle, if you prefer. With *One-Word Storytelling*, each storyteller speaks only one word at a time to formulate the story.

- Each storyteller speaks only one word for each rotation:
  - "Once"—"upon"—"a"—"time" . . .
- Storytellers should listen actively for ways to guide the story along.
- Avoid using the word "and" to stall the story and deflect responsibility.
  - Only use "and" if you need it to complete the story— "my grandmother made me a sandwich of peanut butter . . ."—"peanut butter and jelly" is a natural progression that moves the story along; don't use "and" as a way to avoid committing to the task.
- Don't be afraid to end sentences!

Connecting Text

I introduced *Connecting Breath* along with its variations in Chapter 5. In the rehearsal room there is another variation to explore: *Connecting Text*,

196 Actuating practice

which builds on the *Connecting Breath* exploration and should follow that exercise seamlessly.

> Begin by having the group move throughout the space, first drawing their attention to the body in space, then expanding the awareness to include the rest of the ensemble: making eye contact first, then sharing an inhalation and exhalation of breath. After that foundation has been explored, introduce the next parameter: when they stop and share the next inhalation and exhalation with a partner, each partner will share a short piece of text (a line or two) with the partner. Allow the text to emerge spontaneously. Encourage the actors not to predetermine what they will share, to allow the exchange to reveal the text. They may repeat text, if the impulse demands it. Connecting to the partner with both breath and text fosters the sense of trust and vulnerability they share between them. Allow responses to be there; if they have a reaction to either speaking and sharing their own text, or receiving and listening to their partner's, they can acknowledge their response rather than suppress it. As they continue to move through the space, you can shape the exchanges by offering prompts:
>
> - share something secret with your partner;
> - protect something;
> - confess something;
> - convince your partner;
> - convince yourself;
> - ask for permission;
> - instruct your partner;
> - illuminate beauty.

These are only a few suggestions; you can tailor the nature of the text you ask them to share in order to maximize your rehearsal process or to address challenges you face within the play.

Platt in Action

In Chapter 1, I discussed the Elizabethan "Platt," the placard hung backstage that outlined the key events that happen in the play and the foundation for what we now think of as "plot." *Platt in Action* utilizes the architectural skeleton of the play as a means for creative exploration.

First, create a list of the events that happen over the course of the play. You can begin broadly with a list of the events broken down by scenes. Later, you can get more specific within each scene by breaking it down into beats. For more intimate scene work, you can go further still and break it down into exchanges between the partners.

- Hang a bullet-pointed list of the scene's events (with a clear beginning, middle, and end) in the upstage, stage left, and stage right areas (if you are working in the round, you can include the downstage area, but keep the number of "Platts" to a minimum so that the ensemble must work with the "Platt" as a collective rather than as a group of individuals).
- Have the group improvise freely, moving through the sequence of the play. This free improvisation can be wholly organic and need not include any elements of the play besides the plot. Improvised text is encouraged.
- Between each scene, and when "offstage" the group should consult the "Platt" in order to understand what must come next.

Platt in Action: variations

- *Introduce a time limit for each scene:* enact the Platt in 5 minutes, 3 minutes, or 1 minute per scene (depending on time, you can choose one or reduce the allotted time incrementally). Use a timer to keep within the given limit.
- *Textual variations:* include some iambic text in the exploration, no iambic text, or explore exclusively through iambic text. (If you are exploring *Platt in Action* with only iambic text, make sure to specify that the text cannot appear exactly as it does in the scene; it is not a run-through, but an enacted version of the events told through verse).
- *Relationship Platt:* focus your attention exclusively on the shifts in relationships between characters.

There are many ways to explore *Platt in Action.* It can be used at any stage in rehearsal, with varying degrees of complexity, and is a useful companion to scene study. I particularly like to work on the time limit sequence because it forces the ensemble to distill the essence of the scene with greater and greater economy.

198 Actuating practice

The Pied Piper

The Pied Piper builds its foundation on classic clowning techniques. It promotes a free and expressive body and encourages risk taking. These exercises are inspired by my study with master Lecoq teacher, Norman Taylor.

This exercise works best in an open space.

- Begin by establishing several lines across at one end of the room (depending on your playing space, it works best if the lines form in front of one of the shorter/shallower walls so that the group has a longer diagonal path to cross to the other side).
- The lines should be orderly, and each person should be clear who their companions are on either side of them.
- On a rapid count of eight, the first group will move across the floor with an impromptu "funny" walk. Encourage them to be ridiculous, grotesque even. You can clap out the beat, use percussive instruments, or play music.
- That first group moves across the floor with their "funny" walk. They are part of a group of funny walkers, but each person is doing his own walk.
- When you get to the second count of eight, the next group of funny walkers begins to cross the floor.
- When the first group reaches the other side, they begin to form another line, and hold there until all walkers have completed their journey.
- Repeat several times to encourage greater risk-taking and creativity.
- Add vocalization to the walk as they cross.
- It doesn't matter what the walk is; the most important thing is to commit to a repeatable walk and to take it from there.

  o Let the body inform the walk!
  o Don't predetermine the "right" thing to do!
  o Be willing to look foolish!

After the group has loosened up, segue into *The Pied Piper*.

- The group can stay in their "funny walk" lines.
- Have one "Piper" come to the front of the group and demonstrate his walk. Have the "Piper" walk solo to start.

Rehearsing the part **199**

- Once the "Piper" has crossed the room, the "Piper" returns to original side to lead the group across the floor. The group embodies that "Piper"'s walk as they cross the floor.
- After the group has crossed the floor, the "Piper" will lead again (with the same walk).
- The group now *exaggerates* the Piper's walk, making it bigger, bolder, and funnier.
- As soon as the group reaches the other side of the room, they will once again traverse the floor. This time the group *interprets* the Piper's walk; the Piper watches the interpretations.

This sequence follows a classic structure of beginning, middle, and end. The Piper introduces the walk, teaches it to the group, and hands it over. The group learns the walk, builds on it through exaggeration, and then personalizes it.

The Pied Piper of Verse

This variation builds on *The Pied Piper* and includes a line of verse.

- The group can stay in their "funny walk" lines; you can change their positions for variety, if you have not yet done so (you can choose to rotate earlier, during *The Pied Piper*, if you'd like or if the group needs a change).
  - Have individuals who remained in the middle move to the front, the group in the back rotates up to the middle, and the original group in front moves to the end of the lines.
- Have one "Piper" come to the front of the group and demonstrate a movement/gesture to accompany one line of verse.
- Have the "Piper" walk solo for 2–3 repetitions of the movement/verse phrase so that the group has time to follow and repeat that gesture/line.
- The "Piper" will continue to repeat the gesture/line, to lead the group as they join in.
  - The group should join in by following each gesture/line as the line advances.
  - For example, the Piper repeats the sequence three times as he travels across the room. On the fourth time, the first

200 Actuating practice

> group advances along with the Piper, on the fifth time the
> first and second group advances, on the sixth time, the
> third group joins the rest, etc.
>
> o   This continues until everyone has repeated the gesture and
>   verse line and a new "Piper" begins to lead.

The Pied Piper sequence helps to cultivate a sense of play in the studio. It
can be used at all stages in the process: in callbacks it helps to introduce new
artists to each other and to assess how a group may work together; in the
classroom it helps to pave the way for exploration and dispel any pressure to
perform; and in rehearsals, it infuses the process with play and camaraderie.
Once you are willing to feel and appear foolish before a group, you find a
sense of fearlessness that ignites everything that follows.

The World According to Me!

The World According to Me! distils the character's story into a sound bite. It is
the "elevator pitch" of a character's arc, told in the character's own words. If
you have characters within your ensemble that don't have much dialogue to
choose from—a messenger, for example, who only has one line of text—he
can position that delivery line in the middle of two pieces of text that sum
up the play before he arrives and after he leaves.

> Assemble the group in a semi-circle that follows the configuration of
> a clock from 2:00–10:00. The space from 11:00–1:00 is reserved for
> the actor/storyteller.
>
> •   When each actor has the impulse to do so, he will step up to
>   the playing space, in the "upstage" area of the semi-circle.
> •   The actor/storyteller will summarize the world of his character
>   in three sentences: sharing the beginning, middle, and end of
>   that character's journey.
> •   At the conclusion, the actor will finish with some kind of
>   "button": a flourish, a bow, by saying, "thank you"—any
>   acknowledgement of the audience who has shared in the story.

For example, the actor playing Romeo might say:

O she doth teach the Torches to burn bright:

But Romeo may not, he is banished.

Well Juliet, I will lie with thee tonight:

Rehearsing the part **201**

The actor playing Benedick might say:

Then is courtesy a turn-coat, but it is certain I am loved of all Ladies, only you excepted: and I would I could find in my heart that I had not a hard heart, for truly I love none.
    This can be no trick, the conference was sadly borne, they have the truth of this from Hero, they seem to pity the Lady: it seems her affections have the full bent: love me?
    "I do love nothing in the world so well as you, is not that strange?"

Or, since Benedick's lines are in prose, the actor might condense it to:

for truly, I love none

This can be no trick . . .

I do love nothing in the world so well as you . . .

Like *Platt in Action*, you can use *The World According to Me!* at any stage. You can use it to explore the character arc of the whole play, or you can break it down further to explore an entire act, a particular scene, or a beat within a given scene. Actors can embrace a different "world," a different beginning, middle, and end to see what discoveries can be made. It's more about capturing the essence of the character's journey than it is about establishing a dramaturgically "correct" series of statements.

Confession Circle (via Rose Burnett Bonczek and Beverly Brumm)

The *Confession Circle* provides an opportunity for an actor to tap into his own vulnerability and command a deeper connection to his text. The "confession" is something that must be shared with the partner; it does not necessarily need to be something that is secret or private (although it certainly can be). The key is that whatever is spoken is something that must be so at that moment of impulse.

- Begin with the group in a large, open circle.
- One person begins in the center of the circle.
- The center person crosses to someone in the circle and invites that person to join him in the center.
- When both actors are in the center, the first actor confesses something to the listener, using a piece of Shakespeare's text.

202 Actuating practice

> The "confession" can be anything that the actor wishes to speak to his partner, whether or not the text is actually "secret."

- When the confessor has confessed, that actor takes the place in the circle left vacant by their partner.
- The partner/listener becomes the new confessor and invites a new person to join the center.

  - If the listener wishes to respond to the confessor, he may not do so while that person is still in the center; the first person must return to the circle and then be invited to join again in the center.
  - The actors must maintain the ritual of inviting, sharing, and releasing the partner before any new confessions can be revealed. It must not turn into a scene between two partners.

The actor playing Lear, for example, might invite his Cordelia to the center and speak:

Nothing will come of nothing, Speak again.

He might later invite Regan into the circle to share:

O reason not the need: our basest Beggars

Are in the poorest thing superfluous,

Allow not Nature, more than Nature needs:

Man's life is cheap as Beatles. Thou art a Lady.

Confession Circle: variation

> After using Shakespeare's verse to release the confession, you can vary the parameters so that the center person may speak to or ask anything of the partner, using any form of text. Again, the partner may not reply; the partner only receives the speaker's message or query.
>
> If you are working on *Much Ado About Nothing*, Hero might invite Claudio to the center and ask:

> How could you have believed them?

It is not important for the receiver/listeners to reply to what is said in these "confessions." It is important for invited one to really listen to the partner, to consider what is shared, and to allow the speaker the opportunity to be truly heard.

Emotional/Spatial Dance

Chapter 2 introduced ideas about the spatial dynamics at Shakespeare's Globe and how those concepts can help inform performance. The *Emotional/Spatial Dance* exercise offers a series of choreographic options for exploring these ideas in practice. This exploration is particularly well suited for solo and partner work, and is also useful for directors to consider as actors explore blocking.

Select a piece of text to explore—for a solo performer, a duo, or large group.

- Move closer to the audience (or downstage, depending on the spatial configuration and actor/audience relationship) when you identify moments of vulnerability.
- Move away from the audience (or upstage) to enhance your power or status within a given scene or to gain the upper hand.
- Shorten the distance between you and your partner (or cross towards them) if you address them by "thee" or "thou."
- Lengthen the distance between you and your partner (or cross away from them) if you address them as "you."
- When you identify a mask or a moment of the divided self, switch the energy or do something very different physically to distinguish the difference.

    - *Vary your tempo*: fast/slow; sudden/sustained; fluid/staccato.
    - *Vary your weight*: heavy/light; grounded/airy.
    - *Vary your direction*: curvilinear/straight; direct/indirect.

- You can explore this variety either through physical action or through your intention; you can manifest this "dance" both internally and/or externally—with the body, with the text, or both.

Through this *Emotional/Spatial Dance* you may find discoveries that directly inform your blocking, or you may find indirect inspiration that pulses beneath the spatial framework that already exists for your scene.

Suggestions for solo work

Just like the actors in Shakespeare's company, many actors find the need—or the desire—to work alone at some point in their process. You may have

204 Actuating practice

already figured out ways to apply some of the ensemble explorations to solo work. I'll also make suggestions for you to do that. First, here are some ways to begin to work on a piece of text. These exercises should be done with the text in hand. It is important to work from the page at this stage in your process, even if the text is memorized—you will want to work directly from the orthography to maximize what you discover.

Basketball Shakespeare

- Begin with this basic exploration of Shakespeare's verse to see what you discover.

Walk the Punctuation

This is a standard exercise that you'll find in many other places (Cicely Berry, Patsy Rodenburg—and many, many others—recommend this one), and I always include it in my process. It follows *Basketball Shakespeare* beautifully.

- With text in hand, begin to read aloud as you move through the space.
- Each time you arrive at a piece of punctuation (commas, colons, semi-colons, question marks, periods—or full stops—and exclamation points) you change direction completely.
- Make each shift distinct, a sharp turn in a different direction.

Walk the Punctuation helps to reveal the shape of the character's thoughts, and how the arguments are developed.

Speak Only Consonants (via Cicely Berry)

- Read the text aloud, but vocalize only the consonants in the speech.
  - o   What alliteration do you discover?

Speak Only the Vowels/Diphthongs (via Cicely Berry)

- Read the text aloud, but vocalize only the open vowel/diphthong sounds.
  - o   What assonance do you discover?

Rehearsing the part **205**

Speak All of the Verbs

- What action appears throughout the speech?

Speak All of the Adjectives

- What descriptions appear in the speech?

Read Aloud the Capitalized Words

- Do the capitalized words in the text reveal anything?

Physicalize Antithesis

- Do two wildly different gestures for each of the components of the antithesis.
- As you compare the two, make one huge physically and the other small, for example:
  - Play with making the two distinct:
    - high/low;
    - gentle/rough;
    - fast/slow;
    - sneaky/bold.

Cast the Audience

- What role does the audience play at this particular moment?
  - confidante;
  - co-conspirator;
  - mirror.

Personify Shakespeare's World

- Are there any elements that take on human qualities in your text?

Solo Breath

This is an adaptation of *Connecting Breath* for the solo explorer.

206 Actuating practice

Since we are able to shift our awareness through self-direction, and because we constantly breathe, we can train our relationship to our breath at any time. In *Connecting Breath*, you breathe to, and with, a partner; in *Solo Breath* you breathe to, and within, the surrounding environment.

- *Indoors:* begin in a corridor or staircase—someplace where the walls are relatively close to you.
    - ○ Feel your feet come in contact with the floor.
    - ○ Release the tension you observe within the body on the first exhalation.
        - ○ If you need more time or breath to release, continue until you are ready to build and expand your awareness.
    - ○ Breathe in, with an awareness of your breath filling the sides and back of your body.
    - ○ Exhale easily, sustaining the breath—this is an easy flow in and out of the body.
    - ○ With the next inhalation, expand that awareness beyond the sides of the body to radiate outwards to reach the surrounding walls.
    - ○ Breathe to the walls around you.
- *Outdoors:* If you are in a natural environment, expand your breath to connect to the trees.
- *In a large group:* This is especially useful when you are running out of patience (try it when traveling, shopping, or anywhere you are forced to wait).
    - ○ Select someone to breathe to, and expand your breath to connect to that person.
        - ○ Did that person turn to look at you?

The more you practice this kind of mindful breathing, the more it becomes a form of standing meditation.

Each production, each classroom, and each ensemble is different. Some of these suggestions flow easily into others. The outcomes of certain explorations are enhanced by what precedes them, but unlike components of the training, there is greater flexibility to pick and choose what to explore and the order in which you do so.

AFTERWORD

It is not the fashion to see the Lady the Epliogue:

(As You Like It 5.4.173)

It is fitting that Shakespeare places a colon after "Epilogue," right at that moment of poise: colons help to clarify thoughts, to create intimacy and honesty; precisely the things we wish to do as we enter into a relationship with Shakespeare and with our audience. Throughout *Unearthing Shakespeare* we've explored ways of working that enable us to do just that: to get very specific and intimate, to embody Shakespeare's text in such a way that it becomes wholly our own. I hope that you will always embrace your own "what if," and that you are ignited and empowered by the possibilities before you. Your toolkit is filled with instruments. Dig in and "Play on!"

Appendix A
EXERCISES FOR THE CLASSROOM

Chapter 5

Connecting Breath

Radiating Box

Radiating Box: Distance and Vertical Space

Status work

    Status Exploration

    Elizabethan Chain of Being Status

    High-Status Exploration

    Middle-Status Exploration

    Equal-Status Exploration

Chapter 6

Blind Shakespeare

Blindfolded Shakespeare

Backwards Shakespeare

Chapter 7

Open Mic Poetry

Moving Target: Whole Text

Moving Target: Random Text

Find It Here

Chapter 8

Elliptical Energy Training

    Elliptical Energy Training Part I

    Elliptical Energy Training Part II

    Elliptical Energy Training Part III

    Elliptical Energy Training Part IV

    Elliptical Energy Training Part V

        Elliptical Energy Training Part V: variations

Chapter 10

Iambic Storytelling

Counting

Volleying

Group Storytelling

One-Word Storytelling

Connecting Text

The Pied Piper

The Pied Piper of Verse

The World According to Me!

Emotional/Spatial Dance

Appendix B
EXERCISES FOR REHEARSAL

Chapter 5

Connecting Breath

Radiating Box

Radiating Box: distance and vertical space

Status work

    Status exploration

    Elizabethan Chain of Being Status

    High-status exploration

    Middle-status exploration

    Equal-status exploration

Chapter 10

    The Rolling Line

    The Stacked Line

    Basketball Partner Pass

    Iambic Storytelling

Counting

Volleying

Group Storytelling

One-Word Storytelling

Connecting Text

Platt in Action

    Platt in Action: variations

The Pied Piper

The Pied Piper of Verse

The World According to Me!

Confession Circle

    Confession Circle: variation

Appendix C
EXERCISES FOR SOLO PRACTICE

Chapter 7

Open Mic Poetry

Find It Here

Chapter 10

The Stacked Line

> The Stacked Line: variation

Emotional/Spatial Dance

Basketball Shakespeare

Walk the Punctuation

Speak Only Consonants

Speak Only Vowels/Diphthongs

Speak All of the Verbs

Speak All of the Adjectives

Read Aloud the Capitalized Words

Exercises for solo practice **213**

Physicalize Antithesis

Cast the Audience

Personify Shakespeare's World

Solo Breath

INDEX

actor/audience relationship: 24, 30, 121, 152, 203; in Elizabethan theatre 12; in fourth-wall realism/naturalism 12; in training 152

actor-manager 7

actor's part, *see* Elizabethan Theatre, components of

Admiral's Men, The 5–6

Alexandrine, The 44, 56–61, 63, 155, 168, 170, 171; notation of 155; shared 59–61

alliteration 41, 62–4, 94; notation of 161, 168

All's Well That Ends Well 57–8, 64–5

Anthony and Cleopatra 123–4

antithesis 76–7, 99, 205; notation of 164–8; *Physicalize Antithesis* 205

apposition: *see process of balance, the*

apprentice system, *see* Elizabethan Theatre, components of

archaeology of performance, the xi, 68, 102, 180; *unearthing Shakespeare* xi

Arden Shakespeare, *Complete Works* 89, 95–7, 101

Armin, Robert 10

Asides 24, 26, 31–2

assonance 41, 62, 64–6; notation of 161, 168

As You Like It 11, 207

audience agreement 12–16

audience etiquette 14–15; expectations of 11; perspectives of 11; roles and functions of: *see* "casting the audience"; social classes of: *see Shakespeare's Social Space*; use of in *Elliptical Energy* training 146–7, 150–1

Backwards Shakespeare 128–9, 146

Basketball Partner Pass 190

Basketball Shakespeare, or "Shakesball" 48– 54, 89, 190, 204

Bate, Jonathan 96

Becoming empowered xii

Berry, Cicely 133, 189, 204

Bevington, *Complete Works of Shakespeare* 89, 95–7, 101; David 96

Blackfriars Playhouse 17

Blind Shakespeare 122–7, 129

Blindfolded Shakespeare 127–8, 129

Bonczek, Rose Burnett 195, 201

'book-keeper' or 'book-holder' 10

Brayne, John 4

Index **215**

breath: capacity 131; relationship to thought 66–7; 130–1

Brecht, Bertolt; conventions of 34

Broadway Theatres 16

Brook, Peter 189, 194

Brumm, Beverly 201

Burbage, James 4

Burbage, Richard 4–5, 21,120

caesura 52–3

capitalized words: *see* First Folio; *Read Aloud the Capitalized Words* 205

Carey, Henry 5

casting in Elizabethan Theatre: *see* Elizabethan Theatre, components of

casting the audience 24–30, 205; the confidante 24–6; the co-conspirator 26–30; the mirror 34–36; 138, 205

Catlett, Mallory 194

Chain of Being see Elizabethan Chain of Being

character 85–7; Elizabethan understanding of 11; *discovering 'Character' through character* 89, 98; titles 38

Chekhov, Anton 25–6

Chekhov, Michael 109

Chorus, prologue to *Henry V* 12–14

coining: "thinking on the line"; images 134–5; *see Find it Here*

Commedia dell'arte 192

community, sense of x, 18, 24, 31, 89, 105–6, 121, 152

Condell, Henry 87

Confession Circle 201–2

Confession Circle Variation 202

Connecting Breath 106–7, 109, 195–6, 205–6

Connecting Breath: Variation 108

Connecting Text 195–6

Costumes: *see* Elizabethan Theatre, components of

Counting 194

court performances: *see* Elizabethan Theatre, components of

Cymbeline 85

decorum: see *Mask of the Divided Self, The Development of Thoughts, The* 157

DeWitt, Johannes 7

diagramming the text: *see Shakespeare Score*

dialogue, inherent 28–30

diphthongs 64–5

discovering the Language 62–6

Elliptical Energy i, 34–6, 103, 138–52, 209; direct use of 141–52; illustration of (fig. 2.4 and 8.2) 34, 139; in performance 151–2; indirect use of 151; observations of 148–51; *Training* 140–8; use of mirrors 140

Elliptical Energy Training Part I 140–3; illustration of (fig. 8.3) 141; *repetition* 141–3

Elliptical Energy Training Part II 143–5; repetition and Shakespeare's text 144–5; impulses 142–3

Elliptical Energy Training Part III 145–6; blank wall 145–6

Elliptical Energy Training Part IV 146; audience agreement 146–7

Elliptical Energy Training Part V 147; thrust configuration 147–8; variations of 148

Elizabethan Chain of Being 113, 115–7

Elizabethan Chain of Being Status game 115–7

Elizabethan repertory system 4

Elizabethan Theatre, components of: actors 4; actor's part 6; admission price 8, 37; apprentice system 4, 10; casting 10; costumes 4, 7; court performances 4; fools 10; neutral platform stage 7, 14, 17–18; patronage 4; performance time 7; players 4, 12; playing companies 5; profit-sharing 5; rehearsal period 6–7, 9; repertory schedule 6; shared lighting 7, 9, 24; social dynamics of 37

Elizabethan Theatre, conditions of 5–11;

216 Index

Elizabethan World Picture, The 115
Embodied performance xiii
Emotional/Spatial Dance 203
empowered performance 21, 28
enjambed lines 95, 97, 157–8; notation
    of 157–8, 168, 171, 180
Ensemble Work 191
Excellent Actor, An 120
eye contact 121–2

Find it Here 134–7
First Folio: and authenticity 87;
    capitalized words 92–3, 163–4, 205
feminine endings 44, 47–8, 52–8, 59–61;
    notation of 155, 168, 170–1, 180
fourth wall: *see* performance paradigms;
    Primary and secondary energy in a
    fourth wall paradigm (fig. 8.1) 139

Globe, The 5
Globe Theatre fire 87
given circumstances 45, 86
Greene, Robert 116
groundlings 8, 30, 37, 39, 137
Group Storytelling 195

Hamlet 4, 11, 87, 124, 132, 155
Hamlet's Advice to the Players 10
Heavens, The 18, 20–1
Hell 20
Hemminge, John 87
Henry IV, part I 79–80, 144, 188–91
Henry IV, part II 68–9, 161
Henry V 12–14, 34–5, 126, 151, 163–4
Henslowe, Philip 5
Henslowe's Diary 5, 6–7
Howard, Charles 5

iambic pentameter 41–2, 44, 54;
    degrees of emphasis 43
Iambic Storytelling 192
if/then 29–30, 52, 91
imagery 58, 77, 96–7, 101, 114, 116,
    125
improvisation 114, 193, 197
index cards: *see* prompt cards

Julius Caesar 20, 33, 67, 158, 162,
    168–182

Kastan, David Scott 96
Kemp, William 10
kinesthetic awareness 105–112, 121
King James I 3
King John v, 73–6
King Lear 10, 38, 83–4, 117, 202
Kings Men, The 3

learning text with a partner 187
Lecoq, Jacques 198
listening 120–9
Listening and Storytelling 192
lists and ladders 41, 67, 71–3, 99, 136,
    157–8, 168; formats and structure of
    71–2
Lord Chamberlain's Men, The 3–5
Lords' Rooms 7–8
Love's Labours Lost 135–6
Lyly, John 116

Macbeth 55–6, 66, 90–102, 145
"magic if" xv
"magic" words 91
Marlowe, Christopher 116
Mask of the Divided Self, The 30–3, 203
Measure for Measure 24–6, 162, 164–7
mechanics of speech: linguistic
    placement 92–5
Meisner, Sanford 140; Repetition
    Exercise 140, 148–9
Memorizing Shakespeare 183–91
"Memory Palaces" or Method of Loci
    186
mental athletes 186
Merchant of Venice, The 31–3, 117, 155,
    157–8, 159–60, 161
metaphors 21, 38, 41, 77–8, 101, 113,
    116, 134
meta-historical 18
meta-theatrical/meta-theatricality
    17–18, 138
meter 40–1; *see* also iambic pentameter
metric deviations 44

Index **217**

microcosm within the macrocosm 17–22, 38, 134, 138
Midsummer Night's Dream, A 91, 191
mirrors: *see Elliptical Energy* use of mirrors; casting the audience
Moscow Art Theatre 11
Moving Target 133–4, 137; *random text* 134; *whole text* 133–4
Much Ado About Nothing 20, 35–6, 86, 201–2
mystery and morality plays of the Middle Ages 5

Nashe, Thomas 116
naturalism 11
neutral platform stage, *see* Elizabethan Theatre, components of
Nine Days Wonder (Will Kemp) 10
notation symbols 155–6

One Word Storytelling 195
Open Mic Poetry 132–3, 137
operative words 53
Ornamentation 17
orthography 86, 88–9, 92; differences in 95–102; *dynamics of* 160;
Othello x, 4, 80–1, 162

paraphrasing 131
parenthetical thoughts 67–8, 162–3; notation of 162;
patronage: *see* Elizabethan Theatre, components of
performance paradigms: at Shakespeare's Globe 120–1; contemporary 12, 14–15; Elizabethan 11, 14–15; fourth-wall 103, 120–1, 138; one-room 103, 121
performance time, *see* Elizabethan Theatre, components of
personas: the public and the private self 31–3
Personification: Casting Shakespeare's World 20, 38, 41, 81–4; *Love* 81–3; *Nature* 81, 83–4, 101; *Time* 82, 84; *Personify Shakespeare's World* 205

Pied Piper, The 198–9
Pied Piper, of Verse, The 199–200
"Pillars of Hercules" 18, 22
Platt 10, 196–7
Platt in Action 196–7
Platt in Action: Variations 197
players: *see* Elizabethan Theatre, components of
playing companies: *see* Elizabethan Theatre, components of
plays: *see* Shakespeare's plays
poetry: *see* verse
Process of Balance, The 164–8
profit-sharing: *see* Elizabethan Theatre, components of
prompt cards: for a single piece of text 184–6; *for dialogue 186*
pronouns, gender use of xiv
prose 40–1; notation of 156–7, 168
Proudfoot, Richard 96
psychological realism 11
Public Theatre, The 37
punctuation 204; colons 69–70; commas 66–8; comparison of 88–9; end-stops, periods 66; exclamation points 66; First Folio 66; performance clues 70; question marks 66; semicolons 68–9; notation of 157–8
pyrrhic 61

Queen Elizabeth 5
Queen's Privy Council 5

Radiating Box 109–111, 120
Radiating Box: stages of 110
Radiating Box: Distance and Vertical Space 111–12
Ralph Roister Doister 116
Rasmussen, Eric 96
realism 17
Red Lion, The 4
rehearsal period in Elizabethan Theatre: *see* Elizabethan Theatre, components of
repetition: ideas 158–60; notation of 158–60, 168; sounds in succession 93,

99, 161–2; words 61–2, 173; *see also* alliteration and assonance

repertory schedule: *see* Elizabethan Theatre, components of

Richard III xvii, 27, 45, 59–64, 66, 167

Rodenburg, Patsy xvi, 189, 204

Rolling Line, The 187

Romeo and Juliet 20–1, 38, 49–55, 76–7, 193–4, 200; improvised iambic storytelling 193–4

Rose, The 5

Royal Shakespeare Company, The (RSC) 194; *William Shakespeare: Complete Works* 89, 95–7, 101

scansion 42, 44

Schmidt, Alexander 97

Schmidt, *Shakespeare Lexicon and Quotation Dictionary* 97

scores, use of color 154

self-awareness in *Elliptical Energy Training* 149–50

"Shakesball" *see Basketball Shakespeare*

Shakespeare fears xiii

Shakespeare, John 4, 116

Shakespeare's Globe x–xi, 105; balcony 18; blocking in 22; decoration of 17–18; muses 18; on-stage spatial relationships 22–3, 203; performance conditions 105; stage roof: *see The Heavens;* trap door 20; spatial dimensions of 120; *see* performance paradigms

Shakespeare's plays
    All's Well That Ends Well 57–8, 64–5
    Anthony and Cleopatra 123–4
    As You Like It 11, 207
    Cymbeline 85
    Hamlet 4, 11, 87, 124, 132, 155
    Henry IV, part I 79–80, 144, 188–91
    Henry IV, part II 68–9, 161
    Henry V 12–14, 34–5, 126, 151, 163–4
    Julius Caesar 20, 33, 67, 158, 162, 168–182
    King John v, 73–6

    King Lear 10, 38, 83–4, 117, 202
    Love's Labours Lost 135–6
    Macbeth 55–6, 66, 90–102, 145
    Measure for Measure 24–6, 162, 164–7
    Merchant of Venice, The 31–3, 117, 155, 157–8, 159–60, 161
    Midsummer Night's Dream, A 91, 191
    Much Ado About Nothing 20, 35–6, 86, 201–2
    Othello x, 4, 80–1, 162
    Richard III xvii, 27, 45, 59–64, 66, 167
    Romeo and Juliet 20–1, 38, 49–55, 76–7, 193–4, 200
    Taming of the Shrew, The 28–30, 117
    Titus Andronicus 162
    Twelfth Night xvii, 10, 41, 77–8, 84, 144, 145
    Two Gentlemen of Verona, The 67–8, 69–70, 77, 82–3, 88–9, 155–7, 162–3
    Winter's Tale, The 72–3, 76, 158–9

Shakespeare's plays: editions of, 88–9; publication of 87

Shakespeare Score, The 168–82; elements of 168

Shakespeare's Social Space 37–9

Shakespeare, William: *Complete Works of* 95–6

shared lighting 120–2; *see also* Elizabethan Theatre, components of

Short and Shared lines 54–6, 59–60; notation of 156

side coaching 129, 135; by partner 189

similes 21, 38, 41, 77–8, 101, 113, 116, 134

soliloquy 20, 24, 28–9, 38, 84, 90, 127–8, 133; *see also Prompt Cards*

Solo Breath 205; *indoors* 206; *outdoors* 206; *in a large group* 206

Southwark 5

Spolin, Viola 195

spondee 61

Stacked Line, The 188; *(solo work)* 188–9; *(solo work, variation)* 189; *(partner work)* 189–90

stacking the Breath, or expansive breath work 188

Index **219**

stage directions, inherent 56
Staging Clues 22–3
Staging Discoveries 22–3
Staging Status 22–3
Stanislavski, Constantin xv, 11–2,
  17, 86, 109, 138; *An Actor Prepares*
  11–12; *Building a Character* 11, 86;
  Creating a Role 11
stars 20–1; *see also Heavens, The*
Status Exploration 113; 'Elizabethan
  Chain of Being' Status Game 115–7;
  Equal Status 118–9; *High Status*
  117–8; *Middle Status* 118
Status Work 112–9; *see Emotional/Spatial
  Dance*
status, friction in 117–9; personal status
  114, 119
Storck, David 195
Storytelling: Group 195; *Iambic* 192; *One
  Word* 195
Stratford 4
Structure of the Verse, The 154
Suggestions for Solo Work 203–6
Swan, The 7–8
syllable length: elision 53, 61;
  elongation 155–6, 171; monosyllabic
  vs. polysyllabic words 92

Taming of the Shrew, The 28–30, 117
Taylor, Norman 198
telescope or *Telescoping* 41, 73–6, 97–8,
  100
tempo 198–9, 203
Thames River 5, 9
Theatre, The 4–5
theatres: Blackfriars Playhouse 17;
  Broadway Theatres 16; Globe, The
  5; ornamentation of 16; Public
  Theatre, The 37; Red Lion, The 4;
  Rose, The 5; Shakespeare's Globe
  x–xi, 105; balcony 18; blocking
  in 22; decoration of 17–18; muses
  18; on-stage spatial relationships
  22–3, 203; performance conditions
  105; stage roof: *see The Heavens;*
  trap door 20; spatial dimensions of

120; *see* performance paradigms;
  Swan, The 7–8; Theatre, The 4–5;
  Wanamaker Playhouse 17; West
  End Theatres 16
theatre vs. film acting 139
"thinking on the line" 26, 103, 131–2
this vs. that 33, 76, 164–7; *see* antithesis
Thompson, Ann 96
Tillyard, E.M. 115–6
titles and names 41, 78–81, 95, 101,
  203; "thee" and "thou" 79
Titus Andronicus 162
trochee 44–8, 53–4, 63, 98, 102;
  mid-line 53, 58
Twelfth Night xvii, 10, 41, 77–8, 84,
  144, 145
Twitter 53, 86
Two Gentlemen of Verona, The 67–8,
  69–70, 77, 82–3, 88–9, 155–7,
  162–3

Udall, Nicholas 116
University of Exeter Drama
  Department xvi
"University Wits, the" 116
"upstart crow" 116

verbs 45, 52, 159, 205
verse 40–1, 62; blank 40; changes
  between verse and prose 156–7;
  distinctions between verse and prose
  40; rhyming 40; *see also Basketball
  Shakespeare*
villians, of Shakespeare 25
Volleying 194
vowels 64–5, 94
vowels, repetition of 92 (*see also*
  "assonance")

Walk the Punctuation 204
Wanamaker Playhouse 17
Webster, John 120
West End Theatres 16
Winter's Tale, The 72–3, 76, 158–9
Wonder, Stevie 77
World According to Me!, The 200–1

Taylor & Francis eBooks

Helping you to choose the right eBooks for your Library

Add Routledge titles to your library's digital collection today. Taylor and Francis ebooks contains over 50,000 titles in the Humanities, Social Sciences, Behavioural Sciences, Built Environment and Law.

Choose from a range of subject packages or create your own!

Benefits for you
- Free MARC records
- COUNTER-compliant usage statistics
- Flexible purchase and pricing options
- All titles DRM-free.

Benefits for your user
- Off-site, anytime access via Athens or referring URL
- Print or copy pages or chapters
- Full content search
- Bookmark, highlight and annotate text
- Access to thousands of pages of quality research at the click of a button.

REQUEST YOUR FREE INSTITUTIONAL TRIAL TODAY
Free Trials Available
We offer free trials to qualifying academic, corporate and government customers.

eCollections – Choose from over 30 subject eCollections, including:

Archaeology	Language Learning
Architecture	Law
Asian Studies	Literature
Business & Management	Media & Communication
Classical Studies	Middle East Studies
Construction	Music
Creative & Media Arts	Philosophy
Criminology & Criminal Justice	Planning
Economics	Politics
Education	Psychology & Mental Health
Energy	Religion
Engineering	Security
English Language & Linguistics	Social Work
Environment & Sustainability	Sociology
Geography	Sport
Health Studies	Theatre & Performance
History	Tourism, Hospitality & Events

For more information, pricing enquiries or to order a free trial, please contact your local sales team:
www.tandfebooks.com/page/sales

 The home of Routledge books

www.tandfebooks.com